ALMOST
independence

the place
between loss
and laughter

BRENT LECHELER

NicAmmon Publishing

NicAmmon Publishing

NicAmmon Publishing
2900 Champa Street, Denver, CO 80205

Printed in the United States of America
First Printing: September 2002

ISBN# 0-9721192-0-5 pc eps

The Independence Radio program and World Wide Web
site address is
http://www.independenceradio.com

Editing by Erin Elizabeth Jackson

Cover design by Linda Wood
Wood Design & Art Studio

To my son Nicholas,
who was but a dream and a longing
when I first began to pen these memoirs.
May I give you every confidence that
you are cherished and loved.

Dad

Acknowledgements

To my stepmother, Louise, who embraced our family when she had no idea of what she was stepping into. Thank you for loving me in ways that I never realized as a young boy.

To Lou Tice, for his inspiration and expertise in converting dreams into reality.

To Bob and Judy Shirk, for their thoughtful contributions during the first readings of my work.

To my wife, Doreen, for her enthusiasm, time and talents in making my story come to life.

To those whose lives have influenced me in ways they may never know. John Wagner, Scott Dimock and Harold Hicks whose faith, perseverance and convictions are poured out daily to enrich the lives of others.

To Jim, AnnaMarie, Doug and Erin Jackson who have become role models for me by making it their life mission to save countless lives throughout the world. In honor of their work, NicAmmon Publishing will donate 10% of all book proceeds to the nonprofit work of PROJECT C.U.R.E.

Chapter I

Have you ever noticed how long a short walk can be when you're running late and in a hurry? It's 9:10 a.m. on a Monday morning, and I'm bolting down the office corridor, late for my nine o'clock meeting. The smell of coffee diverts my attention. I realize that I'm already on borrowed time, but the weight of the aroma against my senses convinces me that this is just the thing to quell the numbness of fatigue.

Funny thing how the mind works. I never really drank coffee until four years ago when Doreen and I got married. I use to tease her relentlessly about her morning addiction. And now I can barely start the day without a cup or two of Java creeping through my veins.

I dart off course and round the corner toward the vending machines, taking the inside track. The closer you are to the inside of a curve, the greater your chances are of cutting three times the amount of travel. Not only is this a standard mathematical fact derived from Pi, but it was the one piece of fatherly wisdom that my dad bestowed upon me before the one and only high school track meet that he attended. That was Dad - all logic, no emotion.

Dang. The line at the coffee machine is two-deep, and the person up front is painstakingly reading every direction offered. I'm thinking, what's there to read? Haven't you seen one of these contraptions before? They're universal. And they've been around forever. You've only got three choices: coffee, hot chocolate and chicken soup. It's like flushing a toilet - pretty standard no matter where you go in the modern world.

Anxiety sets in, and my pulse starts to race as I nervously tap my foot to the rhythm of my heartbeat. I'm so wound up these days. I don't know if it's the common malaise of mid-life angst, or the mounting pressure of responsibilities that I so successfully avoided for the first 40 years of my life. Could it be the swelling insanity of a work environment where the executive team confuses visionary leadership with management-by-crises? For a typically carefree, laid-back kind of guy, these are ingredients for a minefield of cynicism. It seems that everywhere I turn, I'm

1

inundated with the absurdities of the modern rat race. Humor has turned to sarcasm, and I'm desperately in need of a dose of logical sanity.

Minutes pass, and he finally commits. Out spurts chicken soup. It's so watery, signaling that it's high time the vending company returns to replace the chicken wing that flavors the hot water. Fortunately, the guy directly in front of me is decisive. He pops in his coin, presses "Coffee," and, simultaneously, selects "Extra Light" and "Extra Sugar." Boy, if everyone were this efficient in life, things would be so much easier.

The dime in my hand is already warm from massaging it between my thumb and index finger. I pop it in and select "Coffee Black." I grab the steaming cup out of the machine and am on my way. It's stinging to the touch, so I carefully balance it with thumb and index finger around the top rim, supporting the bottom with my pinky. This intricate balancing act was the very first thing, and maybe most important thing, that I learned on my first engineering job out of college. Walt Winters, a burned-out hippie technician with a shaggy beard, versed me on this technique. I've been using it ever since.

I sprint through the main foyer and into Conference Room B. A full room awakens my consciousness, and I make my way to a seat at the far end of the oval table, strategically next to the cinnamon rolls.

"Sorry I'm late, but I had a conference call," an obvious lie, but the common corporate excuse. The meeting is already more than ten minutes old, and everyone has their laptops open, feverishly pecking on the keyboards. These meetings are so bizarre. Everyone gets together so that they can work on their laptops and exchange messages with people who aren't even in the room. Why do we do this, I muse - spend thousands of dollars on airplane tickets and motels to visit our other corporate sites, then sit here and communicate with everyone except those with whom we came to meet?

Fred, from our California office, stares anxiously at his laptop as if it were preparing to lay an egg.

"Imy, we're going over the IP solution versus TDM. We're talking to several vendors about the differences and need to make a decision. We have a mandate to determine the direction for the corporate telecommunication infrastructure. There are obviously many factors to consider when mixing topographies and protocols such as ATM, frame ....."

Fred is rambling on and on about our corporate network structure. The people sitting around the table are from across the country, hand-selected to sit on the technical corporate board. Everyone on the committee has a political agenda. Since the board is responsible for technical leadership, I was selected as the token electrical engineer in the company.

"Imy, what do think the ramifications would be of combining IP with ATM?" Benny interrupts in a hushed monotone voice, as if testing me to see if I am paying attention.

"There are none," I quip. "IP is IP with a whole different protocol than the 52-byte ATM cell. Fact is, you could use routers for either protocol and still acquire flexible bandwidth on demand."

"Well, we just happen to have a vendor who will give us a short presentation which I'm sure you'll find very exciting," Benny says, trying to mask the fact that the decision has already been made but still needs committee endorsement. Since Benny is a VP, and I'm not, he knows that I won't put up much of a political fight.

"Donald, the overhead is set up, and the floor is yours," Benny commands in a warm and friendly tone.

The lights dim, and the visual presentation starts. All eyes are glued on the screen as if it is the Super Bowl. I take visual inventory around the crowded conference table. There is Benny, vice president of Branch Tele-communications out of the Boston office. He's a rather nondescript looking fellow in his mid-forties whose only claim to fame is that of corporate survival. Although he has no technical grasp of the sixty-city operations that he oversees, he manages to climb the corporate ladder by laying low and maintaining status quo. Management by crisis is his forte. Just don't ask him to implement solutions – a decision would be far too risky.

Next to him sits Matt, the soft-spoken, mild mannered network provider, also from the main corporate facility in Boston. Matt is a kind and amiable sort of guy in his late thirties. On many occasions, Matt and I have interacted on technical issues. When a few of the Center Directors have tried to pin the incompetence's of their department on my technical infrastructure, Matt has been there to present the clear-cut statistical facts. We value one another's opinions.

Rudy, Charles, Frank and Dale are on the committee largely because of longevity. They all started in the industry as burglar alarm installers and worked their way up through the ranks. You can tell this by their white, buttoned-down, short sleeve installation shirts. The name patches have been removed in most cases, as is evident by the faint oval silhouette above the left breastplate. This crew really knows how to make the most out of a shirt. Each thread of material is stretched beyond specification in order to cover a generous midsection. What their shirts don't quite get around to masking, their undershirts do.

My daydreaming subsides, and I'm back on course with the program. In no time at all, the presentation is finished, and the conference room lights brighten.

"Well, after an incredible presentation like this, where do we sign?" Benny asks, chiding the vendor.

"Well, I just happen to have a pen right here," the vendor jabs jokingly.

I detect a tinge of hopeful seriousness to his reply.

"Well Imy, what do you think?" They're giving us an enormous price break if we register now, even if we don't implement until later, due to budget constraints."

"How much cheaper?" Dale asks.

"Up to forty percent off. With savings like that we'd be foolish to balk. Any other questions?"

I stare in disbelief as all parties involved slouch in their chair and bang on their keyboards.

"Benny, I want to share three facts that I learned from the last International Telecommunications Convention held in New Orleans. Number one. Internet usage is doubling every nine months. Number two. Of the fiber laid, less than three percent is lit. And lastly, technology is obsolete in eighteen months. So what would an ROI look like on a product that is agreed upon now, purchased a year from now, and installed eighteen months later? Wouldn't that leave us with obsolete equipment that we paid sixty cents on the dollar for?"

"No risk, no dividends," Benny snaps in curt fashion.

I stop the interrogation, sensing Benny's obvious irritation. My cell phone rings, and I pick it up to read the caller I.D.

"Excuse me, I gotta get this."

I hastily exit the conference room thinking timing couldn't be better.

A few hours later, the lunch caterers arrive, transfixing everyone's gaze to the food, except for Benny, who continues to lobby for the endorsement of the vendor's new equipment. A hypnotist couldn't snatch more focus than these two servers waving around steel dishes as all eyes blankly follow.

"Let's break for lunch," Dale yawns with outstretched arms.

Sensing my perfect escape, I suggest that I'll be back in a second.

"Gotta check email."

I take up a full gait as I head back to my office, unwilling to contribute any more real ideas to those who are most interested in toeing the party line, not to mention the dessert tray.

Chapter II

The speedometer needle on my Jeep inches between zero and five miles per hour. I'm stuck in first gear, so the actual velocity reading is nothing more than an affirmation at this point. A quick glance would suffice, but I just need a change of scenery from the idling lanes of rush-hour vehicles. I've been on the road for twenty minutes now and have gotten nowhere. Traffic is at its all-time worst, and I'm already late getting home.

I finally arrive at the culprit – road construction – narrowing traffic to one lane. I crawl past the D.O.T. laborer holding a "slow" sign, as if he's really needed at this point. About a half-mile further, the highway opens again, allowing traffic to resume the speed limit.

And wouldn't you know it, another mile down the road, a policeman points his radar gun at traffic. Just in case you're trying to make up a little time, the cop is there to add to your frustration.

As I enter the homeward stretch, I can't help but smile at the thought of how great it will be just to sit and relax tonight. It's my night to watch Nicholas while Doreen chairs a leadership committee. Seems like every evening and weekend is booked these days. If it isn't a civic meeting, event or dinner party, it's work from the office to be done at home on the laptop via dial-up. And if that's not the case, there's never-ending renovation work to be done on the house or in the yard, both with over one hundred years of neglect. We purchased the historical landmark in downtown Denver a couple of years ago. I wonder if they had grass in my neighborhood a hundred years ago. I know I've never seen any in that back yard of mine.

Anyway, it seems that life is so scheduled and intense. Every day begins the same by getting up early to spend time with Baby Nicholas. I attend to him while Doreen goes for her early morning jog. Then I run to the gym for a quick workout before going into the office. I listen to voice mail and return calls from my Jeep on my drive in. I can access my emails via cell phone, prioritizing them to my level of importance. Since I receive over one hundred of them every day, my commute time is well used. On a rare occasion, I force a glance westward at the Rocky Mountains towering in the background, then regain my composure to maneuver through traffic. At work, it's meetings, conference calls and putting out fires, right up until noon. After a brief lunch, it's back to the rat race. Then before I know it, it's time to head for home where I receive my instructions for the evening from the refrigerator calendar posting the evening's function. But not tonight. Tonight is different. Tonight is a quiet night alone with my son.

Suddenly, my cell phone rings. Only a handful of folks know my number, so my heart starts to pound. The Caller ID indicates that it is from home, and instant relief sets in.

"Hello."

"Hi honey, how far away are you? A static voice asks."

"I'm just about there, why?"

"Can you stop at the store and pick up some diapers? We're out of eggs, and you need lunchmeat for tomorrow, and I really need you to hurry. I have to pick up the delegation at their hotel before my meeting, so I'm a little crunched for time."

"Ohhh, alright. I can see the store from here. Be home in fifteen."

Wow, you couldn't package stress and sell it any better than this. What I wouldn't give just to jump off this carousel for a couple of minutes.

After my second orbit around the inadequate parking lot at Big Kings Food, I finally decide to park on the street about a block-and-a-half away. Now, how much sense does this make? A parking lot that accommodates only a handful of cars, feeding a mega-grocery store.

I know enough to step on the very first part of the automatic door sensor in order to time my rapid pace. It's as if I'm running an obstacle course, dodging old ladies and meanderers who have no urgent mission. I grab a carry basket, knowing that my odds of getting a shopping cart with aligned front wheels are less than fifty-fifty. I run over to the meat counter, immediately selecting a number from the ticket machine. You never know if they are honoring these numbers, or if it's first-come-first served, but past experience suggests that I get a ticket. Better safe than sorry.

"I'll take a pound of turkey, the stuff that's a $1.50 off for Club Card members."

"Coming right up, sir."

Now, there's another thing I can't understand. There are absolutely no criteria for becoming a Big Kings card member. The card is absolutely free and can be obtained immediately. So why don't they just give you the discounted price, rather than punish you, when you forget to snatch the card out of your wife's pocketbook? I tend to think that this is part of a master plot to make our lives more convoluted, increase our stress levels and prevent us from managing our lives logically. From my job right up to the grocery store, things just don't make logical sense to me anymore.

I sprint to the checkout and rush out the door to my Jeep. I fire up the engine and race toward home.

At last, home sweet home. I attempt to open the door with my entire gear, groceries and coffee mug in hand. After a couple of unsuccessful tries, I put several things down and swing open the side door of the house. As I reach back to grab my belongings, I turn and trip over the dog. Since our dog is really a cat in a Chow's body, tripping over her isn't a hard thing to do.

"Sweetheart, is that you?"

"Who are you talking to, me or the dog?"

"The dog, of course. I'm just teasing. How was your day?"

"Oh, same old thing."

"Hon, have you given any more thought to staying in town long enough for Nick's birthday?"

"Not particularly."

"Well, I was thinking, we can wait for the party, but it would be nice for all of us to be together for his very first birthday celebration."

"Honey, I know. We've already talked about this."

"Well, I know that your family was never much for celebrating anything, but I just can't believe that you wouldn't want to be here for his first birthday. You can get to your event a day late and miss the opening party and keynote. They're not so important."

"Doreen, this international T-COM conference has been on my radar screen for three months now. Besides, do you think Nick will remember that I missed his big number one? Come on, does anyone remember who was at their first birthday dinner?"

"No, he may not remember it, but he will certainly know that you are not there. And the photos will tell the story, 'Mr. Logical.' Fine, I know you had this conference planned for a long time, so we'll let it slide. But once he's old enough to ask you to be there for him, try looking into his eyes and giving him your logical analysis."

"Yea, yea."

"Anyway, thanks for coming home and watching Nicholas."

"No problem, how's he doing?"

"Perfect as usual. He just ate, so you might want to hold him for a while. He loves it when you rock him to sleep. By the way, Charlie called. He was wondering if you guys could get together pretty soon."

"Yea, like when? I mean, work is just too busy. I'm gonna call him and put him off for a couple of weeks."

"What about his graduation? You know that he won't come right out and ask, but aren't you planning to be there? That's probably what his call is about."

"It's the same time as the conference. How can I?"

Charlie is an Hispanic kid that I mentor through the Denver Partners Program. I got involved with the program after my last philosophical evening, four years ago. I remember sitting in my apartment one evening soon after turning forty. I began contemplating what life was all about and what was I here for. I thought that I'd give it a rest and turn on the 10:00 PM news. The first story was about a "trust fund" playboy who lacked direction and drive and ended up committing suicide. They were doing a feature story on the funeral, interviewing friends and family. I couldn't help thinking that if I died, what would friends and family say about me? Sure, I have a lot of energy and am fun to be around, but what kind of legacy would I actually leave behind? The piece was over, and the network went to a commercial highlighting the "Big Brothers Organization." Well, I put the news story and commercial together. With a little prompting from my pal, Greg, who was president of the Denver Partners Board, I ended up joining his affiliate, Denver Partners, which is a similar program and was introduced to Charlie. Charlie is a great junior partner, and we're both better people because of our relationship.

Doreen pointed out that he probably wouldn't be graduating if it weren't for the times I interceded and talked with his teachers, helped him with projects and kept him motivated. His family sure wasn't there for him, but I wondered if he would even care if I didn't show up for the ceremony. Do the kids even pay attention?

In my heart, I know Charlie would love for me to be there, but how many directions can I be pulled.

"I'll give him a call and explain the situation. Doreen, you know how proud I am of him and all he's accomplished."

"Maybe you could schedule some time with him after the graduation and after the conference. Hopefully, life will settle down a bit by then."

Doreen gives me a peck on the cheek.

"I gotta run, see ya later. Love you."

Seconds later the telephone rings with a prominent downtown hotel listed on the Caller ID.

"Hello?"

"Hello, is Doreen there?"

"No, she just left to pick up your party for the event. She should be there in about five minutes."

"Thank you. We'll be waiting in the lobby."

I hang up the phone and take a deep breath. On the stove is the care package Doreen prepared for me. She is indeed something special. No matter how busy she gets, she always puts her family first. That's just one of the many reasons I love her so.

The faint noise of Nicholas starting to fuss interrupts my deep thought. He giggles when he sees me, and that alone erases the stress that builds up on a daily basis. I lean over his playpen and lift him up to give him a kiss. I carry him over to our favorite and only rocking chair and hold him in my arms as I watch his smile grow fainter and his little eyelids close. Boy, how precious and protected he is. Little Nicholas doesn't know anything about the world yet. I just hope he can grow up and feel like a kid for as long as it takes. I had to grow up fast; too fast. I don't want him to have the kind of childhood that I had. Not that it was all that bad. It was just nonexistent. To this day, I don't have, in my possession, even one baby picture of myself. I have no way of comparing what I looked like to Nick. I want us to be best of friends, something my dad and I never were.

Slowly, we rock back and forth until he is sound asleep. Meanwhile, my mind is wandering even more than usual today. This constant stress of life just doesn't make a lot of sense anymore. I've always tried to look at life logically, but I seem to be over-analyzing everything today. I've always known that I am destined for something. But what? Here I am, caught up in the same rat race with almost every body else, wondering how to break free. And what is life going to be like for little Nicholas when he is my age? Heck, I wonder what his childhood will be like. What's he going to spend a lot of his time thinking about? How will he perceive Doreen and me? Will he think back on his life the way that I do with mine? Will he and I be close, something my dad and I could never accomplish? We have the same age differential between us as Dad and I had. Dad was forty-two years my senior, and Nicholas is forty-four years my junior. I was the oldest and only son for nine years, and Nicholas is my oldest and only. These questions and thoughts preoccupy my mind tonight as I rock rhythmically back and forth, back and forth.

Life was different back then, and being from rural Wisconsin made it even far more different. There was very little culture, and people either didn't know or didn't care about being politically correct. Then again, life seemed so much easier. I don't know if it was being a child or just life in the 60's, but life was simple and quite unique.

I rest my head against the chair as we continue to rock, and I begin thinking about my dad. I haven't thought about him lately or my childhood for years. But a floodgate of memories seems to be accompanying this welcomed evening of quiet and calm. I decide to surrender to the moment and settle into a past that I had shut out for so long.

11

Chapter III

There was something odd about the town. Maybe it was the last names of the residents, almost all resembling the bottom line of an eye chart. Or maybe it was that guttural Polish accent, showering tobacco-laden saliva every time they spoke. Whatever the aura was, it was quite noticeable, even to an eight year old boy.

It was the summer of '65, and we were in the process of moving to Arcadia, Wisconsin, just 72 miles from our tiny town of Elmwood. My father had just resigned as the business manager of Elmwood Lumber & Grain in order to purchase his very own feed mill. He heard about the mill from his brother, Father Tony, who was the resident chaplain at the hospital in Arcadia. So Dad decided to give it a whirl as owner and sole proprietor of East Arcadia Feed Mill.

Now, there were already two other feed mills in Arcadia. Both were downtown. But Dad thought that having a feed mill on the outskirts of town would be a strategic advantage. He just couldn't imagine any farmer wanting to drive through all that main street traffic in order to grind crops into feed for livestock.

The town of Arcadia inhabited two thousand people, with one long main street connecting the East Side to the West. The town's claim to fame was "Chicken Capital of Wisconsin." The Broiler plant was where the chickens were processed, and it was the largest industry in the area. The whole community was set up to support the chicken infrastructure. Not only were chicken coops everywhere, but chicken trucks and feed mills also played a huge role in providing prosperous times for Arcadians. Even chicken catchers were in high demand, a good one fetching more than six dollars per hour.

My step-mom tried flaunting Arcadia's "dense" population, in order to persuade us to be excited about the move. After all, according to the Wisconsin tourism book, Arcadia had a tennis court, swimming pool and "new" country club, not to be confused with the "old" country club. The New Country Club actually had plumbing, wood paneled walls and electricity. Then there was Sky

a smirk on his ugly mug. He was taking home one more thing to add to his stable of entertainment.

And just another folding chair to my right sat Dad, totally exempt from the anguish that I was feeling. He just continued to read his program, as if editing it for grammatical mistakes. After a quick look as his watch, he stuffed the program into his overcoat pocket. I knew this was a prelude to an exit, so I put on my coat and over-lapped the front of it, holding it close to my body. This was standard procedure for a coat that had a broken zipper and was two sizes too big. However the pockets were warm, and on a freezing night like that one, it brought welcomed relief.

As we walked out of the gymnasium and into the cold winter night, I started to count my blessings. I felt thankful for a coat with such warm pockets. I also started to think that this kid didn't even have to be thankful for that, since he had mittens. And he probably had toys. And he probably had a mom. And maybe even his Dad talked to him occasionally.

The walk to the car in the frigid evening seemed like eternity, as the snow crunched beneath our boots. We got into the truck cab and begged Dad to turn on the heat. The old pickup truck crawled through the parking lot, waiting for people to inch out of the single exit. I noticed Dad staring out of the windshield, as if recounting the evening. I could tell he had something on his mind. I know I sure did. Everyone was quiet, knowing that if a conversation were to take place, it was his to lead. Dad cleared his throat, then turned his head slightly to the right in order to address us.

"Now that was one nice Christmas program."

Things were tough going on the farm, and Dad lacked any medium for meeting suitors in this small town of Elmwood. Mom had passed just over three years now, and Dad needed help and companionship on the farm. Family rumor had it that he submitted an ad in a Catholic magazine for a housewife. Lo and behold, who should answer but a forty-year-old lady from St Paul, Minnesota. Louise Hinderks still lived at home with her parents and had held the same office job for over twenty years. Why Dad placed the magazine ad and why Louise answered it is still a mystery. Neither party would confirm or deny the rumor, so we adopted it as fact. Their wedding was held in May of '62.

17

The only thing they appeared to have in common was that they were both Catholic. Dad was seven years her senior. Louise appeared to be spoiled, accustomed to having all meals prepared for her by her mom. Weekends were all about her, and she spent her time and money purely on entertainment.

Arnold George Lecheler was born in 1915, the oldest of eight children who were all born at home on the farm. Grandpa Nicholas was a farmer who knew nothing other than hard work. Dad grew up helping on the farm, and eventually partnered with Grandpa after high school. After a few tough years, Dad could see the writing on the wall. The farm was barely churning enough income to make ends meet for the large family, and it was time for Dad to leave. Grandpa could have used the help, but he had no money left over to pay him. So, Dad left one day, leaving the farm and family behind. He wound up working in a factory in Michigan for a year. After saving enough money, he enrolled at a Business College in Winona Minnesota. He worked his way through school for three long years, setting pins in bowling alleys during his "off time." His love of farming landed him back on the family farm after he finished school. He moonlighted as book-keeper for the cheese plant down the road in order to supplement his income. A few years later, most of the family had left the farm, and it was ripe to be taken over. Dad worked with Grandpa for a few more years and then WWII broke out. Soon after, Dad was drafted and went to basic training in the Carolina's. He later found himself stationed in a base outside of London. For three years the war raged on, and after the surrender, Dad ended back on the farm. The cheese plant had gone under, so Dad had the responsibility of making the farm into an income producer, and Grandpa was ready to retire, leaving Dad on his own.

A few years later, Dad got married and soon started a family. He worked the farm even harder than his father had and seemed to be keeping his head above water financially. Then Mom became sick, and life became even more challenging. After her death, Grandpa wanted to get out from under the farm free-and-clear, and Dad was running out of time. The payments became too much, so Grandpa decided it was high time to "cash in." An auction was held, and the farm was sold. Dad reluctantly took a position as Business Manager of the Elmwood Lumber and Grain. Shortly before he remarried, my new "mother-to-be" put a down payment on a little house in the village of Elmwood where we all settled.

Getting used to this new lifestyle was tough on all parties involved. Everyone had to adjust, and in retrospect, my new mother had to adjust the most. To me, this was just another housekeeper to stay away from. For her, it was adjusting from being a corporate employee who enjoyed having big city life at her fingertips to living in a town of seven hundred people with no street signs. Louise was used to being catered to by her mom. Now the tables were turned. There were three little kids and a hungry man who needed tending to. I remember walking into the house many a time to the sight of her sitting at the dining room table in tears, sobbing violently, telling me how lonely she was. It tore me up knowing that I was part of the problem and not a piece of the solution.

I always kept a distance from Mom and tried to ignore her bizarre comments. As for child psychology, she was totally clueless. Her "warm and fuzzy" ranking was pretty much next to Dad's, right behind Adolph Hitler. Dad wasn't a bad person. He just had a terrible temper to accommodate his no-nonsense policy. I learned very fast never to slip up in his presence. His face would ignite with fury, and the punches, slaps, and bruising would soon follow any misbehavior. The beatings seemed to make him more angry, as if he was taking the fact that I was alive, out on me.

Because I needed to survive without love, I became quite the thinker and started substituting emotion with logic. I then used humor to totally mask my feelings. Things that were wrapped in emotion left me totally cold, allowing me to be able to make personal decisions in a heartbeat. I started running with the "tough crowd," if you could call hanging with older kids who had a secret club and bubble gum contests, "tough." I could have let this situation depress me, but I got a little help from a friend.

Grandma Rosie was more of a friend than a grandma. She was my real mom's mother, and my sole connection to all of my cousins that lived in the small town. She was pure Irish and pretty much laughed constantly. She was the funniest person in the world, sharing her contagious happiness with everyone. She would let me pick out my own birthday presents, no matter how expensive they were. One time I selected a holster with two toy revolvers. I wore this apparatus all around town and almost everywhere I went. The only time that I didn't think about wearing "my setup" was when Grandma took me to a professional wrestling match. The match was held at the school gymnasium. "The Crusher" was strutting around the ring, chewing cigars and spitting them at his opponent. The crowd went wild when he got pinned, especially since Grandma was leading the frenzy.

Our special relationship continued until Mom felt competition existed. She would tell me that Grandma Rosie was no longer my grandma - that her mother was my replacement grandma. Grandma Rosie saw the friction and gracefully backed out, severing my only umbilical cord to an energetic, loving and positive person. In my anger and hate, I tried to run away twice but barley got a lukewarm response from my parents. After allowing a little time to let things cool down a bit, Grandma Rosie came back into the picture and became my best friend again. I knew I would grow out of this relationship someday, but it was the best thing that I had going. I just hung in there, biding my time, until one day Dad came home from the lumber and grain store and declared that we were moving.

As I turned away from the rear view mirror and focused back on the road in front of me, I thought it was time to think positively about the future. I knew that we needed this move and hoped that it would be a fresh start for all of us.

About an hour–and-a-half later, we embarked on the village of Independence, and I fixed on a tattered road sign that signaled my uncertain destiny "Arcadia 9 miles."
We followed the thin ribbon of two-lane blacktop for the next twenty minutes before entering civilization. A chipped and faded billboard greeted us. Welcome to Arcadia, Home of Arcadia Broiler Days, May 24, 25, 26.

I immediately felt the emotional letdown. Dang, we missed Broiler Days!

Chapter IV

A calendar from a local farm implement dealer hung on the kitchen refrigerator and read June 1965. I remember the month so well because of the image of that huge Holstein cow staring me in the face every time I went to grab something out of the refrigerator. A picture of a country field with a cow in the background is one thing, but a cow's ugly mug straight on; staring at me with his tongue up its right nostril was a little unappetizing. You'd think the photographer taking the shot could have cropped out the other cow standing beside it with its tail in the air relieving itself. However, he chose to shoot it straight on, showing the barnyard nature scene, complete with the rectangle banner nailed to the front of the wooden trough that read, "June Is Dairy Month."

After gulping breakfast and finishing the last of the unpacking, I decided to explore my new neighborhood. We had moved into a rented farmhouse, approximately three miles from town. The square, four-bedroom, brick house was two-stories that offered our family plenty of living space. I knew the neighbors wouldn't be breaking down our door to introduce themselves, so I tossed the old black Schwinn off the front porch and decided to take a spin. I rode on gravel, or "crushed rock" as the natives called it, about one hundred yards up to the tar county road. At the end of the long driveway, I decided to turn right, mainly because there was a farm within sight in that direction.

I was peddling down the road no more that three minutes when the buzz of a tractor approaching rapidly behind me caught my attention. As I slowed down to concentrate on my balance, I hugged the right shoulder as much as possible. The buzz turned into a roar, imitating a tank scene from a World War II classic. A fleet of no less than five tractors flew past me, each one equipped with an above average weight person navigating their farm implement. The last two tractors had fat-faced natives hanging off the fenders, trying to lower and adjust themselves to avoid the early morning chill.   The rattle of metal snaps on bib overalls flapping against their huge backs created an equal amount of noise as they roared past me. Each tractor was green and was pulling another implement behind it. Each towed item had a distinct purpose, and the determined looks on the farmers' faces spelled business.

As the smoke cleared, I detected a faint hum in the distant background. Thinking my ears were still ringing, I proceeded down the road taking in the unfamiliar scenery. When the humming increased in volume, I pulled over to the side of the road and took a look behind me. A small tractor pulling a smaller cart came up behind me, temporarily slowed, and then stopped right behind my bicycle. A short, grossly overweight man climbed off the lawn tractor dressed in bib overalls and brown work boots. His mannerisms appeared mature, but a closer look revealed that he was no older than I. He glanced over at me, strolled over to his cart, reached down beneath the rails and resurfaced with an item that glittered in the sun's rays. He walked over to me, and hollered…"thirsty?"

"Uh, well kinda."

"Here."

He tossed me the shiny object, floating it in the air end over end. I caught it with both hands and yelled, "thanks." He climbed back on the tractor, placed it in gear and rode away, throwing up a spray of gravel from the right shoulder of the road. I waved to him as he stormed by and couldn't help but notice the big red sign on the back of his cart,
June Is Dairy Month.

I took a look at my first received gift from a local. It was an ice-cold can of beer. It seemed a bit mature for an eight–year-old. On the other hand, I guess I was being indoctrinated.

Once the household chores were pretty much behind us, my responsibilities were relieved, and I was reassigned to the feed mill, my father's place of business. I was told that I had to work at least one half-day and could take the other half-day off to do fun things, like help around the house. Being new to the area, I had no idea what was fun, but I sure wasn't going to knock having to work only part-time. So, I chose to work the morning shift at the mill, thus fulfilling my half-day obligation.

that he might be a bit forward, but I soon discovered that most Arcadians are.

"I got ta-dee batches, one fer da feeders, one fer da sows and one fer da cows," he said with a rough and broken Slavic accent. I immediately went to seek out John and steered him over in order to have him make heads or tails out of that statement.

"How big da pigs?" John hollered, hoping to be heard over the loud whirr of the mill motors.

"Bout terdy-six or bedder."

John grabbed a pencil and did some rough calculations on the wooden inside support beam of the doorway. After ingesting the totals, John swayed down the isle looking for the correct bag of concentrate to supplement the grain that was being ground. I returned to the grinder pad, watching this cumbersome fellow transfer grain from his truck.

"How big are yous guy's pigs?"

"Pardon me?"

"Why, 'chu fart?"

"Ahh, no."

"Yous got pigs?"

"Ahh, no."

"How 'bout cows. Got any of dem?"

"Ahh, no. See, we rent a house on a farm. We don't actually farm or own one."

"Well, dare pigs on dat farm?"

"Yes."

"Den, how much do day weigh?"

"Ahh, I really don't know."

He grunted at me and proceeded to repeat the question, this time with so much emphasis that snuff showered from his mouth, raining down on my head. Thank God for caps with long visors, I thought. I shrugged my shoulders and could tell that my lack of husbandry was completely bewildering this man. John sauntered over just in time and interrupted the swine interrogation.

"What do you want in the second batch?"

The man limped over to John in order to be heard over the whine of the motors. I took this opportunity to dart into the mill. I knew it would be an easier task to assist John than to help this farmer. As I passed by the pair, I couldn't help but overhear part of the sidebar conversation.

"John, I don't know what da hell da worlt is comin to, ya know. You got a kid dat lives on a farm but don't farm. Next ting I'll hear is dat he don't even know how to milk a cow!"

It wasn't long before this odd character was in the office to pay his bill. Several times the door flew open and a black streak of tobacco shot across the old wood porch.

After bags of feed were stacked in the bed of his pickup truck, this snuff chewing farmer packed himself back behind the steering wheel, the same place he surfaced from about an hour ago. John and I had already taken our spots on the front porch, talking about the experience and waiting for the next rush. The six-cylinder engine coughed a couple of times and came to life. The truck rolled away from the front porch, traveling about twenty feet before stopping. We gawked as three black streams of snuff spewed out of the open window as if being launched from a main artery. The third missile hit its mark, a tin can lying next to the weeds by the concrete pad. There was a roar of the engine as the clutch was popped, and a huge fist protruded out of the open driver's side window exposing a gnarly thumb in the upward position, as if this guy was doing a victory lap at Indy.

"Well, that's Octi," muttered John.

The rest of the morning raced by with one odd occurrence after another. Ira Moelsy drove up in his '48 orange International pickup with a few sacks of corn that had to be shelled and then ground a particular way for the chickens. Ira was a long drink of water with a sloped, drawn face to complement his lanky torso. His long chin protruded beyond the bill of his farm cap. Ira seemed to agree with everything I said, constantly nodding his head in a show of overwhelming approval. He agreed so vigorously on some occasions that he had to grab his cap to keep it from sailing airborne. I learned two things about Ira as he drove away. One, he had a severe case of cerebral palsy, and two, he didn't have chickens.

"John, if he doesn't have chickens, then what is the chicken feed for?"

"That's corn squeezings, ground up to make moonshine."

I just nodded my head in acknowledgement.

The Cornsolla Boys, Dorsal and Alf, were the next customers in to scrutinize the new ownership.

30

with the top half of the big truck surfacing first, just like spotting a freighter off the horizon coming into harbor. The entire truck would soon emerge and start making its way down the slope, twisting around to avoid the mill and make way for the hard right turn into the concrete plant. Sitting on the other side of the thick dirty windshield was Poopsie, maneuvering this huge hauler as if it were a golf cart. This time, I heard a little more air pressure than normal applied to the brakes, and the monster truck slowed to a crawl, then stopped directly in front of me.

"Dat Buick use any oil?" was the gruff question coupled with an inquisitive expression, as if that thought had occupied his mind for quite some time.

"Ahhh, I don't know, to be honest with you."

"Well, did you ever see anybody add oil?"

"Yeah, I think so," thinking I had better start getting definitive or we could spend hours getting to the bottom of this.

"My Poncho don't use no oil."

"What's a Poncho?"

"You know… Pumpjack."

Now, I knew I'd be here until Christmas if I questioned everything I didn't understand from this mental behemoth.

"Ohh yea."

"Ya Hey."

Now, I knew I was in a battle of wits with a guy five times my age and fifty times my weight. So I didn't quite know how this one was going to play out.

"Dat pigup use any oil?" was the next million-dollar question out of the man's mouth.

"How would I know, that's not our pickup."

"Den who's? Pig Laskie's?"

"Yogart's pickup!"

Just then, the schoolhouse door burst open, and Yogart came bounding out.

"Yogart, how's dat pigup runnin?" Poopsie hollered.

This was my escape route, my meal ticket. Once Yogart made eye contact with Poopsie, I seized my opportunity and skirted into the back room of the mill. There stood John Olsen, staring off in space as if in deep thought.

"That man never wears underwear under those bib overalls," John offered as if he was trying to picture how uncomfortable that would be.

"Why?"

"Well, he says it's cooler, but I gotta think he can't find anybody who makes 'em that big."

I shared a smile with John, then asked, "What's a Poncho?"

"It's a Pontiac." Why?"

"Oh, I'd never heard of that word being used for a car before."

"The whole English language takes on a whole different spin in Arcadia."

Boy, little did I know how right he was.

Dad came walking out of the office headed for the mill in a fast gait and looking all business.

"Let's go talk to Petey."

Petey Picka was a welder on the edge of town and had his own machine shop. If you needed any welding done in town, Petey Picka was the crown jewel. Petey was a small-framed man who usually sported an olive green jump suit. Legend had it that he could weld two cigar boxes together as long as you could get the items to Petey's shop. He didn't weld "on-site." Capitalizing on "on-site" welding was Aloysie Sookla. Aloysie had a truck with a portable welder and would come out to the customer's premises to do the work.

In a few minutes, we were walking through Petey's neatly managed machine shop. Dad had just finished explaining his quandary of reattaching a steel wheel-pad plate onto the truck hoist.

"Arnie, it would just make more sense for someone to weld that thing down at the mill. Since I don't do that, I'm gonna give you a guy's number who can help you on this one. Here's Aloysie's number. Give 'em a call, and he'll weld that 'barney-bar-mule-ea' on for ya."

Now, there's a phrase you didn't hear very often. "Barney-bar-mule-ea." "Barney-bar-mule-ea" meant the same as a "son of a biscuit," another common Arcadian colloquialism.

Although Dad was a good friend of Petey's, it looked as if we had to get Aloysie to come on-site to weld.

We headed back to the mill in order to heed Petey's recommendation. Dad squinted, trying to read the number that was scribbled on the piece of yellow note pad.

"Here, I don't have my glasses."

I gave Dad the five-digit number, remembering that the prefix exchange of 323 could be added together, totaling eight, then followed with the other four numbers. The few people in town that had a dial telephone knew that trick, and besides, it cut down on dial time.

"8-7232."

"Go ahead, ring it up and hand it over," were the orders from Dad.

A voice answered after three rings.

"Tricky's Tavern."

I immediately handed the phone over to Dad, who, in turn, asked for Aloysie Sookla.

"Just a minute."

I could hear the sound of the crowd in the background as Dad rested the telephone handset on his shoulder and filed the new number between two books on his messy desk.

"Aloysie here, who's dare?"

"Hi, this is Arnie Lecheler over at the East End Mill, and I was wondering…."

"If dis is a business call, I'd bedder take it in my office….jist a minute dare, buddy."

Dad patiently waited, as the sound of the crowd muffled in the background.

"Now we can talk," the husky voice barked. "What was yer name again?"

After Dad and Aloysie traded information, a man pounding on the "office" door interrupted them.

"Be out in a minute," came the raucous reply, followed by a flush of a toilet.

Dad hung up shortly thereafter. He gazed in my general direction, as if thinking intently.

"Well, either he is the busiest man in the world, or he offices in a bathroom. I guess he's on his way out."

Twenty minutes later, a pickup appeared on the horizon, slowly swerving as if negotiating a very crooked road. I jumped off the front porch to greet the skilled vendor. I showed him the truck hoist and what was needed to be done.

"Dat pig iron?"

"Ahh, I don't know."

"If dats pig iron, it'll be hell to weld!"

I ran in the office to get Dad, figuring he could answer the technical question.

Dad followed me out of the office to find Aloysie examining the contents of the toolbox in his pickup.

"Dats pig iron, and I'll have to run git a different fuser."

I couldn't help but notice that Aloysie's breath smelled like stale poppy seed coffeecake.

"Kid, ya wanna go fer a ride?"

"Dad, mind if I go?"

"Go head, hurry back," Dad said as he turned back toward the office.

We headed into town, stopping three times to check for a flat tire.

"She seems ta pull ta da right," was the stern explanation for why we constantly threw up road shoulder gravel.

About ten minutes later, we were in downtown Arcadia, driving Main Street and taking in the sights. The wide blacktop conduit was flanked by two-story businesses, with the entrances butted up to the sidewalk. The side view revealed these one-story buildings had false second story fronts, attempting to give the illusion of a big city. The effect reminds me of an old western town, resembling a back-lot studio in Hollywood.

We drove right through the "business district," then took a hard right down a one-block street. At the end of the street, we pulled up to the curb, which wasn't far off since we hugged the right shoulder most of the drive anyway. Aloysie stumbled out, and I followed his lead across the street to Tricky's Tavern. We entered the bar with Aloysie stopping to chat with a bar patron. I jumped up on a stool, tall enough so that I could get a bird's-eye-view of the action. I picked up a match book cover that had a cartoon character of a dog-faced person, dressed with a long stocking-hat with a raised beer glass. The inscription read: "Tricky's Tavern, where good friends meet." I thought, what a great place for an office. You can work where all of your friends are. My thoughts were harshly interrupted by a voice out of nowhere.

"Wha 'chew drinking?"

I looked around, but saw no one engaging me with eye contact. The voice sounded again, this time a little louder.

"Wha 'chew drinking, buddy?"

"I'll take a pop."

In the meantime, I didn't have a clue who was talking to me.

"Gotcha covered."

I looked around in bewilderment, wondering who had said that and where he was. Just then, a can of Coke appeared on the bar and mysteriously slid toward me.

"Hey buddy, dat's on Aloysie," came the voice again, this time distinguishable from behind the bar. As I sat there and watched, other beers magically appeared and disappeared from the bar. Money was traded in a similar fashion, with only brief appearances of flesh.

Aloysie walked up to me with a glass of tapped beer in hand.

"Did PeeWee set 'chew up?"

Aloyzie looked at my can of soda with disgust. "He should have filled er up with Ethel!"

"Yea, thanks. Actually a pop's fine. After all, I'm just a kid."

"Dat's PeeWee Krunk. The best barkeep in Arcadia. Dare are some big shots out dare dat go to college, pass dat dare BAR exam, den don't eben know how ta pour a mixed drink. I don't know where PeeWee studied, but one ting is fer sure. When you say "whisky sour, ta-dee fingers worth," guess what ingredients PeeWee pours in ta-dee fingers high?"

"Well, I bet it isn't the sour."

"You're bettin right!"

"Wow, what a bartender!"

"Ya Hey."

"Yes sir. Sure is."

"Ya Hey."

"OK then. Ahh, maybe we should head back to work."

"Well, let's grab dat fuser and head back to da mill. You can take your pop which yous."

"Sounds good."

The trip back to the mill was uneventful, with Aloysie stopping only twice to check that right front tire. Back at ground zero, Aloysie welded the iron wheel plate back onto the hoist, once again making it "truck worthy." He quickly loaded the welding equipment back into his truck bed, then strolled over to the office in order to invoice Dad. Dad had his head stuck in the crusty refrigerator located at the far end of the narrow office.

"Aloysie, do you want a bottle of pop?"

"Better not drink on da job," Aloysie snorted. "Besides, I gotta get back to da office. You know, bookwork."

Aloysie glanced at me and winked, as if he didn't want anyone else to know about his office environment.

Dad gave Aloysie a check which he put in his truck driver wallet, suspended from his bib overalls.

"Tanks, and when anyting breaks, give me a holler. Number's on da receipt."

Aloysie then bolted for the door as if someone called out "free beer." Dad gazed down at the pink receipt and chuckled.

"Here's some Arcadia marketing," Dad said with a sparkle in his eye, placing the pink slip on the counter. I instinctively sprang out of my chair and perused the paper. I couldn't help but smile as I read the bold face print at the bottom of the sheet.

"If something's broke, and you're feeling needy, you don't have to run to Petey. Just call Aloysie, and he'll come your way. He'll weld that piece while you're baling hay."

Pretty seasonal, I thought, but it sure related.

"Well, let's call er a day. Why don't you go lock up the salt shed, wheel in the bag conveyer, and if no one comes in by then, we'll go home," Dad said while studying his watch.

I didn't have to be told twice as I headed for the shed. I finished my duties and met John at the front door, just as he fixed the padlock and snapped it closed.

"We'll see each other in the morning, good Lord willing," John said, which was his usual closing remark. John brushed the feed off of his long shirtsleeves and strolled to his car.

Another day at the mill was in the books.

Chapter V

The summer was passing quickly, and it was the morning of my ninth birthday. Mom was getting used to the family and was making a concerted effort to be like a mom to all of us. Since it was my birthday, she had baked a cake, and I even received a few presents. My parents gave me a speedometer for my bicycle, and Dad gave me the day off from working at the mill. As I was installing the speedometer on my bicycle, I thought back to my seven-year birthday present that I had received in Elmwood as if it were yesterday.

It was suppertime, and Mom had ordered me to go out to the garage in order to dispose of a tin can. In order to keep peace, I got up from the kitchen table and raced to the garage with it. I opened the side garage door, and to my surprise, there stood a black Schwinn bicycle in front of the big steel garbage can. My older siblings had followed me out to the garage in order to view the excitement, while my parents patiently waited at the table.

A quick test ride was mandatory, thinking that since it was my birthday, I probably wouldn't get grounded for interrupting supper. Due to the extraordinary weight of the bike, acceleration was modest at best. But after driving my legs as hard as I could, I was soon sailing past Bob Peterson's house, a feat that took five times as long on foot. I never stopped peddling until the bread delivery truck pulled out in front of me from an alley. I pushed back on the brakes, only to be catapulted forward from a reverse kick that occurred from the attempted brake action. My feet were thrown free of the pedals, causing me to straddle the bar that differentiated the sex of the bike. The delivery truck came to a sudden stop, while I chose the ditch, and rode it, keeping my balance like a Shriner riding a motorcycle in a slow moving parade. Once this steel tank slowed to a stop, I recomposed myself, shaking from the experience. My excitement from receiving this precious gift was slightly curbed. I knew that if I told anyone about the lack of brakes, Dad wouldn't let me ride it until they were repaired. And I knew that he would never get around to repairing them, so mum was the word. Anyway, who needed brakes, I thought. My first inclination was to go, not stop. I'll worry about stopping when the time comes.

This bicycle opened up my whole word. I could now be even more mobile, able to get from the center of Elmwood to anywhere that I needed to go in a flash. It allowed me to spend even more time away from my family. I could now get across town in a couple of minutes, able to visit my friends no matter how remote they were. But mostly I would ride just to occupy my mind. Being constantly on the run was my defense mechanism to avoid distracting thoughts and emotions. Taking in the redundant sights became one of my favorite pass times.

The telephone clamored inside the house, interrupting my daydreaming. Mom came out and relayed a message from Dad.

"Imy, Dad asked if you want to calibrate your new speedometer and assure that it really is three miles from our house to the mill."

Well, at least the thought was there to giving me the day off, and I could appreciate that, I thought. But I knew that he was busy and could use the help. And after all, he did buy the speedometer, so I caved and headed right to the mill.

Over the summer, I had met both of the neighbors and a number of farmers at the feed mill. I had my first lawn mowing job for the farmer who lived just to the south of us, Lambert Walski. The Walski's had a huge lawn, and it took me five-and-a-half hours to cut it. It was sure worth it, though, when the time came to collect that dollar bill, after a twenty-minute inspection. A buck for all of that work didn't appear to be a lot of money. On the other hand, it could buy twenty "Snickers" Bars.

Although I spent most of the summer working, I really enjoyed it. I didn't have the network of friends that existed in Elmwood, so I passed most of my free time hiking in the cow pasture. I also spent a vast amount of time riding my bicycle without brakes. Once I got my speedometer, I rode all over the area recording the mileage to give my mind a little more diversion over the same monotonous courses. I would measure how far I could ride in an allotted time period, then turn around to see if I could better my time.

One evening I was riding home from Ronnie Grewchowski's farm. I had been watching the odometer for most of the way, paying little attention to the road. When I got home, I walked in the house to see a much familiar sight. Dad was sitting in the brown chair reading the paper, and Ruth was sitting on the couch reading a book. Mom, Linda, and Betsy were upstairs. I stood in the doorway, sticking my thumbs in my ears and wiggling my fingers, trying to make Ruth laugh. I realized that it was nothing more than a wasted effort. I stopped the monkeyshines and walked into the room.

"You know, I just crossed the one-thousand mile mark on my bike."

Ruth lowered her book, then propped it up again, as if I woke her from sleep.

"And you're still here," Dad said, never flinching from behind his newspaper.

Now I guess that you could take that comment two ways. But I took it the positive way, feeling good that at least Dad acknowledged me.

I had grown accustomed to the negative personal comments he offered. Just a week earlier, Dad and I were downstairs in the filthy cellar trying to repair the inoperable blower motor. The basement was accessed through a hole in the feed mill floor by an ancient wooden staircase, seemingly slapped together with wood scraps and glue. The pit was pitch dark, illuminated by a single trouble light plugged into a frayed extension cord. Feed dust crusted this underbelly, literally sprinkled everywhere. Loose ground feed was piled over five feet thick along the walls, diminishing to mere inches along an obvious single path connecting the staircase to the grinder motors.

I was holding the iron casing surrounding the electrical input to the mammoth power plant, while Dad loosened the final bolt that had kept the shroud in place. He had just cleared the flower from around the area when my boot gave way from the shear weight of the massive iron piece. Feed dust dribbled earthward, eroding away one of the newly formed mounds. The pulp flowed, covering the final bolt that was keeping the protecting case prisoner.

"I just cleaned that! Do something useful. Run upstairs and grab a screwdriver. Quick! And while you're up there, grab a shovel so you can scoop more feed into the motor!"

I snapped to attention and immediately obeyed the order. I sprinted up the rickety steps, two at a time. I scrambled over to the grinder control switch, which was next to the bird-poop stained window, overlooking the grinder-pad. On the sill lay four assorted screwdrivers. The Phillip's head could be used for just that, Phillip's screws. Three standard drivers accompanied the Phillip's, all of various sizes. In retrospect, I should have grabbed all four, but I figured that since Dad was working on a big motor, he needed a large screwdriver. Anything smaller might make my ignorance audible. I nabbed the big one and flew down the plank staircase. When I got downstairs, Dad had removed the cast-iron cover from the electrical source. He was studying the tiny jeweler screw that had to be loosened in order to disconnect a wire. I froze, knowing that I had selected the improper tool for the job. Dad stared at my selection while frustration filled his face.

"Is that the biggest screwdriver you could find?"

I bolted back upstairs, taking a little more time. Out of sight, out of mind, I thought.

Learning from past experiences, I graciously accepted any comment I could garner from Dad that didn't involve tension, no matter how derogatory they often were.

Chapter VI

The summer was over, and it was time to get educated. After all, you couldn't leave it up to the farmers at the feed mill, although most of them thought they had all of the answers. It was back to school for the three older kids, leaving Dad a man short at the feed mill, so he hired a man to replace me, and I anxiously waited to see if he'd be a good one.

Baraheep was a young strapping guy, appearing to be in his late 20's. Where he got the nickname, Baraheep, was beyond me. He wasn't the sharpest knife in the drawer, in fact, quite the opposite. It wasn't long after I met him that I realized I had to finish his stories. He would start out with a concocted fairy-tail, get about a quarter-way through and then struggle to continue. Since it was a new relationship, I wanted to remain friendly and didn't want to make waves, so I decided to help.

Once the word got out to some of my pals about this guy, they would ride their bikes down to the mill in order to checkout the "entertainment." My buddy, John Gamoke, was the first to stop by for a free show. Baraheep had just completed his tale of having a fast '65 Chevy when he was in high school. Now it was the fall of 1966, and Baraheep was in his late 20's. So when you run the math, his age and automobile vintage didn't add up, but, then again, neither did most of his stories.

Anyway, he was elaborating about how he would constantly race up and down Main Street in his hometown. Then he'd slow down just to tantalize the policemen. John was pretending to be on the edge of his seat, waiting to see if he finally got caught or simply sped away. That's when Baraheep got stuck. He didn't even know how to finish his fantasy. John kept quizzing him, grilling him like a cheap ambulance-chasing lawyer. Baraheep started to fidget, looking to me for help.

"Tell John about the license plate!" I offered.

Baraheep looked over at me with a vacant gaze. Judging from his lack of expression, I thought that I'd better cover for the guy, and quick!

"Tell John how you had a piece of string attached to a tin plate just above your rear license plate and how you'd pull it when the cop got right behind you."

"Yeah," Baraheep mumbled, with a mouth-watering grin.

"Then the tin plate would fall over top of the license plate, just as the cop was proceeding to take your license number. The tin plate had "I'M GONE" printed in bold letters. Then you'd peel out, leaving the cop in the dust with no plate number."

"Yeah," Baraheep exclaimed, preening so violently that drool started spilling down his chin, plopping on his work boot below.

John sneered at the logical incongruities.

"How did you hide from the cops all those years in that tiny little town?"

"See, they saw the fake plate, not the real one," I interrupted, starting to feel sorry for Baraheep under the intense cross-examination.

"But they had to know the make and color of the car. How many other cars like that could there be in that little town?"

"Uhh uhh. Like Imy said, I'd pull the tin, and the string would go down."

"You mean, the other way around there," I said, trying to nonchalantly correct a nervous Baraheep.

"Yea, like he said."

John gleamed and started going for the kill.

"But, how many '65 Chevy's were really around in 1955, especially in that small of town?"

I could tell John was toying with him, which meant that it was time for John to go. I always thought that if a man wants to tell a story, take it as such. Use it as entertainment, not fact. And besides, I hated conflict. Any conflict.

"Well Baraheep, I think we had better get back in there and clean out the back room that Dad mentioned was starting to clutter up."

"He didn't say anything to me about it, Imy."

Here he was, fighting for his life, and he didn't have the where-with-all to even grab for the life preserver.

John let out a sigh that caught my attention, then winked.

"I better get going. The bike ride back ain't gonna be any easier."

After walking John to his bike, Baraheep came up and started telling us how he had a bike just like John's with a car motor on it.

"I'd' love to hear this one, but I gotta go," John said with a grin. "See ya tomorrow, Imy."

Chapter VII

Finally, things seemed to be coming together in this new lease on life. Dad was doing well financially, netting almost eight thousand dollars annually. This was more money than we were accustomed to and felt that we finally made the big time. Several factors indicated that money was no longer a problem. One was that Mom had started to buy grapefruit, something only the wealthy ate. Another was that we got to throw away the rest of that twenty-pound bag of powdered milk in lieu of the real stuff. And the real sign of affluence was the fact that we were being sent to the Catholic school up on the hill.

My parents were Catholic. I mean, my parents were really Catholic. Arcadia, as a whole, is predominately Catholic. There were a total of four churches in Arcadia, two Catholic, one Lutheran, and one Presbyterian - which never had its lawn mowed. The Lutheran church had a small congregation, and the Presbyterian Church closed down about three years after we moved into the area. The two Catholic churches were located two blocks from each other, which never seemed to make much logistical sense to me.

St. Stanislaus Catholic Church was located on top of the hill, overlooking "Our Lady Of Perpetual Help," which was located at the bottom. "St. Stan's," as we called it, was made up of a predominately Polish congregation, while "OLPH" consisted of a mainly German population. Each church had their own elementary school connected to it, serving grades 1-8. There was no kindergarten offered in the area. The people were firm believers that they didn't have to send their children to school in order to have them take naps. Each school ran completely independent of the other with each school day ending at staggered times in order to curtail kids from getting into after-school fights. Since my Uncle Tony was the hospital chaplain supported by St. Stan's parish, we chose St. Stan's church even though we were of German decent.

48

School was about as good as school could be. The building sat on top of the hill and was a two-story, square brick schoolhouse. The two rooms on each floor were split down the middle by a wooden staircase, enabling access to all four rooms. This same staircase was used to access the basement where the restrooms were located. Each nun was responsible for teaching two grades. These close confines made it easy to meet people, and being from the farm, I needed pals.

In no time, I had gotten to know my classmates, and it was very important to me that they all became my friends. I suppose that my non-existent family relationships drove me to turn acquaintances into friendships, converting them into my "family." After all, it was pretty hard finding love and companionship with two older sisters who hung together, a step-mom who spent most of her time being infatuated with her little daughter and a dad who was totally emotionally detached, period.

To kindle these new relationships, I would ride my bike on weekends to my buddies' farms and help them milk their cows or just hang around. In most instances this many mile trek was accomplished before eight o'clock on a Saturday morning. This ritual began when I was about seven years old, living in Elmwood. Most of the time I felt like a "fifth wheel" to my family. I would keep myself scarce and run with all of my friends, often going over to their houses so early on Saturday mornings that I would wake up their dogs. Every house except my house was where I wanted to be. I would end up talking to my friend's parents while they were stumbling around trying to locate the coffee scoop. I would listen intently and act interested in their lives, so much that they would share with me many family secrets. I don't think they ever caught on that all I wanted was for them to like me. Even if they were slow to respond, I could always get a cookie or piece of pie out of them. Pleasing other people's parents was so easy, yet so impossible with mine.

Late that fall, our school had parent/teacher conferences, which gave students an extra Thursday and Friday off. Dad had given me a reprieve from the mill on Friday, so I could go into town with Mom and the girls to get my hair cut. I had been saving my corn de-tassling money since the summer and decided to finally spend some of that sixteen dollars that I had bankrolled. One day, I spotted a football in the hardware catalogue and had designated a five-dollar bill to purchase it. I had been kicking around the same cardboard box, pretending that it was a football, for several months now. It served the purpose, especially for kicking, but the throwing part was always a challenge. Since I had no one to toss it to anyway, the box sufficed. I couldn't wait to get to the hardware store to make my most major purchase.

The last ball that I had actually kicked was a couple of months ago at Wally Waletzko's farm. Dad and I had just delivered a load of feed on this beautiful Saturday afternoon. Once the feed was augured into the galvanized bulk-bin, Dad went into the house to drop off the sales slip. As usual, I sat in the cab of the truck and waited. It wasn't as bad waiting for a couple of hours when the weather was tepid. But when it was the middle of winter, now that was a different story. The drill was always the same. First, I would observe the interaction between Dad and the barnyard dog and store it into memory. If the canine appeared not to be flesh-eating, I would jump out of the truck on the half-hour and run around until my toes would tingle, reminding me that those two frozen ice blocks supporting me were actually blood-receiving appendages. But this day was gorgeous, and after an hour of staring at the hog barn, I thought a grand tour might be in order. I hopped out of the cab and meandered around the chicken coop. A large rust-colored rubber ball caught my eye, freezing me in my tracks. I made a beeline for it, keeping an eye on the front porch of the farmhouse that Dad had disappeared into. I bounced the ball on the gravel drive to gauge the amount of air pressure inside.

The hot sun had warmed its internal air, making this rubber sphere ripe for kicking. I lobbed it in front of me, planted my left leg and launched the ball skyward. After orbiting under it for a few seconds, the round object increased in size until it ended up in my awaiting arms. Without hesitation, I offered the clay colored ball again, this time sending it over a telephone wire suspended by a pole on the roof of the house. After chasing it down, I saw Dad and Wally on the front porch out of the corner of my eye. Dad was carrying on, using his hand jesters while a patient Wally looked my way. Finally, I had an audience. I needed my best kick for this one. I focused on the ball, concentrating as my plant leg dug in straight and hard into the shale. The ball made a thump sound as it left my right foot. My form was perfect, and I never took my eye off the target. The round, mound of rubber streaked skyward, eluding gravity for a few seconds before it rounded off and stopped in mid air, some twenty feet above the roofline.

"Look at that kick!" exclaimed Wally. "That kid has some leg."

"Now cut that out before you break it!" was the curt retort from a scowling Dad, visibly upset from being interrupted.

I caught the ball after one bounce, placing it gently back in the weeds alongside the chicken coop, right where I found it.

Once again, stupid me was fishing for attention, and received it bathed in anger.

"Mom, let's go to the store first, because I know right where that football is, and it won't take but a minute."

"Well, let's all start with haircuts, then as soon as you're done, you can run across the street to the store."

We pulled up in front of The Beauty Nook and parked. I gazed across the street to see how many people were in Petrick's Barber Shop. There was a glare reflecting off of the bay window from the morning sun, so it was tough to get a perfect count. It appeared as if there were two people waiting, which could be an eternity.

There were two barbers in Arcadia, both on the same side of Main Street about a block from each other. Roman Petrick and Ifner Glanchinski were the two town "coiffeurs," who were total opposites of each other. Roman Petrick was an old bald man, and after all, what did a bald man know about hair styling? I had been going to Roman Petrick since we moved to Arcadia, mainly because he had very few customers and was always available. Roman was known to cut hair until the next guy came in, and with his slow customer stream, it wasn't unusual for a person to be in the chair for a couple of hours. Ifner Glanchinski, on the other hand, was in his late thirties and talked nonstop about everything, especially cars. Ifner had the gift of gab down so well that it was a familiar sight to walk past his shop and see him with scissors in hand standing at the bay window alongside a customer donned in a barber bib, referring to a car.

That was the reason that Dad never set foot in Glanchinski's Barbershop. Ifner was the town gossip, always wanting to know everything about everybody. Word had it, once he got you in his chair, he would interrogate you until you cracked, otherwise he would leave you with crooked sideburns. But with kids it was different. We didn't care what he knew or what he wanted to know. It was just cool to have him cut your hair basically, because he would give it his best attempt to cut it the way you wanted it.

"Mom, I'm going to go into Glanchinski's today. Roman has at least three people in front of me, and I want to get home tonight."

"Well, Vernon's mom said that her son went there one time. When Vernon got home, she told him to get back there so that Ifner could finish what he started."

"Well, can I try him, just this once?"

"Well, just don't tell Dad, and don't go telling him all of our business. He doesn't need to know it."

"You mean the feed mill business?"

"You know what I mean. You know, our business. He doesn't have to know that I'm your stepmother. Stuff like that just doesn't have to be let out."

"Uhh, OK."

"But make sure he takes enough off to please Dad."

"OK."

Great! I thought. Finally, I get to go where the cool guys go.

I ran into the shop and took my place next to the window. Ifner was standing there cutting on a weathered-looking man. Next to him was another barber chair with a guy sitting in it. Another guy was sitting on a chair next to me, reading a car magazine. One of the paneled shop walls was plastered with hair licenses and diplomas, while another had magazine cutouts of assorted cars, dangling from tape. The main wall was adorned with wooden ducks sporting tin wings. A two-tiered shelf rested below this nature conservatory supporting a few shaving products for sale.

Ifner was an average looking man with greasy black hair parted on the side. It was combed straight and draped over his eye opposite the part. Periodically, he would shake his head violently to the side in order to create a vision path for both eyes.

Ifner seemed to speed up the process once I entered the establishment, seemingly because I had taken the last chair. In a flash the customer was granted a pardon from the chair, and the heavy-set balding man took his place moving over from the spare.

"So Eugene, still driving dat antique? Isn't it tough finding square tires fer dat ting?"

"Hey Ifner, as soon as I get my mail-order haircut license, I'll upgrade!"

"Ya hey. Us barbers are rich! How do you want it cut today, Eugene?"

"Well, why don't you shave half of my head, cut it crooked up-top, den take what's left on da udder side and plaster it ober da top."

"What kind of haircut is dat?"

"Hey I don't know, but dat's what yous gave me last time!"

"Haaa… hey Eugene, you're not only losing more hair, but you're gittin funnier. Maybe you'll be a comedian when you're bald!"

After the bantering slowed, Ifner's mood began to grow serious. Ifner glanced my way as if to welcome, or at least acknowledge me.

"Hi partner, haircut today?"

"Yes sir."

"So now, who do yous belong to?"

"Arnie Lecheler."

"Dat's right. Yous bought da feed mill, not?"

"Yes, that's right."

"Heard you paid cash fer it."

"That I wouldn't know."

"So, where did yous guys used ta live?"

"Elmwood. It's a little town about seventy miles away."

"Are you sure? I heard Eau Gaullee."

"We were seven miles from Eau Gaullee."

"I heard dat yous guys owned a big elevator up dare."

Now, here I was, not even close to the chair, and I'm getting drilled. I could leave, but I knew my chances of having enough time to get my football after a Roman Petrick haircut were less than slim to none. I thought I better not divulge any important information. This shouldn't be too hard to do since he acted as though he didn't believe anything that I told him anyway.

An hour later, I was all talked out, and Ifner was all listened out. After my cut, I glanced in the mirror, checking to see if I could tell a difference. I know Dad would never notice, but Mom sure would. I paid Ifner and bolted for the door. Without a moment to lose, I ran across Main Street to buy my new football.

Meanwhile, two of my fourth grade classmates, Oscar Bratski and Mel Woub, decided to take a shotgun out behind the feed mill and hunt squirrels. It was about three o'clock on Friday afternoon when Oscar came running down the steep wooded hill behind the concrete plant.

"Help, help, Mel's been shot!"

John started to jog up the hill behind the Ready Mix plant with Dad in hot pursuit. A few seconds later, Dad passed John and screamed out to him to call the ambulance.

Dad sprinted up the dirt road leading back into the woods with Oscar screaming behind him. Twenty minutes later, Dad came running down the dirt road with Mel slung over his shoulder. Dad's right fist was stuck in Mel's belly to stop the bleeding. He had used his shirt for a tourniquet, but due to the size of the wound, the tourniquet proved useless.

Dad slung Mel into the waiting ambulance as if he were a sack of feed. Then he went down to the creek and washed off the blood. That night, Dad never mentioned a word about the incident. That was just the way he was, emotionless. It wasn't until the following Monday in school that I even found out that Mel had been shot and killed.

"Imy, I heard your dad tried to save Mel, but he just didn't run fast enough."

"Save him from what?"

"Save him from bleeding."

"Why, did he cut himself?"

"He was shot last Friday. Didn't you hear about it?"

"No. But I live out on the farm and don't get to talk to too many people."

"Well, it happened right behind the mill, and your dad carried him down the hill to the ambulance, so you'd think that you would have heard something about it!"

"My dad?"

"Yes, your dad!"

"Whoa."

After a brief interrogation, I exited the conversation, storing all the data in my head. I braced myself for the barrage of questioning that was imminent from my classmates. By midday, I had all the answers to what had happened that fateful day, but it was a vacant feeling, trying to be the proud son of a person who was hailed as a hero, even though I had no clue who this hero was or how he ticked.

The shock of Mel's death made me wonder why God spared some people and called others. While living in Elmwood, I had a close call that should have been fatal. I guess that it just wasn't my time to die.

I was six years old, and it was a winter day the week after Christmas. My friends had come over to pick me up to go sledding.

"Now don't go sledding down the alleys," Mom yelled as I brushed past her. I did the obligatory "OK, Mom" as I walked out the door.

The alleys in Elmwood were seldom used, making them a good path to sled down. The challenge was that the alleys ran perpendicular to the streets. In order to keep your momentum, you had to shoot across a street or two. This calculated risk was reduced by sledding on the East Side of town, mainly because there was less traffic, and that's where the steepest grade was located.

I totally disregarded Mom's heed to caution and followed my friends to the top of the hill on the East Side of town. I looked down the desolate alley as if it were an Olympic luge track.

I hollered over to Greg Seiler as I ran with my sled before slamming it down and jumping on top.

"See ya at the bottom!"

As I picked up speed, I knew that I was quickly approaching the first cross street. I glanced over to my right and saw nothing but snow covered road. Over to the left, I saw nothing but a hedge, totally obstructing my view of the road. I quickly calculated the odds of traffic on this lonely road, and dismissed the possibility due to the undisturbed snow. As I proceeded to shoot across the street, I heard a muffling sound and noticed a lack of sunlight. I pulled hard on my sled runner and skidded to a stop after crossing the road. I jumped up to the sight of a shrieking woman sprinting from her blue International 4-wheel drive pickup toward me.

"Oh my God, are you alright?"

"Yea," I said, beaming from the attention.

She shook violently and continued to scream.

"I ran right over you. You're so lucky to be alive!"

"Wow," I said, looking back up the alley at the kids staring down at us.

"Thanks for stopping, but I'm OK."

I nonchalantly jumped back on my sled and continued the ride downhill. After a hundred feet or so, I stopped and began to feel this lady's emotion. For once, emotion sunk in, and I started feeling sort of sorry for her. This complete stranger was yelling at me, but not because she was mad at me. Her shrill voice and rattled nerves were evidence of her care for my well-being. This was a rare occurrence for me, since I was accustomed to emotion displayed in anger, not love. I didn't mean to put her through this, I thought.

Back at the top of the hill, my friends told me how I slid underneath the truck, just missing the front tires. I had enough speed to exit before the rear wheels made hamburger out of my legs. I felt pretty cool thinking what a circus act I had just performed. What were the odds of perfectly timing this sled and maneuvering it under a moving pickup truck? First, speed of both vehicles had to be synchronized. Any swerve or deviation of path would have been fatal. Second, this feat could not have been accomplished without proper clearance. In order to achieve that, the vehicle had to be a high-clearance vehicle, and very few of these existed before the SUV days. Now, there was only one 4-wheel drive pickup in the whole town of Elmwood, owned by Mrs. Gene Radke.

When I got to my house, I saw the dreaded 4-wheeler parked right in front of our place. Usually this would be a grand sight, thinking that I could actually get a good peek inside of the cab for once. But this afternoon would be different. Once in the door, I was confronted by Mom and Mrs. Gene Radkey. Mom hugged me and said, "Kid, God must love you, because you could have been killed."

After again sharing the story with the family, Mrs. Gene Radkey left.

I walked upstairs to my room, actually feeling, for once, a little warmth on a cold winter day. I finally felt that not only God loved me, but deep down, so did everybody else.

Chapter VIII

I had been around the area for about a year now and had some opportunity to explore Arcadia and the surrounding area.

Arcadia had a population of 2,094 people and just received "city" status for recently surpassing 2,000 people. It nestled between Hooterville and Tammarack, just this side of Square Bluff, which is three miles north of Nuecume Valley. Wamandee is to the West, and the twin cities, Dodge and Pinecreek, are located southwest of town. Pinecreek was the smaller of the two with a couple of houses, a church and two taverns. Dodge boasted a population of almost 300 with five taverns.

Arcadia is a long narrow town, divided into four segments. The east-end of town referred to as the "top of the hill" was on a slightly higher elevation. Traveling westward down Main Street was the "below the hill" area. This was the gateway to the "downtown" district.

Downtown consisted of two-story storefronts lining the main drag through town. This ribbon of asphalt continued on for over a half mile before terminating at a T in the road up at the Broiler Plant. Massure's Shopping Center, a three-store consortium that housed a Ben Franklin store, Skodmo's and Herick's Clothier framed Main Street. The shopping center and no less than ten taverns flanked this street that connected the East Side of town to the West Side.

Exiting downtown on a westward route was the old River Bridge that spanned the Trempealeau River for which the county is named. The area across the river was descriptively known as "across the river."

The town sat nestled in a valley, visible from all points around. Traveling northbound out of town three miles along the river on County A brought you to Three-Mile Bridge. This landmark was a corroded bridge spanning the Trempealeau River. Three more miles ahead, was Six-Mile Bridge. I never measured this distance, but it took twice as long to get from downtown out to Six-Mile Bridge than out to Three-Mile Bridge, so I assumed the distance was fairly accurate. Ten miles north of Arcadia was the town of Independence. Independence had just barely received "town" stature with only 1,000 people and nine bars. Believe it or not, Independence gave the impression of severe inbreeding. One slogan on a bar read, "I'd rather have a bottle in front of me than a frontal lobotomy."

Well, they appeared to have both.

There were a total of fourteen bars in Arcadia, one for every 140 people. Since half of the population were children, well, let's just say that there was no problem finding a barstool to sit on.

Since Arcadia was the metropolis of the county, it seemed to be a Mecca for cultural amenities. Its biggest attraction was the Deer Park located on the West Side of town. It was flanked by the Parkeralla Restaurant and Echo's Implement "Buy Of The Week" farming implement corral. Each week another rusty farm implement was showcased within this tiny barbwire confine.

The farm implement dealership was owned by Coon Sharlow. He would saunter unassumingly behind a prospective customer, eyeing the weekly special. I finally understood why Octi used to sing the Cat Stevens' song at the mill, then pause to laugh.

"I'm being followed by a Coon Sharlow, Coon Sharlow, Coon Sharlow...."

The Deer Park was a 75 by 100-foot wire pen with a tiny dilapidated hut and one deer. There was never more than one deer in it, and I really never quite understood the attraction since you could travel a half-mile out into the country and see nothing but deer. Anyway, people would come to the park and picnic, maybe because it had the only two working public barbecue grills in town. Or maybe people would come just to sit on the banks of the Trempealeau River and look at the sand bar. I don't recall anyone in Arcadia knowing where the Trempealeau River started, but we all knew that it flowed into the Mississippi River at Trempealeau, Wisconsin. The Trempealeau River was so shallow that the locals claimed that the fish had to swim sideways. Occasionally carp would run aground along the banks and be found rotting there. The odor enhanced the picnic experience, stamping a lasting imprint on one's mind.

I would say that the second "tourist trap" in Arcadia was the Lion's Head Drinking Fountain in the middle of town on Main Street. Whenever the family went for a Sunday car ride, we would stop there for a drink. Sticking your head in there to get a drink was quite a risk, and we would dare each other to do it until Dad hollered "enough" from the car.

The best place to eat? Now that was a toss-up. You had the bowling alley, featuring Adolph Chitco's concoction of "Henny Penny Chicken," the Parkeralla and Club 93. You guessed it, out on Highway 93. For ambiance, you had to go with the Parkeralla, mainly because "ambiance" to an Arcadian meant getting a booth next to the wooden ducks mounted on the wall. Not only did it have full views of Deer Park, but the homey atmosphere made you feel like you never left the kitchen, bringing calm even to the most intimidated dining customer.

Located just fifteen miles northeast of Arcadia was the small town of Whitehall, the county seat. I never understood why Arcadia wasn't chosen because of its large populace and urban feel. Why, Arcadia was double the size of Whitehall and was the largest city in Trempealeau County. I honestly believed Whitehall was selected because of its name, since it was the only sophisticated sounding one around.

Eleva was located just up the road apiece, and I had always wanted to know how it got its name. Viewed from the county road, I noticed that the city name was painted off-centered in black letters on a big silver water tower. The name was shifted over to the left, as if they were going to put a logo or other form of art to the right of it.

Dad and I stopped in the tiny village one time to check out one of the many Saturday afternoon auctions. While Dad stopped in town to use the bathroom, I decided to get a better look at the water tower and possibly find out why the name was left of center. I exited the car in order to get a better view. Spotting a man window shopping, I decided to ask him if he knew the history behind this phenomenon. He appeared to be an upstanding, life-long citizen, a bulky man in his sixties. He was using both hands to shield the sun in order to get a better view of the contents inside the store. At first, I thought he was probably staring in the storefront window checking out the price tag on that pretty dress for his wife. This "Norman Rockwell" image was shattered as I took a few steps closer. The man was actually standing outside of Norm's Bar pressing his nose against the picture window trying to make his buddy inside laugh.

"Sir?"

"Just a minute, let's see if Ansel looks over here. Com'mon Ansel, come to pappy, come to pappy old boy, come to…"

"Sir, I have just a quick question for you."

The man never changed his stance, remaining hunched over and peering into the dark bay window with both hands cupped around his face.

"His name is Ansel, and I get him on this every Saturday. I'll go walking by here and first get the bartender's attention. Then he'll tap Ansel on the shoulder, and I usually duck, unless the arthritis in my knee is bad, then I'll just turn around quick. Before you know it, Ansel is so frazzled. Then I go in and have a beer with him. Funnier than hell, not?"

"Ahh, yea, I guess."

"Well, I guess he ain't playing today. Wait a minute. That ain't Ansel, either!"

I started to walk back to the car when the red-faced man approached me, eagerly putting distance between the window and himself.

"Now, what was the question?"

"Well, how did the town of Eleva get its name?"

"For the first hundred years or so, the town had no name. Then about fifty years ago, the first grain elevator was built right smack downtown. Since the grain elevator provided some money for the construction of the water tower, the elevator owners decided to paint the word "Elevator" on the silver structure that served as a beacon for farmers tens of miles away. The elevator employee went up to start painting, and it started to rain. Story has it that it rained for four days. Now, I know that is ten times less than the big one of Noah's day, but regardless, one thing led to another, and the guy left the elevator due to a work-related dispute several weeks later. The two remaining employees were older and not "risk takers." The tower remains today, just like the name of the town, Eleva."

"Wow, thanks."

Dad walked back to the car, greeting me with an angry scowl.

"I just asked the guy how Eleva go it's name."

"You talk too much. Get back in the car."

Chapter IX

The early morning spring dew sparkled on the weeds alongside the corncrib as Dad and I pulled into the feed mill. We had no sooner opened the schoolhouse office than a meat delivery truck pulled up in the dirt parking lot along side of the mill. Dolf Sikowski jumped from the cab of the truck and headed over to the schoolhouse porch where we were standing. Dolf was the previous owner of the feed mill and had decided to supplement his retirement driving a meat truck several days a week. Dolf was a slender built man, about 60 years of age. He was fun to be around, always seeing the lighter side of life.

"Arnie, yous guys gonna be busy today?"

"We're always busy."

"Busy working, or busy doing nutin?"

"Well, I hope busy working."

"Well, I've got da short route today and was wondering if da boy wanted to ride along, jis ta see some country, you know."

Dad fumbled with the key trying to unlock the office door, pretending to be so consumed with the process that he didn't hear the question.

"Besides, yous know Onalaska is puttin' up dat tousand footer to boost dare signals."

"A thousand feet of what?"

"Dat tower in Onalaska. Dare puttin it up fer da TV station, and I guess some farm bureau microwave stuff. Anyway, I go past dare every week, and I tought dat da boy would like to see dat dare son of a biscuit."

"Well, when would you be back? I can't have him gone all day."

"No, we'll be back forenoon. And if he's good, I'll even bring 'em back in one piece."

"Well, OK. Imy, behave yourself!"

"Wow, thanks Dad! I'll really work hard when I get back!"

I was so excited because Dolf was a prankster, not as serious as my Dad was. I scrambled over to the green refrigerated truck and jumped in the cab.

The first thing that I noticed besides the bright green interior was that the truck smelled like sausage. I don't know if the odor was imbedded into the cloth seats or was coming from the back, but it was prevalent. It definitely smelled like meat.

Dolf jumped in behind the wheel and fired up the big olive-colored cruiser. In a couple of minutes we were heading on County Road T.

"Dolf, doesn't the constant smell of meat all day make you hungry? I mean, smelling nothing but baloney with only a hint of diesel exhaust makes my stomach growl."

"Yea, but ya know, you kinda get used ta it, much like a chef in a fancy restaurant."

"What do you think about when you drive this truck all day? I know my mind roams so freely, my thoughts would be all over the place."

"Well, I don't tink about much, mainly cause I stop at a lot of stores and talk to everyone. Lot of times, I'll eben stop and talk to da farmers out in da field. Wit all dat talkin, I don't have too much fer tinking."

A few minutes later, Dolf slowed up and pulled over to the side of the county road. I could see a big dirt cloud with a shinny object leading it as if it were pulling this cloud of dirt behind.

"Dare's not a lot of people I'll waist time talkin ta, but Geo Kouljak always has someting to say. I mean, he doesn't talk a lot, but what he says has a lot of 'meat' ta it. Get it? Meat?"

Dolf pulled the big green reefer off to the side of the narrow road and waited patiently. We both gazed as the shinny object drew closer, as if we were in awe of a UFO. A few minutes later, Dolf tapped the horn. Geo acknowledged with a horn blast of his own from the tractor, with Dolf tapping his horn again in return. Geo hit his horn "honk, honk-honk-honk-honk," with Dolf responding with a "honk-honk" back. Boy, how I couldn't wait to hear this conversation between these two mental heavyweights.

Dolf bounced out of the truck, and I followed, walking up to the barbwire fence. Geo had just put his soiled cap over his face with the bill of his cap pointing straight up in the air. With total control of the steering wheel delegated to his knees, Geo held both arms in the air straight ahead, as if he were steering his tractor with an imaginary wheel. This site got Dolf going, who then proceeded to turn around, facing backside toward the field. Dolf reversed his cap and put his glasses on backwards to give the impression that he was still facing the field. Moments later, Geo must have seen me through the vent holes of his cap because he suddenly put his cap on correctly and began to noticeably blush. Geo pulled up along the fence and reduced the tractor's throttle.

"Looks like yous got company."

"Yep," Dolf said, endorsing the observation. "Dis is Imy. His dad bought da mill from me."

Geo returned with a completely blank stare, either in disbelief, or he just didn't know what to say. I looked down at the gravel on the side of the road as if I was studying a precious stone. It seemed that my being here threw everything off, and I could tell Geo was uncomfortable with my company.

"What 'chew up to lately, Geo?"

"Cultivating. How 'bout 'chew?"

"Hauling meat. She's gonna be a hot one, yea?"

"Yea hey."

"Get any rain lately, Geo?"

"No. 'Chew?"

"Not in town, but I heard dat up in da valley, dey got a little night fore last."

"Da hell."

"And up dare at Skokie's dey got up ta an inch, wit jist a skoach of hail to boot."

"Da hell."

"Yea."

"Yea Hey."

"Well, guess we'd better get going."

"Yea, me too."

"Where yous gonna be tomorrow?"

"Tomorrow? Probably up at da udder place, crimping some hay."

"We'll, maybe talk to ya den."

"See ya later."

I followed Dolf's lead back to the truck, and we headed down the road.

63

"Dat's one of the perks 'bout dis job," Dolf said. "You meet so many exciting people wit all togedder different points of view. And not only do day have important tings to share, but you are always challenged by dem."

"Yea, I know what you mean."

"He was maybe a little nervous wit all da commotion, you know, strangers and all, but in da end he loosened and was da same old Geo."

It wasn't very long before we pulled into a rural town. There were old houses set back on huge sprawling lawns. I glanced at a sign that was planted into the side of the road, supported by two wooden posts. "Welcome to Gilmanton, Home of the Two Story Creamery."

Wow, how spectacular this creamery must be to get signage, I thought.

"Dolf, have you ever seen that creamery?"

"Yep, many a time."

"What's it like? Is it really something special?"

"I'm not even gonna answer dat one Imy, cause guess why?"

"Why?"

"Well, today's yer lucky day. Dat's one of da stops on my route!"

Within seconds, we pulled over in front of an unassuming two-story brick building. We jumped out, and Dolf hurriedly went to the back of the truck in order to retrieve some of the precious cargo. Dolf came out with one small wrapped package and headed into the building with me in tow. We entered through one of the mammoth wooden sliding doors and walked across the old wood plank floor up to a counter that was slightly leaning to one side. Dolf quickly unwrapped the piece of meat and handed it to a rotund lady standing behind the counter.

"Hi, I'm Dolf, so glad ta MEAT you."

"Oh Dolf, you're such a card, you should be dealt with," the fat lady responded back, drawing a chuckle from Dolf.

"And who do we have here?"

"Dat's Imy, my partner in crime fer today, and dat's no baloney."

"That's about as funny as the gas that I had this morning," she retorted.

"Ya know, I was mistaken fer a detective dis morning," Dolf went on.

"How's that, Dolf?"

"Someone drove by and caught me in a "steak out.""

"You're too much," the heavy lady responded, now laughing so hard that she started gasping for air.

"I went in to a fancy restaurant last night and saw da guy next ta me orderin a steak," Dolf said, as if recounting last night's antics. "Da waitress asked me how I wanted my steak. I told her ta cut da horns off, wipe its ass and trow it on a pladder. Da waitress come back wit a very extra rare piece of meat delivering it to da table hardly cooked. I struggled ta cut it, since it was ordered and delivered so rare dare ya know. As I grew more intense wit my knife, da steak slipped off da pladder and ended up on da floor. As I jumped from my chair to da floor to continue my assault on da piece of raw meat, I accidentally farted. Beller, you sons a bitches, I'll cut 'chew up yet!"

By now, the overweight lady was laughing so hard that she was pounding the counter with her chubby fist. During one of her healthy exhales, a little gas slipped out, sounding like someone dropped a small bar of soap on the hardwood floor. This sent Dolf over the edge, forcing him to bend over in search of precious oxygen. Now, I'm thinking that this is pretty funny, not so much for the content, but for the cast and age of characters involved.

The door slid open, and both jokesters tried to recompose themselves. Dolf grabbed the meat order, and I followed him out to the truck to fill it.

"It's a pretty small one today, so why don't you take da quick tour of da creamery. Fulfill a dream."

"OK Dolf. I'll meet you back inside."

"Hey, who's funny now?"

"Excuse me?"

"MEAT you back inside? Get it? MEAT you?"

I gave Dolf an obligatory laugh, then went back in and walked over to the old wooden staircase that was located toward the back of the store. In front of the staircase was a sign suspended by a piece of twine that was tied between the two banisters.

"Historic second floor tour starts here. Costs 50 cents."

"Just go on up and take a look-see," came the voice from the still giggling lady.

"Thank you," I said, ascending the stairs two steps at a time.

At the top, I skimmed the unimpressive Gilmanton tourist trap, walking the narrow catwalk that careened around the big milk tanks. I strode over to a long common wall, noticing some irregularities in the brick. After a closer look, I could tell that some of the mortar was brittle, as if a section of brickwork had been disturbed. This interested me, mainly because nothing else up there did. I extended my thumb and forefinger around a brick in order to gain some sort of grip. I tugged slightly, and just as I suspected, pulled a brick right out of the wall. I stared, wondering if the reduced support would cause anything else to fall. This brick, just like the rest of them in this small section, had no bearing on the support of the wall whatsoever. I took a quick glance around, then started pulling a few more bricks out of their place. They moved begrudgingly, then gave up as if only Father Time had held them engaged together. After extracting six bricks, I could see a portion of an old cast iron safe with the following words embossed on the side of it. Michigan Iron Works 898.

Now, my conscience got the best of me. After all, I didn't even pay for the tour. I thought that I had better put the bricks back and get out of there. But as I placed the small red blocks back in their slots, my curiosity peaked. I knew that I had to get Dolf involved so I wouldn't get into any trouble. I ran down and called to him.

"Come on up here with me and check it out."

"I been up dare before, and I know it's very interesting, in fact, I never seen a two-story creamery before dis one."

"Well, come on up, I just want to show you something."

"Alright den, I'm commin."

We clamored up the old wooden staircase, stopping at the summit.

"Check this big tank out. It's hard to believe there is enough milk in the area to fill it," I said, trying to lure Dolf closer to the mystery wall.

"Yea, I know. I stood here fer close to an hour one day appreciating dat puppy. Well, we'd better get trucking, da morning ain't getting any younger, and I told your old man dat I'd have you back forenoon."

"OK, but there's just so much interesting stuff up here, kind of mind boggling. Like this brick wall, how old do you think it is?"

"I bet dat dare brick could go back to turn of da century. Da reason I know dat is because da old brick plant outside Elk Creek closed 'bout den. Course, I guess it could a been built later den dat, since I saw a new brick house commin into town."

That's what I liked about Dolf. Maybe he wasn't an historian, but he could usually get to the bottom of most things.

"Wow, what's going on here," I said while wiggling one of the loose bricks until I was holding it in my hand.

"Now dat right der says it's old brick, cause I remember my grandpa telling me all da trouble dey were having wit da mortar up here."

"Boy, you're sure right about that one." I continued to pull out the original six bricks and stared in to the secret cave.

"Hey Dolf, look at this, a safe!"

"Better put dat back, before dey tink you're stealing from da till. Besides, we better roll anyway."

"From the looks of the safe, it seems real old. I don't think they even know that it's here. Do you mind if I ask her?"

"Hey, I don't wanna git ya in any trouble. Let's jist brick er back up and hit da road."

"But it may be something really important. I'm sure they don't know that it's up here. What do you think? Can I ask her?"

"Well..., alright den, but member, it's your idea. I had no part in it!"

In a flash, the proprietor was at the scene, trying to help lift the safe out of the wall. It's girth and sheer substance made the feat impossible. She stopped for a moment surveying the situation with a twinkle in her eye.

"We're gonna have to get some equipment in here to get this one out. When we get her out and ready to open, both of you will be on site for the festivities. Hell, this may be the biggest discovery since we found that forty-year-old cheese in the basement!"

Dolf and I both said goodbye, and she wrote down his home number so that she could call when the time was ready. Then she had us pose for a quick snapshot in front of the safe. We jumped in Dolf's green meat truck and headed to our next customer.

It was 11:00 AM, and we were on our way home. All of the deliveries on the northwest side of the route were done, and Dolf had to go back to the plant to load up for the afternoon route.

On the way back, we came upon the towering structure that was being constructed outside of Onalaska. Dolf pretended not to notice, then stomped on the breaks and asked if I wanted to take a look. Of course I did. So we pulled over to investigate.

The tower was being constructed for transmitting purposes by a TV station in nearby LaCrosse. Other companies were also contracting space at the top of the gigantic structure in order to house telecommunications equipment. One thousand feet of steel stacked straight up looked as if it were halfway to the sun. There was a crew of three men working at the top of the tower. The base of the tower was concealed behind a knoll, and a safety fence had been erected around the perimeter, keeping curious onlookers at bay. At the top of the knoll, in front of the restricted barrier, were huge schematics and design fact sheets that displayed issues pertinent to the construction. The documentation stated that no more than three men could be on the tower at once. The crew got up and down via a tiny triangular elevator built in the middle of it. The tower was just about finished, and Dolf estimated that the crowd of onlookers was slightly larger than usual.

"Hey Imy, look over dare, a TV camera. Let's go over and ask what da deal is."

I followed behind him, sometimes jogging just to keep up.

"So what's all da fuss about?" Dolf asked, interrupting a news reporter.

"They're just about done with construction, so we're out here doing a little clip," the newsman replied.

"Well, I'm Dolf Sikowski, da meat man from Arcadia, and I been stoppin off from my route for da past six months ta ….."

"Sir, I'm here to just shoot some footage, and maybe get a few candid statements."

"Just say when, and I'm ready ta go," Dolf shot back.

Just then a scream was heard, and a body came flailing out of the sky from the tower. Everyone watched in horror as the man gained momentum earthward. The workman was in a horizontal position, motionless, as if at any instant a parachute would come out of his red vest and save him. People watched, mouths gaping, as his hard hat floated slightly above him, following him to the earth below. It was evident that gravity was going to win this one, with the only saving grace being the knoll that masked the view of the actual impact. A thud was heard, sounding louder than I would have expected from a body hitting the ground from no less than one thousand feet up.

Stunned, the newsman next to me clicked on his big microphone and held it up to Dolf.

"Holy Shamoly, I bet dat hurt like hell!"

Dolf paled in complexion, his eyes popping out as if he had walked by an AA meeting in downtown Arcadia. A hush fell over the crowd. The vision of the hard hat floating next to the falling victim etched into my brain.

Not more than twenty seconds later, the workman emerged at the top of the knoll. He bent over, retrieved his hard hat, dusted himself off, and looked up to the top of the tower. He waved to his work mates at the summit to acknowledge complete composure. He disappeared from sight for a moment as he walked to the base of the tower, jumped on the tiny elevator and ascended the steel structure. The crowd was dismayed, obviously happy for the worker, however feeling slightly confused by the outcome.

"I fell off a ladder one time, and it hurt like a son of a biscuit, but I walked away from it," Dolf said as if trying to put some sense behind what we had just witnessed.

"That was the most unreal thing I have ever seen," I said, still shaking from the experience. "I can't believe what just happened! I guess it just wasn't his time."

Compared to that, the trip home was uneventful. After a morning like that, I was ready to get my feet back on solid ground, or better yet, my butt on the solid mill porch.

Later that evening, the TV news reported that once it was learned that the media was going to make an appearance, two of the construction workers took a dressed mannequin with them to throw off the tower. It seemed a bit extreme, but I guess Arcadia humor was as rough as it's dialect. Anyway, as I look back, I learned something important that day – it was my first lesson in "seeing ain't believing."

Chapter X

It was a beautiful Saturday morning, and Dad and I were half an hour from getting our faces fed. It was eleven thirty in the morning, and in approximately thirty more minutes the padlock would be closed on the mill, and another business day would be in recorded in the books.

Saturdays were a bit of a dichotomy. The good thing about Saturdays was that we only had the mill open for business for half of the day. Lunchtime was an entire half-hour earlier, and what a lunch it was. Chicked beef over toast, guaranteed, along with leftover fish sticks from the Friday night before. The bad part about Saturdays was that once lunch was over, Dad always had to go back to the mill and repair or tinker with something, and it usually meant more work without customer intervention. Most of the fun at the mill was derived from the characters that would come in to do business. But, since Saturday afternoons were not open for business, I was usually sentenced to be alone with Dad in the dark and dingy mill until suppertime.

Occasionally, there would be a Saturday afternoon that had a bit of adventure to it, especially when we got to take a road trip somewhere. One month, Dad and I spent four consecutive Saturday afternoons constructing all four of Alphonse Schbella's round, corrugated tin, pig feeders. We had sold these to Alphie, complete with installation. I remember looking at these in the magazine, and they didn't appear to be so large. Each sheet of tin had to be attached to the other with nuts and bolts, approximately one inch from each other. You would swear that you were mounting jet fighter wings with the quantity of fasteners that were provided. Being smaller than Dad had its advantages, but not for this job. It was easier for me to get inside of the cavernous bin. We couldn't get the electric drill inside the bin due to cord restraints, and, of course, Dad got to use the electric screwdriver, so a month later my cramped hands no longer needed the verbal reminder, "righty tighty, lefty loosey." Let's just call it on-the-job training.

Another Saturday at the lunch table, Dad mentioned how good he used to bowl when he was putting himself through school. He worked in a bowling alley in the little town of Sleepy Eye, Minnesota. When we finished eating, he asked me if I wanted to go for a car ride with him, and we ended up three hundred miles later at this bowling alley.

What magnified the time was the one-way farming conversation that he used as a monologue the entire way.

"Farmers don't know how to farm anymore. They plow, then disc, then drag, mulching up that soil so much that it can't hold moisture. When it rains, it runs off, causing erosion. Then they sit around and pray for rain again. Man oh man…"

This conversation continued the entire way, stemming from overspending on farm machinery to poor overall milk production. Of course, every time that I would try to change the topic, he would never answer; he'd just look out of his window as if gathering more crop data.

By the time we reached our destination, I was getting pretty excited to visit with anyone who would talk about anything outside of farming.

I didn't wait for an invite, probably because I knew that I wouldn't receive one. I followed Dad out of the car and headed into the dingy bowling alley. Inside the dark, stale smelling bar, we were greeted by a thin, greasy-haired, man with a potbelly.

"What can I get for you, boys?"

"I'm Arnie, and I used to work here before the war. I used to bowl a heck of a game with this old black ball that was here. Any idea where it could be?"

"Today is my first day here, so obvisouly you've caught me off guard. Let me ask the owner."

A few minutes later a lanky, pocked-marked man came walking in, heading toward the bar.

"You Arnie?"

"Yes. Was wondering if you would have any idea on the whereabouts of the bowling balls that used to be here before the war?"

"You know, I've only owned these lanes for about five years. I did hear that the owner before last took all of the balls, chopped them up and took 'em to the dump.

Want anything to drink?"

"Yes, I'll take a pop."

"Sounds good to me, too."

It felt so good to say something. It had been so long that I was wondering if my vocal cords still worked.

After drinking our sodas, we jumped back in the car and headed for home. I remember thinking all the way home how bizarre Dad could be. Sometimes "Mr. Logic" was anything but. Oh well, it was an experience. And besides, I had another five-hour opportunity to see if Dad wanted to talk about anything but farming.

"Well, so much for the bowling ball, eh Dad?"

"Yea, but it was a nice ride, though. It's always good to get out and see how the farmers work the land on this side of the Mississippi."

So here it was, another Saturday at noon, with no plans but to eat my chicked beef over toast for lunch.

"Let's go for a car ride," Dad said while mopping the rest of that creamy white sauce with his last piece of toast.

"OK, sounds good," I said, selecting one of my canned responses.

Deep down, it didn't sound good at all. I was wondering where the heck he was going to take me today.

We jumped into the car and didn't say a word to each other all the way to the mill, which was standard protocol.

Dad went into the office and tore down the auction bill that was stapled onto the thick, wood paneled door. He held the rigid poster in his hands, studying it intently. He walked over to the car and handed me the frayed, thick sheet.

"Let's take a ride over the hill to Waumendee and see what they're selling."

After forty miles of curvy roads through the plush countryside, we embarked on Waumendee, a village of about a hundred people. On the outskirts of town was a farm, with cars and pickup trucks lined up and down the county road for close to a mile. We parked, then hiked down the road a spell, turning up a gravel driveway. Farm implements lined the gravel on both sides, paving a skinny walkway up to the farm as if we were on our way to OZ.

A good-size crowd of at least three hundred anxious buyers hovered around a guy who stood a head above the rest. He was standing on a peach crate and cradling a microphone in his right hand. Dad and I walked up close to the front row in order to check out the festivities.

All around us were people in bib overalls, men and women alike. It looked like a fashion show for barn wear. The crowd appeared to be either poor or just fashionably underdressed, but one thing appeared to be certain, there was no dentist residing in the area. I mean, if there was, then he was apparently handing out sugarcoated jawbreakers after every visit. And I thought our mill dog, Jasper, had bad teeth.

The man with the microphone was a skinny drink of water, standing about normal height and weighing less than I did. He was wearing blue and yellow wide-striped pants, complete with a checkered flannel shirt and necktie. His necktie was so wide that it resembled a dinner napkin, the end protruding over his "cattleman" belt buckle. In fact, the necktie was so wide that it actually displayed a scene of an archer with an empty quiver over his back, shooting his last arrow at a herd of deer. The caption below read: "I only need one arrow, because I'm a straight shooter."

This fella's black eye glasses were so incredibly thick that Petey Picka could have used them for welding goggles. In an attempt to conceal his baldness, he combed his black greasy hair over to one side of his head. The wind was his enemy today, flapping this matted wad of human fabric air-born and giving the impression that his hair was waving to the people in the audience.

"Is this guy gonna recite poetry?" I asked Dad sarcastically.

"Recite poultry," came the amplified voice from the man with the microphone, who obviously overheard me.

"I'll recite some poultry. Baauuck, baaauuck, baaaaaauuuuck," came the whiney voice, trying to imitate a chicken.

Dad looked at me as if someone had taken his supper plate away, and I knew that my sarcasm that lead to the shenanigans severely struck a nerve.

"OK, let's get on with it," the man with the microphone said, as he started to bellar in a pig-calling fashion.

"Dad, why does that guy talk so fast?"

"He's an auctioneer, and he's supposed to."

"How come you can't understand him?"

"Well, if you come to enough of these, you learn the lingo."

"Why is there a lingo? Maybe if he slowed down so that everyone could understand him, he'd sell the equipment at a higher price?"

"You talk too much. Shut up and listen."

"OOOOOOOOOOKEEEEEE, we got a JD four row, now whatcha gonna give fer it? Will ya start at a five-five-five-five-five, how 'bout a ten-ten, I mean a hundred dollar bill, comon hundred... hundred give me a two-hundred-two-hundred-two hundred and a fifty...."

People were standing at attention and listening as if Abraham Lincoln had made a brief appearance from the grave, rereading the Gettysburg Address.

I glanced over at the rusted, flat-tired, farm implement.

"The shape that that corn picker's in, you'd think they would give it away," I whispered.

The auctioneer then stopped, and the crowd went numb. Total silence dominated as the man who stood slightly taller than the crowd turned his head to one side, covered one nostril with his first couple of fingers and blew out of the other one, jettisoning a lime green object so noticeable that the farm dog standing next to me watched its flight. The green matter launched out in a perfect arc, end over end, as a gooey middle membrane kept the two harder ends intact. It shot across the blue sky, landing on the hay baler next to him. The Auctioneer promptly resumed his pig calling, without missing a beat. The audience returned their gaze back from the lime green flight show. This interruption garnered about as much reaction as the fly that buzzed around my cap. I waved my hand to shoo away the flying pest.

"Hip," the auctioneer said while pointing at me.

"Bout a four... 'bout a four... 'bout a four... SOLD to the young man in the green cap."

"Who in God's name would buy that piece of junk?"

"You!" Dad snorted in an angry voice.

"Me?"

"Well, should we go home, or do you want to hang around and buy a tractor to pull the corn picker with, as long as you're on a buying spree?" Dad sneered.

Once it became apparent that we had a problem, the auctioneer intervened.

"Son, did you know you were bidding on this farm implement?"

"Ahhh, no. I don't even own a farm. Even if I was old enough to own one, I wouldn't. However if I did, I would surely come to your auctions and buy equipment from you, because, as you can see, you are so good at your profession that you almost sold something to kid who had no intent to buy."

"We'll let 'er slide this time son, just keep your hands in your pockets for the rest of the auction."

The ride home from Waumendee that afternoon seemed like eternity. Since the car radio didn't work, the only sounds resonating from the old Buick were the purr of the engine and an occasional crop comment from the "farm king."

Huddled around the supper table later that night, I brought up the fact that I had been the proud owner of a rusted-out, dilapidated, four-row corn picker. I quickly explained how it happened, and since I didn't know what I was doing, nor had any money, I was excused from the obligation. But once again, the demographics of my target audience were such that several were too young to understand, several didn't care, and one was so busy eating that nothing else seemed important. It really made me wonder how my family couldn't see all of this free entertainment going on around them. Instead, everyone seemed to be locked in his or her own little bothersome world with little chance for happiness. Well, that was their problem, not mine. I was just going to sit back and continue to observe the Arcadia way, because it just doesn't get much better than this for a poor white boy trapped in rural America.

Chapter XI

It was a damp, cool, Wisconsin summer morning, with the early sunshine breaking through the haze, revealing sparkling crystals on the dew-laden grass. I had just ground out a job for Clarence Thomas, the only other guy in town with two first names besides Tom Bill, proud owner of the junkyard. I had just taken my position on the perch of the old mill porch, right next to Smoothie Waldera.

"She's gonna be a hot one."

"Yep," I replied back, reinforcing the obvious.

Smoothie Waldera was one of the many hired hands that came and went. He had gotten his nickname as a kid because he loved Reese's Smoothie Peanut Butter Cups.

Smoothie had just gotten out of the service and didn't quite know what to do with his life, so this was as good a place to be as any.

I heard the sound of a click, and I saw Jasper's ears perk up. From my vantage point, I could see the rack of two colored lights sitting on top of a car parked next to Dolf's mailbox on top of the hill. It was the mailman. The car came down the slope and stopped at the mailbox across the street from the mill porch. At first glance, the car appeared to be driver-less. However, careful study produced the bill of a cap peaking through the steering wheel.

"Smoothie, who is that mailman, anyway?"

"Dat dare's Cleo Stajeek."

"Why is he so short?"

"Why do race cars go round da track counter clockwise?"

"I don't know, why?"

"Well, I really don't know either, but I do know dat dat side of da Stajeek family is short. Dey call his brother Short Pecker, cause he's even shorter than Cleo."

"What does he do?"

"He used to reset pins down at da bowling alley."

"I bet he was good at that, being so close to the ground and all."

"Yea hey, he was one of da best."

76

"Does he still do it?"

"No, word is he used to swear at ya if ya bowled a strike, and wit all da good bowlers in town, da swearin would offend some of da ladies. And besides, da Ojamphras put in automatic pin setters once dey bought da alley."

Cleo Stajeek had just finished putting the mail in the box, and drove off. I sprang up, stopping to stretch my legs, then proceeded to the mailbox to retrieve the mail for Dad. After gathering it all, I walked up on the rickety schoolhouse porch into the office. I plopped the mail down on the counter, and Dad rose to his feet to start going through it. I left the office quickly to avoid another farm lecture and took my seat next to Smoothie, waiting for business to pick up.

A few minutes later, Dad walked out of the office, heading for the mill porch with a newspaper in hand. He held the folded paper in front of my face.

"You know who that is?"

I looked at the picture of a farmer sitting on a big tractor pulling an eight-bottom plow with a caption below: "Oscar pulls an 8 bottom down to the river bottom to get to the bottom of his weed problem."

"Ahhh, not really," wondering why Dad was making such a fuss about this "Oscar" guy.

"No, the picture below that."

I adjusted my gaze southward, and lo and behold, there was a picture of Dolf, myself and a fat lady standing in front of the old safe. The caption read: "Contents still unknown of mysterious historical safe."

"Imy, I guess that they're looking into a safecracker in LaCrosse to come up and see if he can open it. They really want to protect the old thing, just in case the contents are not as valuable as the old safe itself."

"When are they going to do it?"

"There is no date yet, but they'll invite you, Dolf and the media before it's officially opened, especially since you found it."

"Great!"

"Imy, what do ya tink's in dare?" Smoothie asked.

"I don't have a clue, Smoothie. Could be money, gold or valuable papers. Hard telling what people considered valuable back then. Smoothie, what do you think is in it?"

"It may be pirate shit or money from Jessie James or some type a valuable beer."

"Well, whatever it is, it'll be an interesting surprise," Dad said, always optimistic, but never allowing his hopes to get too high.

Suddenly the bell in the mill sounded, signaling that the phone was ringing in the office. Dad high-tailed it in, while I continued reading the article in the paper. Dad came out a few minutes later with a big smile on his face.

"Now that the newspaper article hit, people want to know what's in it, I guess. That was Apolinary Ruecorn. He wanted to know what you thought was in it."

"That's funny. Like how would I know?"

Just then a loud roar of a truck laboring to climb the steel hoist pads interrupted our conversation. Smoothie and I ran to greet the customer. Out popped Pauncho Poohalla, a short, heavy man stuffed in bib overalls. Pauncho had so much tobacco in his mouth that you couldn't understand a word he said. Even without a load in his mouth, you couldn't understand Pauncho. But today he was at his snuff limit. Smoothie and I exchanged a knowing glance, both detecting the tobacco overload.

"Imy, he's got 'er packed in today."

"Why would someone load that much into their mouth at one time?"

"Well, maybe dare discontinuin' dat dare brand or sometin like dat."

"Good point, Smoothie, but if that were the case, he could have just stocked up on it for later. I bet he got down to the end of his can and had just a little left over. It wasn't enough to save for another batch, and he couldn't stand to throw it out, so he put in a batch-and-a-half this time."

"Ya know, dat reminds me; dares ta'dee tings my old man warned me about in life dat I'll never forgit. One is dat you never pet a dog dats eatin meat. Da second one is dat you always keep an eye on a guy who's chewin tobacco."

"What's the third one, Smoothie?"

"I jist remembered dat I forgot it."

Just then Pauncho waltzed over as a cautious Smoothie slithered backward toward the shelling pit.

"Hey boys, let's shell dis here, den lits grind er up fer da steers."

Now since I was somewhat paranoid of what Smoothie had just told me, I couldn't help but notice Pauncho's stream of tobacco oozing out of both corners of his mouth. Suddenly, Pauncho's face contorted, while he struggled, trying to grab for a rag in his rear pocket that was hooked to the pocket snap. Smoothie froze with a panic stricken look on his face.

"Oh shit, he's gonna sneeze!" a frantic Smoothie screamed.

I reeled to see an excited Smoothie ducking for cover behind one of the crooked support beams that was giving its best shot at trying to hold up the grinder-pit canopy.

I jumped back briskly, far enough out of harm's way, still able to witness the explosion. There was black gook everywhere. The white rack flanking the bed of his pickup looked as if it had been parked in the Bronx for two years, assaulted with graffiti. Black goo was on the corn and in the oats. But that wasn't the disgusting part. When Pauncho turned around to finish the conversation, he looked as though he had stuck his face in a coal-burning chimney. I could hardly make out the snot that was stuck to his left cheek.

I reached to untangle the oil rag that was stuck in his rear pocket.

"Turn around, let me unhook that bad boy."

"Why, do I have any on me?"

"Ahh..just a little bit."

"Dat's funny, where's my snuff?" he asked, referring to the tobacco that once infested his mouth.

I left that one unanswered as I ran in to the mill to give Smoothie a hand.

It wasn't long before Pauncho was in the office settling up and discussing farming with Dad. The two of them were in there with the owner of a black pickup truck whom I'd never met before. Smoothie and I had just taken our seats on the old mill porch when on the horizon a yellow pickup headed our way. The pickup pulled over right in front of the mailbox across the street, and an inquisitive Apolinary Ruecorn bounded out.

Apolinary Ruecorn was one of my classmate's fathers.' He was a wiry, older man, probably late sixties, wearing thick round glasses. He was the most inquisitive man I had ever met, constantly interrogating everyone he came across.

"Need jist a little bag of milk replacer."

He issued the command as he stared Smoothie in the eye making it apparent that he wanted Smoothie to retrieve it.

Smoothie walked into the back room to execute the order.

"Now what da heck is da deal 'bout dat safe in G-town?" Apolinary asked, referring to the safe in Gilminton.

"Well, we found it, and they're going to get a safecracker in LaCrosse to open it."

"When dey gonna do dat?"

"I don't know, but they'll call me as soon as they're ready."

"What do ya tinks in it?"

"I just don't know. Could be anything."

"I was telling Ogar, I wonder how heavy dat sons of bitch is?"

"Oh, it was real heavy."

"You know, like I was telling Ogar, if a guy knew da weight of da safe when empty, den weighed da sons a bitch now, you'd know den da weight of da shit inside of it. Dat could be valuable information."

"That's quite the way to think, Apolinary."

My peripheral vision suddenly picked up Dad who happened to walk over to us. I immediately tried to change the subject before he could challenge my facetious comment.

Dad gave me one of his sideways looks. At least he showed some emotion, I thought.

"Now Imy, don't be a smart ass."

I knew that Dad was just asserting the fact that Apolinary was a valued customer, and at no time should any customer be treated with disrespect. I knew this as well, but it would have been kind of cool, just for once, to have Dad chuckle or side with me.

"You know, I was telling Ogar dat between da two of us guys, we git some dynamite …."

"That's why they are having professionals do it, so the safe isn't harmed," I quipped.

I could feel the irritation starting to set in and knew that I had better find a new attitude, or I'd better exit.

"Well in any event, we'll be notified, and we will find out in due time," Dad said in a stern voice, terminating the conversation.

That night around the supper table, the air was more tense than usual. Typically, the family was fairly quiet, with the kids knowing that Mom and Dad were tired after another hard day. Mom had two young children to raise, and she wasn't exactly a spring chicken. Dad was usually tired from throwing feed sacks and shoveling grain most of the day. I was suddenly distracted by Tom, who started flailing his arms while bound in his high chair. He started to cough, then looked at me through his big brown eyes while managing a smile. I smiled back at him, however, suspecting something wasn't right. His smile soon faded along with his waving arms, and I noticed a bluish hue consume his face. I immediately realized the gravity of the situation.

"Dad, I think Tom is choking!"

Dad stared at him for a moment, then stood up, grabbed the high chair and inverted it with Tom hanging upside down, supported only by the tray in front of him. Dad nonchalantly pounded on Tom's back, while Tom coughed up a piece of hardened cracker. Dad put the high chair back on its legs, sat down and speared the top piece of sliced bread from a plate stacked high with it. He resumed eating in spite of the shrill of Mom's screams.

"He's alright, pass the gravy."

That was Dad. Totally unmoved by the human race. The only time his emotions surfaced was when he was in the middle of a temper tantrum. His temperament could go from cool, calm and collected to flat-out rage. This side of him was only displayed when angered by one of us "little people." He had absolutely no tolerance for so-called "nonsense," and any behavior out of his acceptable parameters was dealt with harshly. It was not uncommon to receive a blow to the side of the head, or any other part of the body, if you weren't quick enough to instinctively cover up in time. However, when it came down to sheer pressure, no one could handle it like he could. Being so emotionally cold allowed him to save a life so easily, where most people would have failed. It enabled him to think fast and act logically, remaining totally isolated from any feeling.

As days passed, many of the farmers asked about the safe. It was interesting how some would ask a lot of questions about how the safe was found and what the stored contents could be. It was also surprising to find out how many farmers didn't have a TV set or never read a newspaper. As time went on, the stories grew, some beyond belief. One of the finer hypotheses evolved from a conversation that took place on the front porch of the mill between Poopsie Sokup, Punski Krunk and Dolf Sikowski.

"What do yous tink is in dat dare son of a biscuit, Poopsie?" Dolf asked.

"Hey, I may not know what's in dare, but I sure know what da hell ain't, Dolf."

"What's dat Poopsie?"

"My pliers. I used 'em dis mornin.'"

"Poopsie, dat's why I ask you deese things. You're always tinkin."

"Dolf, maybe it's da old man's spreader," Punski chimed in.

"Not da spreader," Poopsie exclaimed.

Now, they were starting to talk over my head, which kind of took me by surprise.

"What's a spreader, Dolf?"

"You know. Honey Wagon."

Poopsie sat there in deep thought. "Did dat ting still run?"

"Dolf, what's a Honey Wagon?"

"Yea hey, she ran good, till da old man got da new, used one..."

"Dolf, what's a Honey Wagon?"

"Manure spreader."

"Den he seemed ta lose dat spreader," Punski said with a far away look in his eye.

Dolf sat there with a big grin on his face.

"Boys, da safe ain't dat big! Punski, ain't it funny dat your dad lost everyting except his beer?"

Dolf stood in front of the crew while depicting the size of the safe with crude hand jesters.

"Like I said before, da safe ain't dat big."

"Well, what else valuable could it be, unless it's a valuable beer?" Punski added.

"Well, day may even be putten dis on TV, so I'll let yous guys know as soon as I know when da safe will be opened," Dolf followed.

A week later, the anticipated call arrived. The Gilminton Creamery called on Thursday with news that the opening of the safe would be Friday morning at 9:30. Dad and I dressed for the occasion. I put on my good jeans and sported my clean tennis shoes. Then we drove the forty-minute, windy road over to Gilminton. I was so excited and wished I had someone to share the excitement with. Dad was excited too, excited that the corn was doing so well on the other side of Independence. They had had a dry spell up there, seemed like hardly any rain fell north along the Trempealeau River for about a month. After igniting a few one-way conversations, I finally gave up, growing tired of answering myself. I stared out the window, watching as the miniature rows of corn in the fields flew by. I guess Dad was right. The corn did look good.

As we arrived at the creamery, a short line of people stood outside the building waiting to get a view of the opening ceremonies. I cut through the line directly to the front door with Dad in tow. Dad ducked slightly in order to clear the wooden, homemade sign swinging in the doorway suspended by a piece of baler twine that read: Only Creamery Customers in Dire Need of Supplies May Enter.

I looked around, and oddly enough, it seemed as if everyone had run out of milk that Friday morning. The creamery was packed full of people, everyone waiting for the cameraman from the TV station to arrive. I think people thought that if they stuck around, they may hit stardom since the event was to be aired on the six o'clock news. In the thick of things was Apolinary Ruecorn talking with a short, rotund man. His gut protruded so far that he had extensions sewn on the straps of his bib overalls.

Dolf was there talking to everyone, exaggerating how he encouraged a timid boy to uncover the safe and expose it to the store owners and general public. There were people bragging about how they knew what was inside, but didn't want to share the news, knowing how that would spoil the excitement. And then there were folks who were not quite as creative, just milling about pretending to be actually shopping for creamery products.

"Maryanne, where da heck did you hide da milk?"

I looked over at an older man with extremely bad posture who acted visibly shaken.

"Stoltz, you've been in here every day for the last week buying milk. You'd think you'd remember where the hell it is."

"Well, I always remember it being over dare next to da cheese...."

"Stoltz, how long have you lived here?"

"Oh... 'bout seventy-six years, give or take ten."

"How long has this creamery been here?"

"Oh... 'bout as long as I can remember."

"Where's the milk always been?"

"Dat's right, in da cooler across from da cheese."

"Now git your saggy ass over there, grab your milk and step outside so others can shop. We just don't have the room for all of this foot traffic today."

The outspoken, heavyweight proprietor noticed Dad and me standing by the milk cooler. She slowly walked over to us.

"It's been this way all day today. People in here dragging their feet, trying to be the ones "shopping" when the safe gets cracked. I can't wait till this thing is over. It better be good, cause it sure has been hectic around here the last couple of weeks."

Dad listened to her while appearing to be in deep thought.

"Well, at least it must have been good for business."

"Now who are you, I don't think I've seen you in the store before."

"I'm Arnie Lecheler, owner of East Arcadia Feed Mill over the hill. Imy is my son who found your safe."

"Oh, so you're his dad."

Smiling conspicuously, the lady stroked her badly styled, shoulder length curls.

"I know we've talked on the phone, and now I can finally put a face with the name. And a good one at that."

Her flirtation was brutally interrupted when another customer screamed to have a half-pound block of cheese sliced thin enough for fifty people to enjoy.

"Damn it, Yoggy, you know you always buy your cheese in five pound packages because you have all them grandkids. Why in God's name do you want only a half-pound cut up like that? What the hell do you think that cheese is made of, gold?"

"Well, I could buy a little more if you could cut all of dat up fer me..."

"Guess what? I ain't your mom. Besides, you always have cut your own cheese. And if you don't get da hell out of the way, I'm gonna really cut the cheese, then we'll all be in trouble!"

I noticed her face reddening. She was so overcome by emotion that she forgot we were standing behind her.

Hearing all the commotion, Dolf drifted over and stood next to the milk cooler. Dad had walked over to take a closer look at some of the cheese prices.

"What was dat about?" Dolf asked.

"That guy wanted her to cut the cheese."

"Well fer her, dat should be an easy task."

"Dolf, don't start," the heavy proprietor warned.

"Oh, I tought you said 'Dolf, don't fart.'"

Dolf then glanced around the immediate area, like a baseball pitcher checking the base runners before pitching the ball. Then he raised his left leg and let out a spurt of gas, sounding like a bee with volume control. It started out low in volume, and as more pressure was applied, it increased in decibel level. I was quite amazed with his sphincter talent. He was able to regulate it in order to put on a show for the immediate audience. The fat lady appeared embarrassed, sensing that Dad could be within earshot.

"How dare you fart before me!" she retorted.

"Hell, I didn't know it was your turn!" Dolf responded.

"I'll be right back."

With that, the lady waddled to the front of the store, as if something of greater importance had just caught her eye.

The old oak sliding door rumbled as I noticed a cameraman trying to get his bulky equipment through the partially exposed entryway. People were being ordered to exit the store in order to accommodate the equipment being set up to record the action. The safe cracker from LaCrosse was present and had already surveyed his challenge. He oozed confidence, implying that his skills would be ample to open the iron box. After a signal from the cameraman, the opening ceremonies were ready to begin. The fat lady, Dolf and I were instructed to stand next to the safe for a shot and quick interview. The news reporter from the big city held the microphone and talked into the camera, setting the stage. Once he was done, he turned to us to start the interviewing sequence.

"How was the safe discovered?"

"Well, Imy, dar, saw, it, dar, and ober dar we went and told about it to Maryanne who den came ober dar by us..." stammered a nervous Dolf.

"And where do you live, sir?"

"East Side of Arcadia, dis side of Nort Creek, udder side of Nucume Valley."

Dad noticed the puzzled look of the news reporter and decided to step in.

"Arcadia, Wisconsin."

After a brief summary by the reporter, the signal was given, and the safe cracker moved into position to work his magic. The crowd was told to keep the utmost of silence. If they could not uphold their responsibility of quiet, then they would be asked to leave.

The safe cracker was a wiry, middle-aged man wearing miniature round rim glasses. He carried a cache of little files and sharp-pronged instruments in a large leather pouch that he yanked from his worn black leather bag. The last item retrieved from his bag was a stethoscope that he wrapped around his neck like a doctor about to do an examination. This antic seemed to amuse the bystanders.

Standing close to the front, about two rows back, was an obese man with rancid breath talking to a slightly smaller bald man.

"I tink he's taken her pulse, hey."

"Delbert, dats so he can hear da tumblers, you dumb shit."

"What's next, put a termometer in da key hole?"

"He'll have dis baby cracked in no time at all, dare. I seen dis on TV before."

The safecracker seemed a tad frustrated and started digging in his bag for more tools.

"Maybe he should put his fingers on dat old handle and take her pulse, hey."

The news reporter shifted his weight to the other leg as if slight fatigue was setting in from balancing the recording equipment that was strapped on his back.

Fifteen minutes later, boredom replaced anticipation, and the crowd became slightly restless. The reporter put up both hands, then lowered them in order to hush the audience. The crowd recomposed itself, and once again dead silence prevailed.

The safecracker kept working the key lock and combination, but to no avail. The only silence breaker was the slight clicking of the combination dial on the front of the safe.

"Hell, if you can't open da bastard, let's blow dat sons of bitch to pieces!"

I didn't have to trace the voice back to the mouth because I recognized that that was none other than Apolinary Ruecorn.

"He's got a point!" another onlooker yelled from the back.

"Bet you even got dynamite in dat dare pickup of yours, Poly!" heckled another.

"You bet your ass I do!"

"People, please, I'm recording here, and had he opened the safe with everyone talking, we would have had to cut the sound. If you can't keep quiet, please leave so the rest of the people can enjoy this.

"Yea, like he would have opened it! I'm just glad dat my Christmas presents ain't in dare, or I'd really be screwed!"

"Yea, hey, what if, like my wife was in dar, or worse than dat, how 'bout if my beer was in dar, den what would I do? Da way he's going, I'd have warm beer, or even worse, stale beer!"

The rotund proprietor stepped away from the safe in order to address the crowd.

"That's it, everyone out. The safecracker cannot work unless it is quiet, and the TV people need silence, so everyone out!"

Apolinary begrudgingly walked past her toward the door.

"Well, you know where I'll be."

"Yea, driving me nuts."

Everyone spilled out on the roomy front porch, with some standing vigil in front of the two picture windows in order to continue the watch.

An hour passed with absolutely no news. Just a small group of chosen people were allowed to hang around inside to watch the safecracker who now was spending most of his time on the telephone. You could see that the number of noses pressed up against the windowpane had diminished. People were starting to lose interest, and most of the masses had left. The camera man had stopped recording, and the reporter was sitting at the counter writing on a paper. I was standing over next to Dad leaning on the milk cooler when the heavy owner came forward interrupting all thought.

"Well, we could always let Apolinary give it a whack," I said.

"We decided to call it off. Looks like they're gonna take it to LaCrosse to a demo place and pop the door off."

Dad took a look at his watch.

"Oh well, heck, it's time for lunch anyway. Might as well get a bite to eat then head back over the hill."

Dad and I grabbed a cheese sandwich, then jumped in the old green Buick and headed for Arcadia. I was hopeful that maybe Dad would ask to see if I was disappointed. Since I knew he wouldn't ask me on his own, I thought I would prime him a bit by setting the stage.

"Dad, I'm a little disappointed."

"About what?"

"About the safe not opening. How about you? Are you disappointed at all?"

"Naw, not really. I hadn't had a cheese sandwich this good for a long time!"

That was Dad. He'd find joy in finding a penny in a manure spreader. Always enjoying the little things life had to offer, no matter how miniscule.

About a week later, Dad got a call summoning us to LaCrosse for the grand opening. But Dad decided it wouldn't be feasible for us to attend. After all, LaCrosse was fifty miles away over several hills that we had never traveled before. Besides, it was hard to get any time away from the feed mill, so we'd just have to wait in order to discover the contents of the safe. And after being let down once, the thrill wasn't quite as monumental anymore.

The following Thursday, Dolf's blue, Chevy Impala descended the hill and stopped in front of the mailbox. I was in the mill cleaning up a bag of sow cubes that were ripped open by the sharp prongs of a feed cart. I watched as Dolf sprang from his car, grabbed the mail out of the mailbox and headed straight across the road and into the office. Since this peaked my interested, I walked out to the porch to see what Dolf was up to, even though I was quite sure what his intent was. A minute later, Dolf emerged out of the office and headed straight for the mill with Dad strolling slowly behind. I stepped off of the porch and met him halfway.

"Wanna go to LaCrosse ta see what's in da safe dat we found?"

"Dad, can I?"

"Brush the dust off on those trousers, and we'll see you when you get back."

I didn't need a second invitation. I stood up and vigorously attacked the dust on my jeans.

"Dad, are you coming along?"

"No, someone has to stay here and run the mill. You found it. You go. I'll see you when you get back."

"Wow, well thanks, Dad. And thanks, Dolf."

"We should be back sometime before supper. I'll just drop 'em off back here."

We jumped into Dolf's car and sped away, leaving Dad standing in the middle of the road studying his mail.

LaCrosse was a metropolis that I had always heard about but had never visited. My cousin, who told me that he lived there, had told me about the stoplights at intersections, lights at railroad crossings and buildings even taller that the co-op chicken-food plant out on the dike road. My eyes were gawking out the window, taking in the unfamiliar scenery.

"How do you know where you are going?"

"I ain't got a clue. Actually, I been dare a few times in da past, with da help of a road map. I asked quite a few people before I headed dare da first time, but nobody I knew had ever been dare before."

"How long ago was that?"

"Bout five years ago. Dat's why you're so lucky. You're young and already will have been dare."

"Wow, I guess."

About an hour later, we hit the outskirts of town. Dolf immediately turned down the stock report on the radio in order to concentrate. Besides, why did we need to know the current price of cattle, when there wasn't a cow pasture within sight? Suddenly, we were on an extra wide road with two lanes going each way.

"I've never seen a road this wide before," I said marveling at the freeway.

"Yea, eider have I. I usually go da back way."

"What do you call this?" I asked, anxiously awaiting the definition of this foreign type of roadway.

"Lost!"

We continued down the road a stretch when we saw a sign that read, George Street, Right Lane.

It was evident that Dolf was starting to get frustrated.

"How da heck ya know what lane is da right lane?"

"Uh, I think they mean the right hand lane."

"Oh, I guess dat makes sense."

We exited on George Street and followed it into downtown LaCrosse. After a turn on to a street that produced front grills of parked cars and backsides of street signs, we quickly did a U-turn to join the proper traffic flow.

"We're getting there, 'by George,'" I said trying to add some levity to a tense situation that might loosen up Dolf.

Dolf never responded as he concentrated ahead, waiting for the stoplight to turn green as if he were a drag racer.

Several stops later, some for stoplights and a few for directions, we arrived at the demolition company in the warehouse district next to the river. The sign above the rusty tin shed read, Blow Your Socks Off. Along the rutted city street was a train of parked cars, and we drove a few blocks before we found a parking spot. Dolf seemed quite astounded by the number of vehicles.

"Wow, Imy! And I thought the Gilmanton Creamery had a lot of people!"

Behind the tin shed was a concrete bunker where the actual explosion was going to take place. This bunker was approximately a ten-foot by ten-foot concrete box, appearing airtight. The safe was sitting on a small portable lift in a parking lot just outside of the bunker. A mesh-wire perimeter fence with spools of razor wire installed at the top surrounded the half block area. A security guard stood at the gate, keeping all spectators at bay. Dolf and I were ushered into the "commons" area once we convinced the sentry who we were. Inside the mesh stood a small gathering of people, no more than twenty, along with two cameramen and a couple of reporters, all unfamiliar faces. One reporter was talking to the hefty owner of the Gilmenton Creamery when Dolf and I walked up. When the reporter was done interviewing her, he turned his attention to us and asked Dolf his name.

"Daaa--ollllf."

"Sir, I've got the sound off. I just want to find out your name for the record and your association with this. Then we will record this for the noon news."

"Well, I'm Dolf Sikowski, and I was da one who helped find da safe."

"What do you think is in it?"

"Could be money, could be gold... something valuable."

"And who is this young man?"

"This is Imy, my partner in crime. He was wit me when I found da son of a biscuit."

"The word safe could be used as well. Hello Imy. I'll be recording the action here today for the noon news. How do you feel about this whole situation?"

"Well, I was with Dolf when the safe was found and am very excited to be here in LaCrosse watching this together with TV 8."

90

I thought that if I plugged his station, he wouldn't be intimidating. I remembered when watching the news how belligerent some reporters could be to people who weren't very cordial.

The reporter seemed pleasantly surprised with the fact that I had TV station familiarity.

"Well, we're just delighted to be here interviewing you and very honored to share this wonderful experience."

We were suddenly interrupted by a man wearing a white button down shirt that was hanging out of his pants, along with a loose wrapped necktie. He was making a beeline for us, and it appeared as if he ran the show.

"We're on and ready to roll," he commanded.

"Let's get the safe in the bunker and let her buck!" The cameramen for both stations were set up and ready to go.

After a signal from one of the reporters, the cameras rolled as a reporter made a long-winded statement about the findings of the safe. The reporter summoned the rotund Maryanne over for a quick interview, then motioned Dolf and me.

"Please tell me your name, and where you're from?"

"I'm Doolllfff, and I, I live half way between Nort Creek and Nucome Valley, just dis side...."

I knew in order to spare the geography lesson, I had to think fast to help my struggling counterpart.

"Arcadia."

"And who do we have here?"

"Hello, I'm Imy, and I was with Dolf when the safe was found."

"Well, what do you think is in it?"

"If I had a dime every time someone asked me dat, I'd own a bar in Waumendee," Dolf interrupted.

"Well, we're about to find out. I heard we're ready to go. So boys, if you don't mind taking the safe over to the bunker, while we...."

"Blow dat sons a bitch to da moon."

I craned my head in order to locate the unsolicited comment. Whoever yelled it had his poker face on, and everyone else in the crowd appeared baffled by the origin of the voice. The safe was wheeled into the bunker, and we were ushered outside of the thick mesh security fence.

My mind couldn't help but wander, wondering what could possibly be in this thing. I remember how curious I was when I first discovered the safe, wanting to open it immediately. I thought that it might contain money or some other valuable commodity. I wondered if I would have any rights to the contents since I found it. If so, I would buy a new bicycle, one with real brakes that actually worked. However, after seeing the politics involved here and remembering past experiences, I knew that it was better not to get my hopes up. Besides, as more time elapsed and through all the commotion, my interest had slowly waned. Had I not found the safe, I wouldn't have cared a wit about the contents within. But it was very interesting to me to see how many people were watching this spectacle. It was hard to believe that this many people didn't have better things to do.

Minutes later, we were ushered behind a concrete wall located beyond the perimeter of the commons area. A muffled explosion reverberated in the bunker, and a demolition crew went in to check out the damage.

"Eddie, I'm gonna buy yous one of dose chambers fer yer birtday," came a yell from one area of the crowd. "Dat way, yous can eat all da beans yous want before yous come ober ta play cards," he continued. His heavy guttural voice sounded as if he were clearing his throat while talking at the same time.

"Yea hey," responded a medium-built guy on the other side of the crowd, as if proud to be addressed in this fashion.

"Yea hey," was the raspy response returned from this class-act orator.

"Well, sounds like we have a good showing from Arcadia," the reporter piped in, identifying the lingo and trying to deflect the verbal jousting.

Just then, the safe was wheeled from the bunker and placed back in the commons area where the interviews had taken place. Wispy gray smoke seeped out of the front of the iron structure, where a stubborn door had resided. The same small crowd of people was summoned back in, including Dolf and me. The door was hanging off the side of the safe, dangling by the top left-hand hinge. It had been burned by the blast, blackening the left side of the safe closest to the hinged door. I bent down low to get a better view of the stored contents. There was only one package, appearing to be about three inches thick, a foot wide and ten inches deep. The packaging was lime green in color and badly crumpled. The proprietor of Gilmanton Creamery bent over and nervously retrieved the green package. As soon as the crowd of people behind the fence saw green, they saw "green." I mean, they saw money. The rumor circulating the crowd was that it was cash and lots of it. Marryanne held up the green parcel to the excited crowd.

"Well, I think we know it ain't beer! So a lot of you guys got some settling up to do."

A murmur came over the crowd as some reached for their wallets, reluctantly transferring money to others.

"Why are they doing that, Dolf?"

"Dar settling bets. A lot of people tought dat dare was rare beer in dat safe."

"Now, how dumb is that?"

"Come on Dolf, you ain't exempt!" The voice belonged to none other than Apolinary Ruecorn. Dolf blushed and waved him off, saying that he'd talk to him over a beer later that night.

The green package was cautiously ripped open. I could smell the moldy paper from where I was standing, reinforcing the fact that whatever it was, it was ancient. Marryanne examined the contents, completely puzzled. Crowd noise fell to a hush as she passed the paper contents over to an older, heavy acquaintance of hers standing next to her in bib overalls. He looked it over, and after a quick review, handed it back to her to make the announcement. The main reporter walked up to Maryanne in order for her to announce her treasure to the crowd.

"Milk records."

The reporter stared at the fat lady, appearing very confused.

"Milk records?"

The acquaintance stepped over to the microphone and verified the finding.

"Milk records."

The acquaintance took the packet and started to study the contents further.

"Well, not jist any milk records, but Otto Pronchinski's milk records."

"Can you expound on this?"

"Eh?"

"Well, tell us in laymen's terms, what are milk records?"

"I don't believe I ever met Laymen's Terms, but my definition of milk records is a show on how much milk each cow gives. Udder wise, how da hell would ya know? The cow sure don't!"

"I see, sir. Go on."

"Well, everyone in da Gilmanton area knows da Pronchinski's. One reason is dat dare are so darn many of 'em, ya gotta know one of 'em. Anyway, da Pronchinski's always had top cows in da area. I know my grandpa lost in a 4-H milking contest to Otto's boy. So who knows why dees records got in da safe but.....shit....look at dis."

The fat guy was deeply engrossed and surprised beyond belief.

"If I had milk like dis, I'd put dees records in a safe, den put da safe in da bank. Dees are unreal!"

The crowd started to dwindle, while the fat guy read on. About a third of the crowd actually appeared interested in the data, many from Arcadia, and prodded the fellow to continue. As he stumbled on, the reporter was disconnecting his sound equipment while the cameramen packed up and rolled up their cords.

"Well, Imy, let's head back over da hill."

I followed Dolf unceremoniously to the car, and we drove off.

The entire affair was beyond disappointing. It was plain dumb, I thought. Now I know why Dad never gets his hopes up about anything. I wondered if the whole world was this bizarre, or if this was just Arcadia. I was determined that someday I would find out.

Back in town, Dad was just walking away from that familiar black pickup that appeared from time to time, as we drove down the hill and parked next to the mailbox. We jumped out of the car and met him on the porch.

"I already heard."

"Yea, isn't the whole thing stupid?" I commented.

"Well, you know, what's valuable to some people isn't always valuable to others," Dad philosophized. Besides, that's probably why he hid the safe, so that no one would find it, since people who see a safe usually think something of value is inside. But I do have to say, with records that incredible, I wonder what the heck they fed those cows. Those might not be individual state records, but I know that these records break the state record for the total herd category."

The telephone bell in the mill clamored, indicating a phone call. Dad ran to the office, and Dolf headed for the car. I took my position on the front porch by myself, gazing straight ahead. Jasper emerged out of the old, setback corncrib and trotted across the road, heading over to the office. Nothing seemed to matter to that dog except the essentials of food and water. At least humans can enjoy all aspects of life. No matter how strange or uncontrollable the events. It's pure pleasure to be a part of them. Disappointment is just a byproduct of expecting something great, isn't it? The thrill in life must be the ride, not the "end result." I figured that must be why Dad's so logical and unemotional. Maybe he's secretly enjoying the thrill of life's events without dwelling on the material outcome. People who can live life this way seem to enjoy it, instead of living for a desired outcome. Kind of like living in Arcadia. We'll never strike it rich here, but the experience of it all is priceless.

Chapter XII

Winter hit Arcadia with frigid air and very little snow. An average winter day could be as cold as 20 degrees below zero, with an even colder wind chill. Dad suspected that since Arcadia was 72 miles south of Elmwood, this might be normal winter conditions. I was hoping he was wrong. I didn't think relocating a mere ninety minutes south could make that much difference on snowfall totals.

I couldn't wait to go sledding down the hills that were just a snowball's throw away. Since I didn't have a sled, my plan was to draw from a cache of empty paper feed bags to use as my mode of transport down the intoxicating hills.

Since there wasn't much snow that first year, sledding was replaced with ice-skating. Mom had a pair of racing skates that she had used in high school some 25 years ago. I would put on multiple pairs of socks until I had a tight enough fit to support my skinny ankles. Access to the Trempealeau River was just on the other side of the cow pasture. On the river, I could skate in either direction for miles. Not only was this great exercise, but the view of the different farms from the river instead of the road was breathtaking. What a difference it was viewing a barn from the back, I remember thinking. In retrospect, I was starved for scenery.

Even though I enjoyed ice skating thoroughly, the biggest and most popular winter sport in Arcadia during the middle of winter was ice-fishing. This was a sport that was meant only for the rich, and since I didn't have the money to buy the proper equipment, I was reduced to being a spectator.

Fisherman would take their small icehouses and pull them out on the lake with their pickup trucks. The houses would sit out on the lake all winter long. Most were approximately twelve feet by twelve feet and had all the amenities of home. A swank icehouse would have a furnace, small appliances and, of course, four holes. Gas powered ice augers separated the big dogs from the wannabees. It was truly chic to entertain in your icehouse, flaunting your lifestyle by pulling cold beer from your miniature refrigerator. This sport seemed to offer something for everyone, the sportsman and old codger alike.

Each year, most of the small towns in the area would sponsor a contest. At Lake Independence, an award was given for the catch of "Big Bugler." This was a fish that nobody ever actually saw, but everyone talked about. At Third Lake in Trempealeau, an award was given for the muskie with the biggest teeth. However, the Trempealeau River was too shallow to drill, so Arcadia was exempt from hosting an event.

Festivities would crop up around the area weekly, with the mega-event being held down in the village of Dodge. Dodge was the bigger town of the renowned "twin cities," dwarfing its sister city of Pine Creek by a couple hundred people. Dodge was nestled in the hills about fifteen miles south of Arcadia. Dodge's claim to fame was having the longest chicken barn in the world. Dodge seemed to have almost as many taverns as it did people, making it evident why it was second-to-none in playing host to the biggest ice-fishing contest in the county.

It wasn't unusual to see thousands of people on the pond on ice-fishing Sunday. Icehouses would be packed together like sardines, with roof eves touching each other resembling a row-house project in a major city. Where there wasn't an ice-shack, there was a hole drilled in the ice with a short pole dangling over it. The lake was so perforated that it was hard to comprehend what was holding everything up.

Willard Yaski, a buddy of mine, invited me to go with him and his dad to the Dodge ice-fishing contest. His dad had a shack set up there with no intention to fish in the contest.

"Willard, why would you go then, if you're not going to fish?"

"To see Stogic."

"Who's Stogic?"

"That's Polish for grandpa. My uncle and Stogic are fishing this year. They won the casting contest in Trempealeau, so they get the shack this year."

"What contest?"

"The casting contest. Every year when we're out on the boat, we pick a day when the wind is calm and have a casting contest. The person who casts the longest wins the heat. The heat winners then compete in the elimination trials. Once you make the quarterfinals, you are guaranteed a hole in the ice-shack the following winter. Of course, it's still important to qualify for the semifinal and go on to win the championship."

"Well, if you win the quarterfinals and a fishing hole in the ice-house, why would you need to win the championship?"

"Because, then you can pick the hole."

"Ahhh, OK."

"See, this year Grandpa took the trophy, so then he'll get the hole right next to the refrigerator."

"Ahhh, OK."

"See, makes sense now, doesn't it?"

"Yea, I guess so."

"So you've never been?"

"No."

"But I thought your mom was from the Twin Cities?"

"That's the Twin Cities, as in Minneapolis and St. Paul."

"Oh. Never heard of 'em."

Willard and his dad picked me up that Sunday after church, and we made our way down the curvy road that leads to Dodge.

"Jis wait till ya see da house!" Willard's dad repeatedly exclaimed.

About a half-hour later we arrived, overlooking a sea of red. It was interesting to see how fashionable red deer-hunting jackets could be. The crowd was so immense that I couldn't tell where the pond was. Evidently, a few other people had the same problem.

"I can't wait till ya see yer first icehouse. Once ya see one, it jis kind of stays wit ya fer awhile."

"I can't wait, Mr. Yaski."

"So yous probably been here fer dis a lot, since your mom is from da area dare."

"Acutally, no. Believe it or not, there's another twin-cities, located in Minnesota."

"Dat down buy Beloit?"

"No, that would be Northwest of us, across the Mississippi River."

"Hmmm. Never heard of dat. Day ice fish up dare?"

OK, this geography lesson probably isn't going anywhere, I thought.

"Wow, check out all the people!"

We parked and stepped out of the car. There was a six-foot human object completely dressed in red, drilling on the road shoulder with an eight-foot gas powered ice auger.

"You ain't gonna find no fish on da road dare" Willard's dad said with a grin.

"Hey, I ain't drillin on da road."

"Well, da lake's ober dare, dis is da road."

"Maybe dis is da lake, and everyone else is fishin on da road, ever tink a dat?"

Willard's dad stood there, expressionless without a retort.

"Got 'cha tinking, din't I, ole buddy?"

"Yea, you got me tinking dat you're drunk."

"Well, I mite be, cause if I wasn't, I'd chase you with Auggy auger, and I'd drill fer more dan water….."

In order to avoid confrontation at all cost, I started to walk away with Willard and his dad following suit. Mr. Yaski could be a character, sometimes pushing things to the limit.

I met Willard's dad for the first time when I was in downtown Arcadia one day. Dad had to run to the post office and asked if I wanted to tag along. Since I hadn't looked at the new fishing poles in The Coast-To-Coast store for awhile, I thought that I might as well go. I had just come out of the hardware store when I noticed a scaled-down milk delivery-route truck appearing out of nowhere, swerving violently down Main Street. My eyes remained fixed on it, as I walked backward towards Dad's car. About ten seconds later, this door-less milk wagon was up on the sidewalk chasing me down. The miniature van made a beeline at me, occasionally riding up on people's lawns in order to circumvent the saplings that were planted in the medium. The horn was a study blare, controlled by this crazed delivery route driver. I now sensed danger and bolted for the car. I ran down the sidewalk, leaping in the passenger seat of Dad's car while the truck screeched to a halt.

"Yous Arno's boy, not?"

"Yes," I responded, "gasping for breath."

"I'm da town's milkman. I got a boy at home 'bout your age. Maybe you know 'em. His name is Bill. But we call him Willard."

"Yea, he's in my class."

"Welp, better git back ta work. And da cow tinks he's got it bad."

Just as fast as the scene developed, he was gone. I sat there dazed by what had just happened. I couldn't wait to tell Dad, although I knew that I would get the same response as I would if I had told the dashboard.

We were walking out on the lake amidst this vast sea of humanity. Every square inch of ice-covered water was occupied by a hole, house or hoof. And everyone had a flask of his or her favorite "cough syrup." We made our way over to the Yaski icehouse.

"How do you know which one is yours?" I asked.

"Ours is da one wit da Green Bay Packer banner on it."

I gazed over the plethora of ice shacks and still wondered how they could tell them apart. Literally hundreds of icehouses had Packer paraphernalia hanging from them. Championship banners from years past flapped in the wind resembling a patriotic, polar expedition settlement. I shrugged my shoulders and followed the Yaski's to their ice shack.

"Here she is."

Willard pushed on the door but met too much resistance to open it. So Willard's dad pushed for all he was worth, and made little headway as well.

"Too many people in dare. Dat one guy is gonna have a tough time pulling dat door knob out of his butt."

We stood outside of the ice shack for awhile, hoping some folks might exit so that we could go in. I looked around and saw a short pole bending drastically that wasn't even close to a hole in the ice. The fishing pole was supported with a wooden device called a tip-up. The owner of the pole stumbled over, grabbed it, and pulled up on it with both arms. He tugged so hard that the empty fifth of whiskey in his pocked came tumbling out. I couldn't help but notice the hook that was lodged under the unassuming man's snow boot. He continued to pull so feverishly that he finally tipped himself over.

My sideshow was soon interrupted by a fever-pitched scream coming from one of the ice shacks nearby. The shack emptied almost immediately, with a frantic crowd crying for help.

"Eider someone farted, or we got a problem," Willie's dad stated.

"Mr. Yaski, I think that's one in the same."

We darted over to see if we could render help, and when we entered the house we laid eyes on the most prehistoric fish emerging from the ice-hole. I had seen some ugly ones, but this was, by far, the worst. I caught a garfish in the Treampealeau River one time that was so ugly that I threw the whole works away on the spot, pole and all. Another time, I saw a guy pull a 100-pound channel catfish out of the muck of the Mississippi backwaters that actually had shoulders. The grotesque creature had to be dragged in with a hay bale hook.

Without a doubt, this one took the cake. This fish had a set of teeth on it that resembled an alligator. Its snoot was waving wildly in the air as if it couldn't wait to get on dry land and start eating people. The excited fisherman didn't know what to do except to go and look for a club. Suddenly, the door of the icehouse sprang open, and a man came rushing in as if to provide help. The man grabbed the jaws of this missing link and proceeded to pull it up out of the water and into the icehouse. The icehouse owner had seen enough and ran toward the door. Another man ran in with a tire iron ready to defend himself. At this point, the man who was personally dealing with this creature had it totally wrapped up, still struggling to land it on the floor of the house.

"Put that tire-iron down. That's my dog!"

"Your dog?"

"Yea. My dog fell through a hole in the ice over there and just started swimming. I knew he'd surface, but didn't know where."

I watched as the man lifted the matted Golden Retriever out of the hole and held it close to him in an effort to keep it warm. Mr. Yaski glanced at me nonchalantly as if disappointed by the outcome.

"Well, let's see if we can git in our icehouse again, boys."

I followed them out of the door, thinking that, after what we just witnessed, Willard's dad was right. My first impression of an interior ice shack experience would stay with me for quite some time.

Chapter XIII

The hard winter had broken and the warm weather signaled inklings of summer. I had been out of school for over a week now, and the end of May was approaching. This was my all-time favorite month, mainly because three long-awaited events converged around this time. A long, hard school year had come to an end, and I was looking forward to a well-deserved school break. This time of year also meant summer was finally around the corner, ending the spring mud season that usually followed a stark, frigid, Wisconsin winter. And last, but definitely not least, the Memorial Day Weekend signaled my first Broiler Days festival.

I had read about the infamous Broiler Days Festival before we even moved here and had to listen to the natives talk about it for an entire year. Finally, the anticipation was coming to an end, and the festival was only a few days away.

I had intently studied the poster promoting the event that was stapled up on the inside of the mill office door. Friday night was the kickoff, with the carnival in town and beer tent opening at 5:00 PM. Chicken grills would be setup between the carnival and beer tents, serving barbecue chicken or "yard bird," as the natives called it, until midnight.

Saturday morning started off with the "kiddy parade" at ten o'clock that went through the east side of town. Immediately following the parade, the usual water fight was staged, with the volunteer fire department providing the trucks and high pressure water hoses. Saturday noon was the start of the softball tournament, and the horse-pulling contest was scheduled for three o'clock.

The evening billing was Actina's Accordion Amplifiers, a husband and wife accordion band. Everett C. Skribner, not to be confused with the other two Everett Skribner's in town, and his wife, Actina, played at weddings around town and were the band of choice. Actina played the accordion, and Everett C. mastered the drums. I had seen this musical duo before and was mildly impressed by them. Actina was a large framed woman, making the squeezebox that she played resemble a slinky. Everett C. would nonchalantly bang out rhythm on the drums. He usually leaned back on his steel folding chair until the front legs were airborne. During the "instrument only" sections, he would "kick-back" and converse with his two kids playing under the drum set.

As I read down the banner, I came to the bold print, capital letters that would catch the eye of even the most casual observer. SUNDAY-SUNDAY-SUNDAY.

Obviously, Sunday was the mother-load. I mean, it's hard to top a softball tournament so competitive that you would think they were playing for beer. The horse pull and BBQ chicken were also tough acts to follow. How can any other small town outdo that? But all these events were just a prelude to the grand finale.

GRAND PARADE SUNDAY 1:00 PM - RAIN OR SHINE!

Not only were some of the units listed, but some of the farming implements that would be appearing were noted as well. A horse shoe contest followed, along with several other peripheral events taking place concurrently.

Sunday evening was to be special. Starting at eight PM, was scheduled the annual tractor pull, and all farmers were encouraged to enter.

Tractors were a huge topic in and around Arcadia, each with an intense patriotic following. The name brand manufactures were the likes of John Deere, International- Farmall, Massy/Harris, Case, Oliver, Minneapolis Moline, Allis Chalmers, White and Ford. My observation was that the main competition existed between John Deere and International-Farmall. First of all, no one on any farm in the area had a White. I didn't know why and never asked. It was just fact. The Fords were small tractors with Volkswagen-sounding motors. Everyone called the Minneapolis Moline, "Mickey Mouse," which was not very masculine. Allis Chalmers made a smaller tractor, good to pull hay racks or run the blower when filling silo. Besides, farmers referred to these tractors as the "Alice," once again not a very manly name. Oliver hadn't made a new tractor in ten years, or no one from the Arcadia area had bought a new Oliver in ten years. So the only Olivers existing were just that, "existing." Besides, Oliver was the name of the farmer on Green Acres, a TV show, and nobody wanted to be equated to him. Massy's were tractors supposedly seen on the East Coast. Through process of elimination, the last two heavyweights left standing were John Deere and International-Farmall. These tractors could be distinguished by their distinctive colors; the John Deere doused in all green, and the International-Farmall painted totally red.

Now there were leaders and there were followers in Arcadia. It just so happened that the Bleezna boys all loved "Big John." Since there were so darn many Bleezna's, John Deere had quite the following up on Barns Bluff. It was rumored that Adolfus Sopenski started with John Deere, and whatever Adolfus does, Bleezna's will copy a week later. That goes for plowing, planting, harvesting, etc. Dad used to joke, saying the Bleezna's spent more time watching Adolfus Sopenski than watching their own crops.
Aloyizie Pirzina, Alfred Woletzco, Roger Potzner and Lambert Walski were just some of the big names around the area that rode "Big John."

Then there was the other side of the tracks, the International-Farmall boys. They were more the renegades, living life a little more on the edge. Farmers like Punski Krunk, Shorty Borgy and Adrian Krysner were found to be siding with "Big Red." Their farms were not quite as pristine, maybe a few more weeds around the milk house, or a couple of obsolete implements sitting out along side the barn. At any rate, the tractor controversy in the Arcadia area ranked a close second to the beer brand wars.

The alarm clock read seven thirty. I had set it for seven o'clock, but the alarm switch must have pushed itself back in when I casually bumped it against the back of the bookshelf. I just lay there thinking that I should have learned that lesson from last week. In fact, last Saturday, I had it set at 4 AM to be at Ray Urbec's to help him de-beak turkeys. The same thing had happened, and I ended up being an hour late. He still paid me for all the time I worked, but he chose not to send home with me that fourteen-pound turkey that he had set aside in the freezer. Oh well, I got home so late, I couldn't eat it anyway. At least, that's what I remember thinking. Besides after cutting off two thousand turkey beaks with a heated guillotine, my appetite for a turkey dinner wasn't there.

After clearing the early morning fog from my head, I leapt out of bed and rushed downstairs to greet the day. I had been waiting for this day for almost a year now. Broiler Days were here, and we were going to the parade.

Dad was already up making breakfast. The crackle of bacon popped in the electric frying pan, and the smell of burnt toast permeated the kitchen. I rounded the corner, greeted by two pieces of overdone, charcoal-colored bread sitting on a small plate.

"Imy, better get some butter on those sponges, before they dry up completely."

"No problem, Dad."

"How many eggs you want?"

"What are you having?"

"Three."

"I'll take two."

I went to the refrigerator to grab the butter, then stopped dead in my tracks, distracted by the calendar depicting a green monster 4020 John Deere tractor headlining the month of May.

"May is when we plant," was the inscription printed below the sparkling implement.

My heart skipped a beat, as I anticipated the tractor pull coming up later today.

As I closed the refrigerator door, I stared at the mighty farming beast again, imagining the incredible power at one's fingertips. As I was about to return to my buttering task, a quick thought prompted me to flip over to the month of June. Just as I thought, a picture of a big Holstein cow blanketed the calendar with the inscription below: "June is Dairy Month."

At least they were consistent.

"Wait any longer, and we can use this toast for a sanding block," came the impatient voice of Dad.

"I'm coming, Dad. How many pieces of toast do you see yourself eating?"

"None, if you don't get butter on 'em pretty soon!"

Mom was just making her daily shuffle in from the bedroom, coughing up a storm.

"I'll butter the toast, if you want to get ready for church," she said in between hacks.

"Not a problem Mom. I'll only be a few more minutes anyway."

I knew I couldn't have her spewing up lung chunks over the toast, since it would grossly remind me of Saturday lunch.

"Why don't you just have a seat at the table, and I'll have this wrapped up in a flash, Mom."

An hour later breakfast was over and the entire family got in the old Buick and headed to 10:30 mass at St. Stans. St. Stans was a blond brick, stark structure built sometime in the 1940's. It dominated the summit skyline, standing alone at the top of the hill. The interior was cavernous and cold. The rows of wooden pews were flanked with holy statues, and the marble floor amplified many a heel. We entered to a surprisingly large crowd, with the usher, Stosh Sikowski, actually having to point to a place for us to sit.

"Dare's room by Billy Bert."

Now that was a commonly made mistake. Ushers should never sit friends of our age in close proximity to each other.

As soon as we entered the pew, Billy's hands went over his face, trying to conceal his devilish grin.

The usual people were there, all fidgeting slightly, waiting for Mass to start so that they could get in their obligatory hour of worship for the week. In front of us was Father Subchuck's housekeeper, Julia Pirzina, a tall shrewd-looking woman who was swiveling her head like a predecessor to Linda Blair who later starred in the Exorcist. Slightly to the right and in front of us sat the entire Lavern Suechea clan, with the bald dome of Lavern already listing port side, bobbing like a fishing bobber on a waving lake. Lavern had an uncanny knack for sleeping during the time the congregation sat, yet springing up whenever the congregation rose. In the front pew sat Uferzine Rebarchick. Uferzine was an ornery-looking woman in her late seventies. She walked to church every day from beyond the corner store, at least a two-mile journey. She attended every funeral, and we were sure certain that it was just a plot to get a free meal that was always served after the service in the church basement. We didn't know much else about her, except that she couldn't be trusted. She would point to us with that crooked index finger of hers and tell us how she was going to report us to the nuns and priest. Well, let's just say that she never gave any of us a big "warm and fuzzy" feeling.

The church bell rang, and the parish stood and sang "Ave Regina" in unison with the screeching choir. Of course with Julia Perzina standing directly in front of us, Billy and I changed the refrain "Ave, Ave, Ave, Regina," to "Julia, Julia, Julia Perzina." Julia turned her head in a complete 180-degree rotation, glaring down Billy and me. We were both standing, heads down, convulsing with laughter, trying to look inconspicuous.

As the Mass started, we regained our composure and started to chant back the proper prayers that were listed in the Misilette. We sat down for the first Reading, and Billy let a little gas slip out. Of course, I was anything but suprised. The fart began with a subtle tone, then started to grow with intensity and amplitude. As it grew loud enough to distract a few nearby parishioners, the expulsion kept rhythm with his laughter. Each violent exhale prompted another sporadic blast, making every moment funnier than the last.

Just when I thought I couldn't take it any more, I looked up at the pulpit, trying to think of anything but the present. Once I regained control, my eyes focused past the priest, and my heart stopped. My blood pressure rose, turning my face so red, a tomato would have paled in comparison. I stared ahead in horror, noticing only one altar boy serving Mass. Since I was an altar boy, I knew the solemn oath that I had taken. One of the stipulations was that, if at any time it appeared that you were needed, you had to go and serve. Absolutely no exceptions were allowed. I anxiously looked to see who I would be sharing responsibilities with, and it didn't look good. I saw the goofy look of Bimbo Klonecki staring me down, as if daring me to come and serve with him. Dad gave me a sideways look, knowing he had to put an end to all the shenanigans.

"You better get up there."

So I genuflected and headed up the side isle to the vestibule in order to suit up.

I knew that I had my work cut out for me being up there with Bimbo. "Bim," as we called him, was a good friend but quite an instigator. He always played a trick on someone, usually backfiring on everybody. One time, just minutes before serving for the "Way of the Cross," five of us alter boys were lined up in the side vestibule, looking at the altar and waiting for the church bell to ring. Heading the lineup and standing in formation was big Lard Pheler carrying the long-stemmed cross. Behind him were Bim and Korps, each with a prayer book. Bringing up the rear was Wayne and myself, each holding lit candles. Hospital Chaplain, Father Papiernick, was standing behind us. Bim started talking about a bee he was watching flying around the altar and holy statues. He had all of our attention by now, pointing with a rotating index finger, as if to follow its intermittent flight. Even Father Papiernick, the hospital chaplain was interested and had taken up the search. The longer that we stood there looking for the bee, the more leery we became, thinking Bim was fibbing, since no one else could see the elusive insect.

"There it is, right on the microphone!"

Bimbo simultaneously passed gas, mimicking the sound of a bee buzzing the mike.

"Here....here....that's enough," came a monotone reprimand from Father Papiernick. Just then, the church bell rang, and we were out the side vestibule door like a bad parade, all five heads bobbing from laughter. I couldn't keep my candle lit until the sixth station, extinguishing it with every laughing exhale.

I quickly threw on my cassock and went out to stand next to Bim, not even exchanging a glance. I knew once I acknowledged him, it was pretty much over. I wasn't going to allow him to get in my head. Besides, with Mass almost half over, what could he possibly do to me? As my confident stature was reaching a peak, a loud whisper interrupted my composure.

"Hi monkey nuts."

This phrase was followed by a choppy exhale of air out of his lungs, resetting the tone of the moment. Now logically, I knew that voice could only have come from one of two people in close proximity, Bim or Father Subchuck. If I were a betting man, odds were it came from Bim. I pretended not to hear it. I listened deeply to the Gospel, then took my chair for the sermon.

This is really going smoothly, I thought. I wondered what communion prayer Father would select. Eucharistic Prayer I was very long, and III and IV were middle-of-the-roaders. But Prayer II was the short cut. Should Father select it, this Mass would be in the bag.

The sermon was going just fine until movement out of the corner of my eye caused me to rotate my head and take notice. At the back of church, Stosh Sikowski sporting his white usher uniform was giving the wind up signal to Father. His right arm rotated as if he were a pitcher during a "fast pitch" softball game. He would stop periodically and feverishly point to his watch. This commotion continued for about two to three minutes before Father acknowledged the signal.

"Well I'm getting the wind-er-up from Stosh, and because of the parade and festivities in town today, we'll use Eucharistic Prayer number II."

A sigh of relief fell over the crowd.

"Let us stand."

Wow, this is just too easy. Just the offertory, communion and final blessing, and we're out of here. The offertory had just gotten under way, and we jumped up to get the water, wine and chalice. Bim went for the chalice, and I went for the cruets, vehicles for the water and wine. Now Father Subchuck was a large Polish man who walked around with a laughing box during bingo night in the church basement. He was never known to turn down a drink, and it was customary for us to have one cruet filled to the brim of wine and the other about a quarter full with water. After a glancing examination of the cruets, everything appeared to be consistent, so I grabbed them and met Bim at the altar. Bim had retrieved the chalice and had a suspicious grin on his Polish mug. I glanced over, returning the grin, only amplifying his. I knew something was up, but didn't have any idea what it was. Father Subchuck grabbed the chalice from Bim, took off the little linen that covered the top, and while praying out loud, rotated on the balls of his triple E Oxfords, stopping in front of me. He was holding the cup steady in order to receive my precious gifts of water and wine. I glanced down so that I could pour the wine first, since that was tradition. To my horror, the wine and water cruets had been reversed. I could only take the quarter-full cruet of wine and pour it all into the cup.

It is a known fact from the alter boy training manual that when the Priest wants more liquid, he continues to lower the chalice until he raises it abruptly, thus ending his want for more. After emptying the entire quarter cruet of wine into the chalice, the chalice continued to lower, then bob as if floating on a restless ocean. I don't know who was more disappointed, Father Subchuck or myself, but the look in Father's eyes said it all. The congregation had just finished another obligatory song, and it was just Father and me, with Bim smiling in the background.

"You better run and get more of the good stuff, son."

The command seemed to come from God himself, appearing to vibrate the shingles on the roof.

"Yes, Father."

I was off in a flash. I wasn't two steps into my dash to the refrigerator in the vestibule when my cassock caught my shoe, and over I went, head first into the side of the altar. Luckily, the sides of the altar were indented and draped with a starched white linen, salvaging my thick noggin, but not my pride. Recomposing myself, I walked off to execute my task.

The rest of Mass went off without a hitch. Afterwards, Father Subchuck softly scolded that we all make mistakes, and my mistake was coming to serve with Bim. Bim's face went pale for a second, but Father patted us both on the back. "You're both good kids, and God will bless you for it."

I guess that's why Father was like "The Father." He commanded all respect, however, he did nothing but love and forgive.

With Mass over, we headed back to the farm to change clothes, then off to the grand parade.

The weather was warm and sultry, and a threatening sky loomed overhead. May's weather could really be a crapshoot, anywhere between 50 and 90 degrees, from a constant rain to a cloudless sky. Thinking that we may get some rain, I donned jeans and a tee shirt and ran out of the house to wait in the car. Then I remembered that Mumpsy, our farm cat, had just had a litter of kittens. So I got out of the car and ran over to check them out under the front porch. After a quick review, I ran back to the car, not wanting to be accused of being the delinquent one who caused the family to get bad seats at the parade. Minutes later, everyone reported in, and the big green Buick was off to downtown Arcadia.

Dad kept his eyes open for a place to park. A bicycle went by with an old man peddling. He was wearing tweed pants, and his long white hair flowed well below the collar of his plaid shirt. I waved to him, since that was the culture of Arcadia. But he returned with a jester that surprised me. The warm friendly look of his face just didn't rhyme with the deliberate middle finger that he stuck out. He retracted it quickly in order to balance his two-wheel ride, then waved it again at me as if to assure that I got the message.

"Dad, who's that?"

"That's Ignuts Waldera. He goes to our church."

"Well, at least he goes."

A few minutes later we were parked. I was slightly taken aback by all of the excitement and activity.

People lined Main Street as if it were a New York City Ticker Tape Parade. Farmers from all around the area had driven to town for the festivities. Parade-goers were lined sometimes two deep throughout the one mile parade route.

The parade began on top of the hill at Margaret's Store, then it came down one block, turning left onto Main Street. The parade proceeded down the hill through town and terminated just across the river.

We chose a curb right in front of the City Library, a small, one-story brick building located across the street from the high school. No sooner had we sat down on the stained cement then the high-pitched wail of a siren pierced the air, taunting a chorus of howling dogs. An old style fire truck went whizzing down main-street in the opposite direction of the parade route with three wildly waving firemen hanging off the fender stoops, resembling bandits trying to rob a stagecoach.

"Gee Dad, they sure look like they know everyone."

Dad appeared annoyed by the volunteer firefighters.

"They're drunk, and they're just trying to hang on."

"Then why is the driver going so fast?

"He's drunk too."

Just then, one of the men riding on the rear fender flew airborne as the truck negotiated a curve to ascend the Main Street hill. His leg appeared to become detached and flew end over end, separating from his flailing body, hurling lifelessly through the air, sending a chill down the parade spectators' spines. This spectacle brought loud cheers from the crowd, until the apparent appendage was identified as a long boot, which hit a taboo target. The boot landed on a full cup of freshly poured beer that had been mindlessly abandoned on the curb. It was apparent that this newborn, unassuming, twelve-ouncer was truly the victim here. An eerie still came over the crowd, and howls and hoots turned into whispers. A couple of disheveled men behind me were among those in the crowd who were curious about the outcome of this spectacular event. One of the guys was donning a dirty seed corn cap and had a face that looked like ten miles of bad road. The other guy was just plain fat.

"I wonder whose beer dat was?"

111

"I seen Myron, K-wamp and Gubba up dare, and yous know if K-wamp is up dare, den dare is beer up dare."

"Hey, I been drinking with Gubba and doz boys, and none of dem would ever leave a lonely beer."

"Hey, it all depends what dare drinking. Maybe if K-wamp bought dat cheap stuff, Gubba set her down for some better beer."

I didn't recognize any of these names, except for K-wamp, of course. It seemed that everyone had heard of him. K-wamp was a teenager from Independence with a huge beer gut and earned the nickname when trying to do a swan dive at the downtown pool. He completely undershot the dive and did a total belly flop, displacing so much water that the pool had to be evacuated because the pump sensors had automatically been deployed to add water. I guess the noise that he made when his belly hit the water earned him his name.

"Hey, do yous tink dat it was a total waste, or do yous tink dat dey can salvage something out of her?"

"Forgit it. Dat beers dead."

"Not da cup, hey. Yous can still use dat!"

Another shrill siren of a Cadillac ambulance soon interrupted the cerebral side bar, and the two debaters staggered up the street to get a better look.

After the accident scene was cleared, a loud cannon sounded down main street signaling the start of the parade.

I felt goose bumps all over. Finally, after a whole year of built up anticipation, the wait was over. The parade had started.

The first unit was the Color Guard. Dad stood at attention, snapping a tight salute with his right hand, leaving just a half-inch of insulating air between his hand and forehead. I took off my cap and held it over my heart, following suit after most of the men in the crowd. I didn't know what to do with my left hand, since I wasn't holding a beer, so I let it fall lifelessly at my side.

After the Color Guard passed, a large squeal pierced the air. The Dairy Princess float, pulled by Eugene Adank's convertible, seemed to have encountered a problem. With the load of humanity sitting in the convertible, it was quite ironic that the trouble stemmed from a bad wheel bearing on the hitched hayrack rather than from the over burdened car. The float was one of Beenie Studt's hayracks, and I'm positive that the left rear wheel hadn't seen a grease gun in years. Eugene pulled over and waddled out of the cockpit of the crowded drop-top to inspect the wheel.

The next unit was a John Deer tractor pulling a nicely decorated hayrack with a huge plaster cow that stood approximately twelve feet tall. The float was sponsored by Dears Sausage with a banner along the side of it reading: "Nobody makes Deer Sausage like Dears Sausage." The tractor and cow ensemble pulled over behind the Dairy Princess float, offering assistance if needed. After a brief discussion and quick analysis of the situation, it was readily apparent that the crowd of oversized dignitaries riding in the convertible could not make room for the Princess, nor was anyone willing to walk. As soon as the logistics were worked out, they assisted the Dairy Princess to her lofty perch on top of the Dears Sausage cow amid a standing ovation. The hayrack was unhooked, and the big convertible continued its trek down Main Street with the entourage continuing to drink beer and wave to the townspeople as if they were an important attribute to the parade. They were followed by the Dairy Princess hanging on to dear life by clutching her hands to the cow's rubber ears as if they were handlebars. Since she couldn't get a wave off in this position, people just stared back at her as if she was from another planet, or county for that matter.

More units continued to roll past our vantage point. There was the winner of last year's car demolition derby riding shotgun in a tow truck, hauling his smashed and dented trophy car behind him. Then there was the "Sportsman of the Year" car, which was nothing but a Cadillac with a big set of deer antlers tied to the front for a hood ornament. Eli Andry's beer truck seemed to garner the most applause, with a proud Eli driving with his left arm out of the window clutching the side mirror and gaze fixed ahead as if he were piloting an F14 fighter plane. The band from Ettrick walked by without playing a note. Word had it that the drum major missed the bus, so the only noise produced was from the tuba players verbally taunting the parade patrons sitting curbside. Of course the clowns were a spectacle to watch, not only for their candy throwing, but also for the intensity with which they targeted it. The clowns would select their victims, then hurl small pieces of individually wrapped hard candy at their respective beer cups. These victims were apparently outsmarted by the cunning clowns and would run for cover once the plot was figured out. This ploy allowed the kids to end up with the candy, as it should be. It was amusing to see so many out-of-shape people flex so many body parts while keeping their beer cups undisturbed. Full beer cups hanging from limp wrists appeared as if attached to a gyroscope, always finding a perfectly balanced horizontal plane. Hardly a drop of the golden substance was lost.

Following the Women's Auxiliary car, a lime green, eight-door, extended taxicab went by, with the caption spray painted on both sides "The too drunk to walk club." Right behind this prestigious click came the Woobsey Boy's driving their sports cars, with the rear ends jacked-up a couple of feet. Their windows were sprayed with foam touting their auto repair business. "Don't need jack in order to jack, just call Jack." I guess it meant that one could get the rear of their car raised at a very reasonable price through Jack Woobsey.

Some out-of-town units appeared all clumped together since Arcadians seemed afraid to mingle with foreigners. One of these floats went by adorned in so much crape paper and flowers, that I couldn't tell what kind of hay rack it was. The Shriner's followed, driving little motorcycles in formation, breaking only to do occasional figure eight loops. Surprisingly, they seemed to be the only sober parade performers.

The local motorcycle gang "Joe Can and the 12 Packers" roared by in low gear, each member sporting some type of beer-wear. The gang was sporting their "colors" which was merely the empty cardboard 12-pack container each was wearing for a helmet, using the little front flap as a visor. People clapped as they went by. The gang responded with a "thumbs up."

After a few even more meaningless parade units passed, the roar of heavy farm machinery thundered in the background. A fleet of no less than twenty-two tractors slowly roared by in low gear. This maneuver prompted a crawling pace, while, at the same time, their revved up engines could be enjoyed by all.

After the tractors came the combines, a six-row corn planter, and even a threshing machine. The next unit to come down the pavement was a one-handed farmer aboard an old Allis Chalmers tractor pulling a manure spreader. Both pieces of equipment were quite unspectacular, and the guy driving the small tractor wasn't even drinking a beer.

"Hook, what 'cha do, get stuck in da parade coming back from da field? I'd get da hell out or you're in deep shit," an unkempt observer yelled out.

"Yah-hey, went out to spread some shit and got caught up in dis shit!" the one-handed farmer hollered back.

We stared, as Dad seemed visibly annoyed by the vulgar comments.

"That's Hook Shabella. He owns the farm just outside of town by Chico Gooza, and he's probably just trying to get back home."

Ruth glared at Dad, aghast by his use of the word "hook."

"That's so sad that a person with a pronounced handicap has to be labeled with it."

"Well Ruth, that's Arcadia. Take Stubby Opps, for example. He has one arm ending just below the elbow. I recently learned that his real name is Ararea. And the weird thing is, he owns the shoe store in town. He can tie a shoe faster than me. And look at Hook Geebler. I don't even know his real name."

"Does he have only one hand as well?" Ruth asked.

"No, he has two. They call him "hook" because of his huge bent nose."

The stomping hooves of the horses interrupted the conversation, signaling the end of the parade.

"Well, I guess that shoots another parade in the ass!"

I turned around to view an overweight man dressed in trousers and a sport shirt, struggling to get up from the curb.

"Mornin, Mayor," was one of the greetings extended to this man as people walked by. Another person stopped to exchange pleasantries.

"What a parade, Mayor. Right when you think that there's no way you can top last years,' Hook goes by on his Allis. Can you stand it! Wow, I can't wait to see next years'!"

"Dad, I thought Hook was just driving through and got stuck in the parade route?"

"He did."

"Then why did that guy just ask the Mayor…."

"You talk too much!"

I knew that was my key to shut the heck up, so I did.

"Dad, how does the Mayor know that it's the end of the parade anyway?" an inquisitive Ruth asked as if to fill in for me.

"Just wait till the horses go by, and you'll figure it out."

115

After the horses plodded past us, one of the equestrians slowed down to a crawl, responding to a pair of drunken men who were shouting to the horsemen.

"Hey horseboy, did you know that a horse show is where horses show their asses, and horse's asses show their horses?"

Both mental heavyweights shared a simultaneous hearty laugh while the horse seemed to roll its eyes as if it heard this one before. Then the "Quarter barrel drinkers" on quarter horses continued down the street in formation, leaving the pickled pair gasping for air and laughing. When the herd of half-breeds were past us, I learned why they put this act in the back. One glance at the street provided all the proof that I needed. The odor, which was becoming more unpleasant by the second, was as good an indicator as any that the parade was over.

"Anyone hungry?" asked Dad. "Let's head down to the pits and get some chicken."

"You betcha," I replied.

"Well, not after that!" Ruth exclaimed with a disgusting look. "Not only does it look gross, but it stinks, as well."

"Well Ruth, then don't look over there," I chided.

"Besides, we'd better walk down there before it gets too late. In fact, after looking over the girth of most of the people here, change that 'walk' to a 'run.'"

My sisters each grabbed the rest of the blankets used for curb seating, and we all headed down to where the festivities were to take place.

With the smell of chicken permeating the air, we didn't need directions. At the front of the food line was a long, wooden plank suspended by a steel barrel at each end. We scooted up and waited anxiously for someone to take our order. Behind the lumber counter was the chicken pit area. It appeared that there was enough grill space for hundreds of pieces of chicken. I couldn't help but notice how serious and organized the men were when managing this fowl fry. Two men were always in position to manage the massive grills, using winter work gloves as hot pads. One guy would call out a cadence, emulating the White House Marine Drill Team. When the order was barked out, both men would grab their respective giant, grill-handles and flip the huge rack of chicken in one felled swoop. The event looked choreographed, as if it were practiced for hours. The exposed veins under their rolled up shirtsleeves popped out every time they did this. The "flip master" walked back and forth, inspecting the barbecue like a pit boss in a grand casino. The sternness on their faces said it all: Arcadia means chicken, and we mean business, and today, chicken is our business.

A grossly overweight woman waddled over to take our order. She stared me down as she flipped up a page on her disorderly note pad.

"Are yous related to Pompoos?"

Her voice was raspy, as if stifled by a throat full of phlegm from breathing in the smoke of the barbecue.

"Ahh, no," I replied.

"He might have some Walderea in him."

I looked over at an even larger person leaning up against a barrel. This person had on a seed corn cap with the bill pulled down over the eyes, making it impossible to distinguish them from a man or a woman. This person then left their cover and approached the wooden plank, still making the odds fifty-fifty on a gender call.

"Your dad Punski?"

"No, I'm a Lecheler."

"What the heck is a Lecheler?"

"Dad, I don't appear to be getting anywhere here, maybe you'd have better luck."

"Hi, we'd like to order some chicken."

"Light or dark?"

"Well, let's see...we have three...."

"Got tickets?"

"No, where do you get tickets?"

"Emil Stelmach is selling 'em at da next card table over dare."

Dad turned to search out Emil, hoping to get a bearing on where he had to go for tickets. All he saw were card tables set up with people standing around them.

"Ahh, which one's Emil?"

"Right next to Shorty Borgy."

"Now where's Shorty?"

"Well he's a hard one to spot, but see Angus Andrey standing next to Kindro Kutlatch, right next to the Shriber Boys?"

"Ahhh..."

"Well, everyone knows Hindu Schriber. He not only pitches for Tricky's Tavern Softball team, but he's also the best 'over forty' bowler in Arcadia."

Now Dad seemed totally stumped, and even my little sister who was three years old could see that we weren't getting anywhere. We excused ourselves and migrated over to the card tables. Fortunately, the ticket table sat right under a huge sigh that read BBQ CHICKEN TICKETS.

We got our tickets and were soon chowing down on the best-barbecued chicken this side of the Mississippi. Now, since I had never been more than ninety miles from the Mississippi River at any time in my life, I realized that that was not saying much, but it was the best BBQ chicken I had ever devoured. When the feast was over, mom and the girls went over to the carnival, and I opted to go with Dad to the softball tournament.

Now I had heard about the Ferris Wheel operator, Cotton Candy Jim, who could open pop bottles with his teeth and the "Bird Man" who, as you probably already figured out, could make noises like a bird. Even with a talent pool as astounding as this, I opted to check out the big leaguers and the fast pitch softball championships.

Dad and I made our way to the wooden bleachers and found a seat about half way up from the top. The consolation game to determine third place between Hooterville Tavern and the Fall Creek Chicken Chasers was just getting underway, with the championship game for all the marbles waiting on deck. The stands were full, and a competitive spirit began to fill the air. Even though the umpires were ready, several problems plagued one of the teams. The Hooterville Tavern Team had backed into the consolation game because of an earlier forfeit from a team sponsored by YaHoo Woshney's Bar. This had a sweet and sour impact on the Hooterville Team. Because of the forfeit, it appeared that most of the Hooterville Team members played that game in the beer tent, figuratively speaking. The team now had two obstacles to overcome. The first was the pitcher, Cleavon Kalinski, a notorious fast-baller with tons of control problems to go along with his normal drinking problem. The long, greasy-haired, fat-bellied, flat-lander had shown up for the game intoxicated as a result of being in the beer tent all afternoon. The other problem was that their all-star outfielder, Laddie Matchie, had to go back to the farm to do the chores. It wasn't until he returned that he realized he forgot his spiked shoes at home. He'd have to give it a whirl in the barn boots that he was sporting.

The umpire waved his arm in order to start the contest, and to the chagrin of the Hooterville Team, they knew they had to play regardless of their handicaps. Cleavon took his place on the pitching mound, staring down the batter from atop of his perch. Cleavon leaned slightly to the left as if to begin his windup and then fell over. He struggled to get up and kept checking the pitching mound as if the rubber had become loose and forced his quick decent. Cleavon started the algorithm again, this time delivering the ball at a rapid speed over the twelve-foot backstop behind the batter, catcher and umpire. This seemed to ignite the already excited crowd. Jeers started to rain down from the spectators.

"Give 'em another brewski!"

"Don't show 'em your beer, Iggy. If he sees it, he's likely to pitch from here!"

Cleavon got the ball back, thanks to a little help from a kid behind the bleachers that flanked home base. Cleavon wound up and let go of the next pitch way too early, causing the ball to roll on the ground like a high-speed Botchy Ball. The grounder arrived at home plate with such velocity that batter, catcher and umpire all ran for cover.

"Hey Cleavon, how 'bout another worm-burner!"

The crowd laughed hysterically.

Lippy Surrinski, a slightly built man who was playing second base, went over to talk to Cleavon. Now I had seen this team play before and remembered most of the players, especially Cleavon, Lippy and Laddy. But the one thing I never forgot was the choppy, abbreviated steps Lippy took when he walked. It was as if he was trying to touch every square inch of grass in a straight line as fast as he could. The umpire finally stood to call time in order to give Lippy more of the precious commodity.

About ten seconds later, Lippy arrived at the mound trying to calm Cleavon. A few seconds later, Lippy began his painstaking journey back and was close to his position when Cleavon wound up for his next delivery. The pitch was obviously released way too late this time, overcompensating for the last pitch. The ball shot straight up in the air, with the catcher punching his glove once, then nonchalantly catching the ball without leaving his stance.

"You're out of here," the umpire yelled, standing in front of home plate and giving the thumb to Cleavon.

Cleavon stood there with a big smile, thinking he had just gotten the big out, not quite sober enough to follow the actual chain of events.

"No, you're drunk, and get the heck out of here before someone gets hurt!"

"Hell, if you guys don't want to play fair, I'll just go and drink beer!" Cleavon hollered back.

Cleavon threw down his glove and stumbled over to the makeshift dugout. Lippy then approached the pitcher's mound, finally arriving about thirty seconds later. After a few practice pitches that really weren't too bad, the umpire called "play ball."

The first pitch was swatted right back to Lippy, who ran after it like a tractor in slow gear. The runner easily reached first base and kept taunting Lippy as if he were going to steal second. The next pitch was hammered into right field, sending Laddy on the run. Since Laddy was playing the long, damp grass outfitted in rubber-soled, steel-toed work boots, making any kind of cut for the ball was completely out of the question. Laddy not only slipped and fell on the original cut, he fell while trying to stop, and then fell again while throwing the ball to the infield. Let's just say, it wasn't to be Hooterville's day in the sun.

We watched the softball tournament for a couple of hours until Mom and the rest of the family walked up and asked when we were going home. Tom was starting to fuss, and Mom and the three girls were tired, so they approached with an agenda.

"Arnie, the girls and I are tired. Mind if we go home and then come back and pick up you guys tonight?"

"Sounds fine to me. You know we're going to the tractor pull?"

"Yea, I know."

"Come pick us up at about ten. If we need to come home earlier, we'll give you two longs and a short."

Now "two longs and a short" meant just that when dealing with hand crank telephones. Everyone who lived in town had rotary dial. However, out on the farm, we had to coexist with the other farmers whose telephones had a crank on them. We did have several phone models to choose from, a wall-hanging beauty that had a mouthpiece protruding out in the middle of the long wooden contraption, or the sleek desk design, which weighed a ton and only came in black. Regardless, every farm had a ring cadence, which let them know whether or not to answer the telephone. We shared a party line with fifteen other farms, and the telephone would ring constantly. It became quite a talent to discern your ring code automatically without acknowledging all of the other calls. However, most of the farm-folk would pick up the telephone on all rings so that they could listen in and be privy to all the gossip going on. The problem was that the greater the quantity of people listening to a telephone conversation, the less one could hear what the intended parties were saying. This would occasionally cause a problem, making the caller's voice indistinguishable. All of the farmer's wives loved this system because it allowed them to stay on top of everyone else's business.

Mom hoisted Tom up in one arm while grabbing a blanket with the other. Linda grabbed Betsy by the arm after giving me one of her cute little waves.

"See you guys later!"

It really felt good being there, just Dad and me. It was probably our first time together in a non-working environment. Who knows, I thought, maybe he'll like it, and we can actually do this again sometime.

I remember the last time that it was just Dad and me. It was the Friday before Easter, and a semi-trailer of bulk concentrate feed had just been delivered to the mill. The driver had to leave to get cleaned up for Good Friday church services, so he unhooked the trailer next to the front porch. This permitted easy access to the feed-bin above the broken out second-floor window. A couple of hours later, Dad released John for the day.

"Well Imy, let's get this twenty ton of feed off the semi and into the hopper, then call it a day."

"Sounds good. What do you want me to do?"

"I'll swing the boom-auger into the bin through the window, and you can get inside the trailer and stand on top of the feed. Once most of the concentrate has been unloaded with the 'moving floor,' you can shovel the rest from the sides onto it. The belt will continue to move feed to the front of the trailer to the boom auger. Once it gets empty, don't step in the middle of the trailer. I don't want you to get too close to that moving belt and see you sucked into the auger at the end."

"I'll be careful."

I stared at the gigantic trailer of feed, contemplating every word that was just said to me. For my own safety, I did not want to miss a word of instruction. However, I also didn't want Dad to think I was dumb either, so I knew better than to ask questions.

Dad stooped over to investigate levers that were riding under the mammoth rig's undercarriage. In a moment, he had the boom-auger churning but couldn't engage the floor belt motor.

"Shit. She sheared a pin!"

Now I knew we were deep in it, because Dad very rarely swore and never said the manure word, especially on Good Friday. Little did I know how fast his misfortune would soon be mine.

"Well Imy, looks like we gotta shovel this one. The pin's broken, and since it's Good Friday, our luck of getting anything repaired is nil. I'll take the bin, you take the truck."

I grabbed an aluminum feed-scoop and climbed up the side of the iron hauler. I secured my boots on a horizontal steel ledge while unfastening the top canvas that was secured tightly in place with rubber bungy cords. After peeling back the heavy tarp, I stood on top of this sea of bulk feed, waiting for my task to begin. About twenty minutes later, only a deep crevasse appeared in front of the forty-footer where the concentrate had gravity fed into the exit auger. The scope of work immediately became apparent. I had to shovel the rest of this payload over to the six-inch opening located front-center at the bottom of the rig.

By nine o'clock that evening, an exhausted Dad climbed up the side of the trailer, only to see me sitting in the bottom unable to escape. The rapid movement and loud racket of the overhead auger signaled little resistance from moving feed. Twenty-two ton of bulk concentrate had been manually shoveled, and my arms and back had felt every scoop-full. I sat on the floor of the semi-trailer, too weary to stand. My forearms were burning, while my back ached so intensely that it caused me to feel nauseous. I had broken into a cold sweat, totally drained of all energy. Dad gave me a hint of a grin, after studying the empty box.

"Hungry?"

"Boy, I'd say."

"Thought so. Here. Catch."

I looked up, and in the glow of the mill yard light a dark object fluttered, hitting the steel floor next to me. I reached out for the shadow, grasped it and held it close to inspect. It was too dark to read, but one smell and I knew it was absolutely nothing other than a Snicker's Bar. I tore off the paper and chomped off a bite.

"You did one heck of a job, Imy. I couldn't have done it without you."

This was the pinnacle of our relationship. Just Dad and me. Not only did he just buy me a candy bar, but he was also complementing me. I sat there for a second, letting my senses soak it in.

"No problem Dad. Really, it was nothing."

I stuffed the candy wrapper in my pocket, later pasting it into my scrapbook, thinking there was hope for us yet.

The consolation game was over, and they were well into the championship game. It was Tricky's Tavern up against Gubba's Hut, a bar in Independence, for the big prize. With Hindu Schriber pitching for Tricky's Tavern, it was a sure win.

"Imy, I'm hungry. Let's go and get some chicken, then we'll hit the tractor pull."

Dad stood up in order to start the gradual decent from the bleachers. I followed behind him as we made our way over to the tent. This time no explanations were necessary as we went over to buy our tickets.

The food crowd had started to dwindle as eager spectators swarmed toward the main event. As soon as we were done eating, we followed suit. At last, the tractor pull runway was in sight. We had arrived, and what a scene it was!

As a tractor pull novice, I had done some preliminary research to find out how this contest works.

There are three different weight classes: lightweight, middleweight and heavyweight. And there are two divisions within each class. The winners of the division in each class have a "pull off" to claim a champion for their respective class. Even though three winners would be recognized, only one trophy with any magnitude would be handed out for the heavyweight championship.

The tractor pull takes place on a concrete runway that is approximately twice as wide as a tractor and about two hundred feet long. The object of the contest is to start from one end of the runway and cross the finish line pulling a wooden skid which has a square iron box in the middle of it. This box is filled with a measured amount of sand, weighing several thousand pounds. Additional weight is provided by humans as the tractor makes its way down the concrete slab. A person stands on each side of the runway, ten feet from the starting point. That people pattern is repeated until the finish line. When the whistle is blown, the tractor heads down the concrete slab pulling the sled with a person jumping on from both sides every ten feet. This continues until the tractor crosses the finish line or can't pull anymore due to the added weight of people jumping on the skid.

Occasionally, the tractor pulls the sled and the full complement of people through the finish line located toward the end of the slab. If multiple tractors pull the load through the finish line, more sand will be added to the box on the sled and a "pull off" will occur. The people who are lucky enough to be scattered along the runway get selected through a lottery system and are called "stakemen." You can register for the privilege through most taverns and at Glanchinski's Barber Shop. If selected, not only do you have a chance to make print in the *Arcadia News Leader*, but you can also witness the entire contest from ground zero.

Four sets of bleachers flanked the starting point of the concrete runway, two on each side of the track. Beyond the bleachers, tractors lined up next to each other on both sides. The time was 8:00 PM, and all spectators stood for the playing of the National Anthem, which was amplified from a worn record over the PA system. Farmers stood next to their farm implements with caps over their hearts. Since the absence of the American flag was apparent, most eyes fixed on the big inflatable beer can hovering over the beer tent. Following our nation's song, a rousing round of applause erupted, mainly because the beer man had sprinted out of the tent with a full cooler headed our way. Then the command was given over the PA system.

"GENTLEMEN, START YOUR ENGINES!"

This four-word command sent chills down my spine. The roar of the crowd producing a backdrop for this festival finale sent me into sensory overload. The farmers looked as if they were posing for glamour shots since the breeze from the swamp was fluffing many a mane. The combined smells of diesel fuel, beer and

124

chicken were well known elements for a good tractor pull. And the crowd appeared ecstatic. People in the stands were laughing and talking, definitely psyched up for the mega event of the year.

One by one, the monster farming implements fired up their enormous power plants. Each farmer was given at least 30 seconds to start and race the engine to the overwhelming pleasure of the audience. No one drew bigger applause, however, than Adrian Krysner, firing-up the big Farmall Super M. Adrian was a lean man of average height, with a face that looked like it might be the only thing that could stop his mega-machine. His facial lines were deeply etched, underscoring a strong case for sun tan lotion and facial crème use.

The roar of his engine was enormously deafening, mainly because of the eight exhaust pipes sticking vertically upright in plain view. But the real spectacle was watching the eight empty coffee cans that served as rain covers, placed upside down on top of these pipes. The cans shot skyward as this powerful engine was started. Adrian sat on the tractor seat revving the engine and raising a can of warm beer to the audience which offered a thunderous standing ovation. A cigarette hung out of his open mouth suspended by saliva glued to his lower lip. Following the introductions of these agrarian gladiators, it was time to get down to business.

The spectators had now taken their seats, anxious for the event to start. The farmers were nervous and ready to get this grand event under way. But a commotion was stirring down in front of the cement runway, and everyone could sense a problem. There appeared to be a logistics concern among the stakemen. A pushing contest erupted into a downright brawl, with several groups of men having to be separated by people in the lower bleachers. After the struggle subsided, it appeared that two men were pretty shaken up from the fistfight. I sat there completely astonished, wondering what could be so important about this event that it would cause grown men to fight.

"Dad, why was everyone fighting?"

"I really don't know. Maybe someone said something to somebody."

Dad seemed to be confused by the commotion, too.

A drunken farmer sitting to my right turned to face me, sticking the bill of his cap into the bridge of my nose.

125

"Da're positioning dem-selvès. What some of dose stakemen do here is try to git up front, cause dats where da action is. See, if ya gits too much towards da finish line, a lot of doe's tractors don't make it dat far, so dem guys git no action."

This event commentator then echoed out a huge long belch and simultaneously muttered out the endorsement "Go Adrian."

The crowd grew visibly impatient while waiting for the guy on the PA system to make the announcement. After a few minutes, their hopes were assured.

"WE NEED A STAKEMAN, IMMEDIATELY. ANY VOLUNTEERS?"

The inebriated tractor-pull consultant next to me jumped up as if to yell "Bingo" and fell over as he did. It was amazing how after toppling down three rows of bleachers, he never lost his hat or spilled his beer. Since the distraction caught the PA announcer's eye, I stood up and waived my arms.

"OK FOLKS, LOOKS LIKE WE GOT OURSELVES A VOLUNTEER!"

I looked down at the farmer who was inverted just a moment ago.

"Ahhh, let da kid go, I'm too drunk anyway."

"WELL, THERE IS A WEIGHT LIMIT, LADIES AND GENTLEMEN."

I then pointed to Dad who was trying to act invisible during the whole affair.

"WELL FOLKS, HE HAS HIS DAD HERE. HOW 'BOUT WE LET 'EM DO DA BUDDY PLAN? HOW 'BOUT IT DARE, DAD?"

Now I had heard about the buddy plan. Kids at school used to talk about it for months on end. The buddy plan is when a dad and a kid stand at the same stake and both jump on the skid as it cruises by. The only stipulation is that the dad has to sign a waiver and can't be noticeably drunk. My dad rarely drank anything that wasn't healthy, so we fit the bill.

A weak round of applause commensurated the deal, and Dad and I were down on "skid row" with the rest of the elite.

We started to walk down to the very end of the concrete pad where the lonely stake sat, unmanned. As we started our journey to the end of the runway, a plot crept into my head. I looked for an easy victim to test. As I walked past these men, all with a can of beer in their hands, I looked for an angle. At last, about a quarter way down from the starting line, there was an immense character in bib overalls with a beer can in his hands. His hands were so huge that I couldn't see the can distinctly, however, his vice grip on the container told me it must be beer. This poor guy was on his last refreshment with no backup in sight. Most of the other guys had a stash next to the base of the stake, many of them with coolers. I knew this guy couldn't last through the first round, let alone the entire pull. I had found my victim. I walked up next to him and nonchalantly said hi.

"Yo," came the response, with a hint of jealously in his eye, probably thinking that I didn't realize how lucky I was to get the chance of being a stakeman.

"Yea, we get to go next to the finish line and see the winners as they come across."

"Buuuurrrrrrp."

"Yea, that will be pretty neat, especially when that's where they take the pictures of the winners. But just watching the expressions on those faces as they cross that line of victory will be so worth it."

"Kid, dem tractors in da finals don't git dat far."

Now, I was scrambling, trying to save face and not look like an idiot in front of this guy, which actually appeared to be quite an easy task.

"I know that, but we get to see a lot of them cross, and besides, there's a little less crowd noise, letting you hear the tractors better."

"Go fer it, kid."

As I started to walk away, I glanced over and my eye caught the big inflatable beer can on top of the beer tent. Call it pure reflex, but I thought, I'll go for the gusto.

"Oh well, at least we'll be closer to the beer tent."

This mega pile of humanity studied his nearly empty beer vessel and hollered out to me.

"You know, kid, yous made a lot a sense back dare. I kind a did have dat dare end mapped out, so I tink I'll take ya up on yer offer."

This obese creature started his walk down to the end, muttering under his breath while he walked away. "Damn, dey moved da tent dis year!"

Dad and I took our stand right next to the stake. Dad seemed slightly amused with the whole ordeal, but once again, it was hard to tell. In comparison, he sure didn't appear as excited, loud and obnoxious as the others, but then again, he was sober.

At last, the pull was underway, and the first tractor backed up to the sled. With the engine roaring at full throttle and the crowd screaming in the background, the farmer popped the clutch, and the immense piece of farm machinery lurched forward. The massive rear tires spun as if they were on ice. The tractor ground toward us as the farmer hung on for dear life. The front wheels grew airborne, leaving the steering to be addressed by the rear wheel brakes. From my vantage point, I couldn't tell if the tractor was swerving back and forth out of control because of the lack of friction between the front tires and the runway, or if the navigator had had a few too many.

In no-time flat, the sled was next to us, and it was time to jump aboard. We sprang on, finding a quick post between all the other people pouring onto this contraption. Immediately, we grabbed the iron railing that was welded on the outside perimeter of the center box. You could tell it was a rather veteran crowd. All of the guys were riding with their backs to the box facing outward, serving a three-fold purpose. The first was to be able to enjoy the ride and watch the people in the stands while being hailed as a VIP. The second allowed them to stand with one hand on the grip and the other to freely drink their beers. The final and most important purpose was that this face-forward stance allowed more stakemen to be stacked on the sled, without their huge guts hitting and knocking each other off.

The tractor continued its trek down the runway, slowing gradually with the added weight every ten feet. About three quarters down the concrete pad, the tractor labored, chugged and stopped. The judge, walking beside the choking beast, blew a whistle, signaling the driver to stop. He then measured the distance officially and unhooked the sled. An enormous earth moving implement came out from the starting position, hooked up to the other end of the sled, and pulled it back to the starting line. The stakemen jumped off at their respective positions.

This scenario repeated itself throughout the night until two of the lower class champions were crowned, and the only tractor standing in the way of Adrian Krysner's sure trophy was Adolfus

Sopenski's John Deere. Now this was drama at its best. You had John Deere vs. Farmall. It didn't matter which side of the fence you were on, and believe me, there were no fence walkers here, it was green against red, finesse vs. power, new against old, good vs. evil. The arguing crowd became so disruptive that the final championship heat was delayed. The commanding voice over the PA took charge and instructed everyone to do the same drill that had taken place back in '61.

"ALL FARMALL BOYS OVER TO DA NORTH STANDS, AND ALL JOHN DEERE BOYS OVER TO DA SOUTH STANDS. IF YOU DON'T KNOW WHO TO CHEER FER, DEN YOU AIN'T FROM DA AREA! AND IT DON'T GIT BETTER DAN DIS! BOYS, YOUS GOT TIRTY SECONDS APIECE TO FIRE HER UP AND GRANDSTAND A BIT, DEN IT'S DOWN TA BUSINESS. MAY DA BEST TRACTOR WIN!"

With that, Adolfus Sopenski fired up the green John Deere tractor to a wildly whistling and cheering crowd. He popped the clutch and laid three feet of solid rubber down the grand runway. He then screeched to an abrupt halt and backed up to take the sled.

"Datt makes me wanna wet my pants," came a shout from a stakeman across the slab.

"I guess that's emotion, huh Dad?"

"No, Imy, that's beer."

The intensity on the faces of Adolfus and the stakemen was so thick that you could cut it with a knife. All of the stakemen pulling for Adolfus carefully placed their beer cans down, so not to add any more critical weight that would jeopardize a Big John victory. Adolfus revved up the mean green machine, released the clutch and gave it all he had down the runway. As stakemen jumped on, the John Deere fans all stood on the sled using just one foot, dangling the other off to the side as if that would displace extra weight. The stakemen who were adversaries of "big green" jumped on the sled and continued to jump up and down, trying to add more weight. The scene looked like a bad circus act. Adolfus pulled the sled right up to where the very last stakeman was positioned. It was the very mass of humanity with whom I had traded places. The green monster sneezed, snorted, then abruptly halted after this last load jumped on the skid, unable to inch any further. The whistle blew and a formal measurement was taken, and we resumed our locations for the last pull of the night.

Adrian Krysner jumped on his Super M Farmall, fired it up and held one wheel brake forcing the tractor to fly around in circles. He drew a lukewarm applause, mainly because it was hard to top eight coffee cans catapulted skyward from his engine pipes which he showcased during the introduction.

He then reversed to hook up to the sled. The stakemen were quickly adjusting to their practice of trying to influence the load. All at once, a stern voice came over the PA.

"WAIT A SECOND DARE, HOLD EVERYTHING, WHAT'S YOUR PROBLEM, SIR?"

The crowd came abuzz, with everyone trying to figure out who was causing the delay. There seemed to be a commotion up at the finish line. Word had it that the mammoth stakeman at the end of the track needed to get to the restroom, and fast.

"Why is he running so funny, Dad?"

"First of all, that's a lot of mass to get going. Second, I think he has to get to the bathroom quickly."

The next stakeman overheard our conversation and appeared to be an engineer on restroom logistics.

"Da problem is dat not only did dey move da beer tent dis year, dey also moved da port-o-potties."

While the John Deere people were calling foul, the PA announcer attempted to clear the slate by saying that one trip to the restroom is totally admissible by Trempealeau County code. Now, everyone knew that if Adrian pulled up to this stakeman, and the fella mounted without causing Adrian to stop, Adrian would win. However, everyone also knew how hard it was to pull the sled to the line in a championship heat due to the added weight of sand in the box.

The immense man came jogging out as funny as he had left, returning to his position with a full beer in hand. The whistle blew, Adrian took off, and the crowd fell to a hush. The Farmall labored but never faltered, right up to the last abundant stakeman. He boarded without his beer, and the tractor chugged on a few more feet. With the rear wheels still spinning, the foreword momentum finally fatigued. The whistle was blown, and the judge took the measurement. It was official. Adrian Krysner was declared the winner by six agonizing feet.

Adolfus Sopenski raced over to the bottom of the PA box, waving his arms in disgust. The event announcer scrambled down the ladder ready to confront him.

"Dats plain bull."

"Now Adolfus, he out-pulled cha fair and square, dare."

"Yea, but hadn't dat one guy went to da can, he would have stopped Adrian straight in his tracks when he jumped on, jis like he done to me. I jist want yous ta know dat I'm protesting dis."

"Very well, but this year's trophy belongs to Adrian Krysner."

About a third of the crowd was stunned, another third was cheering raucously and the rest were just too drunk to care.

"Well, Dad, what do you think? Do you think Adolfus had a point? Do you think that the way that guy was drinking beer, he could have removed enough weight to make a difference?"

"Hard to say, Imy. We better go call Mom."

Once again, another warm and fuzzy conversation snuffed out by my uninterested father. Since we both partook of this event that had occupied our lives for the past three hours, one would think that he would have had a better response than that. But that was Dad. He always talked *at* you, never *with* you.

We walked quietly over to the park pay phone.

"Hey kid," came a raspy voice out of the night.

"Yea?"

"Tanks fer littin me take da finish line stake. Yous were right, ders nuttin like it."

"Yea sure, no problem. See you next year."

I watched as the giant silhouette disappeared into the night.

In a few minutes, Mom pulled up.

"Well Imy, what did you think of the tractor pull?"

"Interesting. Very interesting."

As I laid in bed that evening, thoughts of the day occupied my head. I scoured my memory, searching for just one generic guy, but couldn't recall even one. These Arcadians were so immersed in their own odd culture that it didn't occur to them how foreign their ways appeared to this transplanted nine-year-old. And although this town survived on a different set of rules, their logic was sure amusing and interesting to be a part of. Each person appeared to be a caricature of themselves. This town seemed to be few on amenities but big on entertainment. And after all, isn't that part of what life is all about?

I closed my eyes that night with a picture of Adrain Krysner basking in his glory atop the Super M. He was popping wheelies while circling the portable restroom after his victory. Yes, that sure was entertainment!

Chapter XIV

As the months came and went, so did the dogs that came to live at the feed mill. Jasper had unofficially retired and returned up the hill to spend his last days with Dolf. A female mut had wandered in one day and soon had a litter of pups. It wasn't long before all the pups disappeared with one exception. Dad didn't seem to know what had happened to them, nor did he appear too concerned. It wasn't until later that day that I walked into the back room of the mill to pick up a bag of Pig-16. While I was lifting the bag onto a feed cart, my train of thought was interrupted by a whimpering sound. I followed the cry, walking behind a stack of feed bags only to find a large gunnysack moving on the floor. I counted four forms struggling to get out of their burlap prison. I stood motionless, feeling sick to my stomach. I grabbed the feed cart and wheeled my cargo out of the mill into a waiting pickup bed. I knew what was going to happen. Dad couldn't have all those dogs running around the mill. There was no such thing as an animal shelter in Arcadia, so he was going to take matters into his own hands. His lack of emotion proved him to be efficient, but his hard heartedness scarred me. I knew better than to interfere. The last time that happened, I was hit so hard that I bled out of my nose and ear simultaneously. After a quick trip to the hospital for head x-rays, I was back home as if nothing had happened. I'll never forget Dad's response when the doctor asked how it occurred. Dad just offered "with another body."

I loaded the bag of feed onto the truck and wheeled the empty cart back inside the mill. I went and sat on the stoop of the salt shed, patiently waiting, permitting Dad the opportunity that he silently demanded. A half an hour later, I stopped swinging my legs and watched with a nauseous stomach as Dad exited the mill with a wiggling burlap sack, heading for the creek. I jumped off of my perch and tried to isolate the pain and sorrow that I felt. I walked over to the cement plant behind the sheds to find a truck driver to laugh with. That's how I survived. Thank God for Arcadia, I thought. Arcadia helps me live.

133

Chapter XV

The only thing that changed more than the dogs at the mill were the human resources. John Olsen was long retired, and one day during lunch break, Baraheep went to see Emil Stelmach's new chicken barn and never returned. During the interim, Dad hired Ebner, one of the Sookla boys, to help, thinking that Baraheep had walked out and quit. That was the last of the Baraheep show. And as it turned out, my friends missed him more than we did.

Ebner decided to go back to work on his cousins farm, so another position for a hired hand immediately opened. People came and went. Valentine Liwsowski wanted to give it a go, as he had some experience working there when Dolf owned it some forty years ago. He still had the three-pronged system down for starting up the grinder, which was a valuable attribute. But Valentine, or Val as we called him, was in his early seventies, and he smelled like really stale poppy-seed coffeecake. He lasted about two weeks. Dad found his stash of old vodka bottles hidden in the back room and decided that it would be best if Val re-retired.

Vagabonds would continue to apply, help out for a couple of weeks to a month, then be on their way. Dad would give most of them a chance, and, as long as no money was missing from the till, allow them to prove themselves. One such character was Arnie Paulson. The first thing that struck me about Arnie was his normal sounding name. Not only did he share the same name as my father, but some farmers thought he was a retired pro golfer who decided to do something useful. He was an average built man with the standard potbelly, of course, and stringy hair thinning on top and long in back. He was missing both front teeth and constantly wore a construction hard hat. Dad said it was because the butternuts were falling when he started at the mill. When he would sit on the front porch, the husked nuts would occasionally drop on his head through the ever-growing hole in the porch roof.

One day in the late fall, two men were pulled over for a traffic violation just outside of Independence. It turned out that both men had warrants out for their arrest as suspects of an armed robbery in

California. The men were arrested without incident and were being held in the county jail in White Hall, awaiting extradition to California. After three days of good behavior, the prisoners were let out periodically to perform housekeeping duties. A week later, they were let out of their cell to go and put gas in the cop car, and they never returned. A search posse was formed by several farmers and hunters from around the area. All three major roads were blocked, and the Sheriff's Department was making a plea for anyone with a gun to report to their respective American Legion halls to help.

Arnie Paulson decided to join the search, more than likely in an effort to get out of work. The only reason that Dad let him go was because the suspects were sighted only miles from Arnie's house out in Nuecome Valley. Arnie signed up and was told to go to five assorted farmers around the area who may have trouble defending themselves. One of the farmers was a recluse named Buzzie Jarr. Buzzie was physically handicapped and didn't farm, per say, but he did have a few animals stabled in his one dilapidated barn. The Sheriff's Department thought Buzzie needed to be checked on because of his very remote location at the end of the valley, accessed only by a dirt road.

It was early afternoon, and Arnie was driving out to Buzzie's place. Arnie pulled up behind an unmarked police car that was parked where the dirt road met the muddy driveway at the bottom of the hill. The man sitting in the unmarked car looked as nervous as Arnie. Arnie drew his rifle next to him as he pulled behind the vehicle. The man in the car pulled his weapon as well, and both sat motionless during this "sit off."

"Can I help you?" the man called out.

Arnie didn't know what to do, however, he had been deputized and was going to use his authority to the fullest if needed.

"Maybe you can help by getting out of that car with your hands up!" Arnie hollered back.

"And why might that be?"

Now Arnie never missed a "Five-O" episode in his life. Maybe he was a victim of too many cop shows, but it was obvious that he had paid attention.

"I'm here to arrest you!" Arnie called out.

"If there is any arresting to do, I'll do it!"

"You're under arrest!" Arnie screamed back.

"Sir, I'm a federal game warden."

"Yea, and I'm Joe Mannix."

"Sir, I have a badge to prove it."

"Well, I'm part of a posse."

"You're more like a pussy. Not get the hell out of the car, because in the name of the Federal Government of the United States, you're under arrest!"

"Naa uhhh, you are!"

The game warden jumped out of the car, slammed the door and walked toward Arnie's car, obviously aggravated.

"Well I'm a game warden, and I'm here to grant Buzzie's request for a permit to hunt deer from his car since he's debilitated and all. Now exit the vehicle!"

Arnie slowly exited his car, never disengaging eye contact, and walked over to where the dirt road ended and the muddy driveway began. Something then caught Arnie's eye, and he no longer seemed interested by the confrontation with the game warden.

"That's odd."

"What's that?"

Arnie didn't answer as he bolted over to Buzzie's old pickup truck parked at the bottom of the rutted drive. Arnie lifted the hood to do a quick examination of the stalled vehicle.

The warden reached in his car and grabbed his shotgun. He loaded some shells into the magazine of his rifle, pumping a shell into the firing chamber.

"Let's walk up there and have a look-see."

The two men walked up the quarter-mile incline following the dirt driveway to Buzzie's porch. The Warden then raised his hand in order to caution Arnie.

"Hang back here."

The Warden went up and pounded on the old screen door.

Buzzie came to the door, looking excited to see company.

After introducing himself, the warden proceeded to interrogate Buzzie.

"Seen anything funny out here?"

"Just you."

Arnie walked up to the door, knowing they were no longer in any danger.

"What's wrong with your pickup?"

"Notin. Why?"

"Well, we just noticed it at the bottom of the hill and thought with the limited use of your legs, that's one hell of a place to put it."

"Now dat's funny. Let's go take a look. Lemme grab my cap."

The threesome casually descended the hill allowing a limping Buzzie to catch up and do a further investigation of the pickup.

After snooping under the hood and doing some quick diagnostics, Buzzie thought it appeared that the truck had been tampered with. He had his nose in the carburetor while adjusting the linkage next to the air filter.

"She's flooded. I wonder how she got down here in da first place?" Buzzie leaned against the fender, looking quite perplexed. "I tink someone tried to start her, couldn't cause dey flooded her, den tried to jump start her by rolling her down da driveway."

The Warden seemed engrossed in deep thought, processing Buzzie's statement.

"You got any other buildings besides the house?"

"Yep, ders da barn, and dat's pretty much it."

"Let's go up and have a look-see."

The trio ascended the hill, waiting for Buzzie at the summit. Together, they walked into the barn through the massive open door. You could tell by the look in the game warden's eyes that he was starting to feel suspicious.

"That door always open like that?"

"Yep, she's jist too heavy to fight wit, so I don't close her anymore. Besides, I figure it's better to leave dis barn door open dan da one on your trousers."

As they reached the center of the barn, they walked toward a large rectangular-shaped cutout in the ceiling with a ladder disappearing into it. This was used as a staircase to access the haymow or second floor of the barn. The trio casually sauntered over to it, with no one uttering a word. When they got within ten feet of it, they spotted the end of a double barrel shotgun staring back at them, suspended from the cutout ceiling. The three ran for cover, knowing that the suspects would have to scale the ladder to get down on the ground floor to be any kind of threat. The brave bounty hunters sprinted from the barn to the house, with Buzzie leading the way. In the house, guns were drawn, and the cops in Arcadia were called. The suspects escaped from the barn but were captured two hours later in Cottie Gouch's cornfield. Seemed that

137

they picked a bad time to cross the field. The Soppa Brothers were pheasant hunting there, and the gunshots fired from Al and Junior's shotguns scared the fugitives into a corncrib where they holed up. As the escapees were being taken back into custody, the game warden shot Buzzie a solemn look.

"Buzzie, I got good news and bad news."

"What's da goot news?"

"Well, the good news is that there was a reward out on these guys, and you're subject to receiving part of it."

"Da Soppa Boys gitting any money?"

"No, afterall, they weren't aware of the situation. They were just pheasant hunting."

"Den, what's da bad news?"

"The bad news is I'm going to have to rescind your handicapped deer hunting permit. If you would have run any faster, someone would have had to follow you with a fire extinguisher!"

"Well, I guess I had ta do what I had ta do, and you godda do what yous godda do, and dats da name of dat dare tune."

Chapter XVI

I was twelve when Dad decided to move us into town. My older sisters were in high school by then, and with all of the commuting back and forth for after-school activities, my parents thought it would just be easier to live there. We moved to a very old, large house on top of the hill, directly across from the church. The house was divided into three rental units. We rented the first floor of this three-bedroom house with two people sharing each bedroom. Despite the cramped quarters, the location was ideal for me since the Catholic school that I attended was right next door.

Life in the city would definitely be an adjustment. The bright lights and urban sounds were foreign to this transplanted country boy. The lone street light illuminating the church parking lot was pushing the limit, however the clanging church bell every hour on the hour was down rite aggravating. People in the city seemed different, and the kids appeared to have nothing to do. Even the US mail service was odd. Besides, who even heard of a mail woman anyway? Stranger yet, everyone on her route seemed to know the business of the neighbors that had mail already in their boxes. I guess everyone down the delivery chain from us knew our business. Oh well, it gave people something to talk about.

It seemed as if things were tightening up a bit financially for Dad. He knew that he would either have to start marketing himself or provide a service that farmers couldn't get from the big co-op feed mill in town.

In order to soften the financial crunch, I decided to get a paper route to earn some spending money. Cash didn't flow very freely from Dad, in spite of my labor at the mill, so survival meant self-employment. I applied for the *LaCrosse Tribune* route and was fortunate enough to get it. I was so proud of myself, right up until I found out that I was the only one who applied. I remember thinking how odd it was that the salesman from LaCrosse showed me how to fill out the resignation paperwork just after he shook my hand and welcomed me aboard.

YOU AREN'T GONNA KEEP THIS ROUTE FOREVER was etched in my brain from that moment forward.

I took the route over from Dink-Wad, whose real name was Bill Smith. Where he got his nickname was anyone's guess. However, I did not find it surprising that a person from Arcadia with a common name like Bill would need an alias.

I started immediately, picking up my papers at the post office downtown. Since I was the only LaCrosse Tribune paperboy in town, my route extended no less than six miles. It took only a few weeks to realize that this route would become an arduous task in the winter, especially with no car support.

Once I started talking to the other paperboys in town, I learned that the most coveted route was the *Winona Daily News*. I waited for an opening, then grabbed the next available route. This time there was competition, however, my paper delivery experience helped. I now had a route with a defined area where I could utilize my time more efficiently. My route started at the post office in the center of town and took me across the river, ending up at the Mileage Station, a small gas station located right next to the chicken plant. My clientele were regarded as the "poor people" in town, mainly because most of them lived across the river.

Delivery went, for the most part, without a hitch, but collecting a buck and a quarter every other Friday was a different story. There appeared to be three types of customers: the customer that wanted to interact and pay; the customer that didn't mind paying, however, was seldom home; and the customer that flat out didn't want to pay.

I inherited this route from Palmer Hoganberry, a hippie type, city kid who rode around on a banana bike. His real name was Joe, but that was just too normal of a name to survive in Arcadia, so everyone referred to him by his grandfather's name, Palmer.

Palmer had decided to move down his career path. He was trading in his route to take an early morning, part-time job at the chicken broiler plant. Since he lived above Tricky's Tavern, he knew early morning promptness might become a problem.

He had already shown me the air horn that had been removed from a diesel semi-truck that he connected to his alarm clock. Apparently, he had become so accustomed to sleeping through all of the noise in the bar below that he had to create some device to wake himself.

"How does it work?"

"Do you mean how does it work or how well does it work?"

"How well does it work?"

"Pretty good, but the first time it went off, I wet the bed. Now, the truth is, I've become so used to it going off that I can't tell it from a passing chicken truck."

Training began immediately, and it was great to have a few more days of it than Dink-Wad had offered. I was anxious to learn about the new customer base that I had just adopted.

We took off from Palmer's place and rode three blocks to the Arcadia Post Office. About a block away from our destination, old Ignuts Waldera rode his bike past us. Once again, a warm well-received smile dominated his face as he held his right hand high and gave me the middle finger – just like he had done at the Parade during Broiler Days.

"Why does he do that?"

"Do what?"

"You know, why does he offer a genuine smile, then shoot me the middle finger?"

"Ignuts lost his fingers years ago in a farming accident. His only finger left is his middle one. So don't take it personal. He does that to everyone."

As soon as we arrived at the post office, we went inside to find only two bundles of papers lying on the lobby floor. Neither had Palmer's name on them.

"Didn't see any for you guys," came a voice from the stocky man behind the postal counter.

"C'mon Ivan, I got a new guy starting, and I don't have time to screw around."

Ivan Growchon was an abundantly rotund man, and I use the word "rotund" lightly. His short and squatty body made him appear as round as a beach ball. Everyone in town knew Ivan and his great sense of humor. The only thing Ivan didn't find funny was eating.

"No, really, your papers got dumped up at the corner store. Another goof up, I imagine."

Palmer looked at Ivan, shook his head and sighed.

"Ahhh... we're just gonna have to find em. You start looking in all the big mailbox bins, and I'll start over here under the counter. He usually picks the bins, but lately he's been using the counter. And one time he put 'em in the girl's bathroom. He got in trouble that time, though, because the cleaning lady went in there and threw 'em all out. He finally helped me find 'em in the dumpster in the alley an hour later."

"Does he do this often and only to you?"

"Yep, pretty much all the time, unless he's too busy eating, and it's pretty much just me."

The papers were discovered five minutes later, conveniently placed behind a "Federal Property Do Not Touch Or You Will Go Directly To Jail" sign on the floor.

"Let's load up and cruise. Here, I'll show you how to load 'em in those rear side baskets of yours. Always put 'em in with the folds facing the front."

"How come?"

"Don't ask why, just take it from me, a guy with over a year of experience."

So I loaded my bike just the way he showed me, and we were off, heading to our first client.

Monker Markaasock was the first house that we visited.

"Palmer, why do they call her Monker? I know that's her nickname, but I never knew why."

"I'm not sure. I heard that it just seems to go with her last name."

We went through the entire route, with Palmer giving me bits of sometimes useful information along the way. I took copious notes, wanting to get into the heads of my new clients to provide the best customer service in a time efficient basis.

"Watch these guys close." As Palmer threw a paper in the door, the moldy stench of mildew oozed out to greet us. "These are the Krumholtz brothers. They are two old farts that own two farms and still farm both of 'em, but live in town. They are the cheapest people I have. They drive an old rusty Chevy and probably still have the first dime that they ever made. When you come here to collect, they will always try to prove that they have already paid."

About ten customers later, we came up to Lambert Rook's place.

"You can collect from him at Siepal's Bar between three and seven, or at Barky's Big-Mouth-Bass-Bar from seven to eleven. Best to catch him at one of those two places before he runs out of money."

142

About an hour-and-a-half later, after delivering eighty papers, we were at the end of the route, finishing up at the Mileage Station.

"Watch this one, she's kind of crazy."

We got off of our bikes and headed in to make the last delivery. Palmer dug in his pocket for some loose change.

"Want to catch a pop?"

"Sure. How much?"

"It's only a dime here, but you have to sit here and drink it, cause she wants the bottles back at that price."

We sat back in the stained, over-stuffed chairs drinking our pop and recounting some of the customers on the route.

"Well, just a couple of days, and she's all yours."

A week had passed, and Ivan was getting smarter about hiding my paper stack. He was very creative in concealing 80 copies of a daily edition. One day I found them behind a plastic bin marked with a green magic marker DON'T TOUCH THIS OR IVAN WILL SIT ON YOU, THEN EAT YOU. I was starting to get a bit irritated spending up to twenty minutes trying to find my stack when the rest of the paperboys would grab their bundles and run. I also found it troubling when the signs got more threatening. One time he had put the official government sign on my stack that read: Removal of government property is prosecutable by 1 year in prison and a $1,000 fine.

"Ah, Ivan, the newspapers aren't government property."

"Well, if you think about it, your papers are in the post office which is a government office, so they automatically become government property."

"Whatever."

One day, I saw Wayne Kampa on his route. Wayne was a schoolmate and acquaintance of mine, although I didn't know him that well. What I did know about Wayne was that he was a real instigator and jokester, constantly laughing. Wayne thought most things were funny and possessed a very nonchalant attitude. He was always late picking up his papers, and I knew that his route intertwined with mine. He asked if I wanted to trade some of my customers with his to make both of our routes easier. I concurred, even though I knew that I was at a disadvantage. Wayne knew his customer base, and since I didn't know mine, I knew that he would probably try to unload some of his problem customers. That was a chance that I was willing to take because I knew that he delivered to Ivan Growchon's house.

"I'll give you a Lester Kutt for your Lambert Rook, just because it's easier for each of us if we both don't have to go down the same street," Wayne said, starting the negotiations.

Though, I didn't know much about my customer base, I did know that Lambert was what we called a "stool percher," and they were considered good customers. They didn't really care if the paper got wet, because they were always in the bar and didn't read it until the next day, if at all. I also knew Wayne was a seasoned veteran and had "stool perchers" that he collected from. Since Wayne had time on me, I felt that he had a pretty good idea of some of my "golden customers." There was no way I was going to let him cherry pick my best people.

"I tell you what, since I have to run past Lambert to get to Taplins, why don't you just take Minortzs and Wachinskis, and I'll take Lester Kutt off your hands and let's say... oh an Ivan Growchon."

"Sure, you just want to keep Rooks because of Sonja."

Sonja was a homely girl that was a couple of years older than Wayne and me. She always wore the same clothes, and because of their apparent poverty, kids made a lot of fun at her expense. I didn't appreciate the critical tongue, however, I wanted to maintain a cool head during my first business transaction.

Wayne stared straight ahead as if still digesting the last option that I had just thrown at him.

"No, that just ain't gonna work too good, how 'bout ...."

"Hey, I delivered to Lester Kutt on the LaCrosse route, and I know how difficult he is. You have to get off of your bike, walk in the garage and put it on top of the freezer. I just thought, logistically, that it would work better for both of us, even if I ended up with Lester."

"OK, OK, deal," Wayne said. "You get Ivan and Lester, and I'll do Minortizes and old man Wachinski."

It was hard to control the happiness bubbling inside of me, but I maintained my poker face and continued to deal until our routes made more sense. Only a total of eight trades were made, but both of us felt as though we had won. I was terribly proud of my first "win-win" business deal.

The next day I picked up my papers that were hidden in the oversized garbage can in the back of the lobby. I strutted over to Ivan with one of the soiled editions.

"Since I'm your new paperboy, do you want your delivery here or at the house?"

"What happened to Wayne?"

"He decided to unload some of his problem customers," I retorted with a gleam in my eye.

Ivan's blank stare turned into a sheepish smile, and I returned it two-fold.

"You can drop it off on the front porch."

I loaded my papers quickly and was on my way. My new 5-speed bicycle and assembled saddle baskets were a real convenience to me. I could now jump off and on my bike with ease without having to lug eighty newspapers over my shoulder in those worn cotton bags that they provided. I had saved enough money on my last paper route to buy my Schwinn along with this delivery aid.

The eight paper trades that Wayne and I made seemed to work out for the best. The only one that I got snookered on was Dr. Moscana who resided at the top of a hill. It was bad for two reasons. The first was that it was the only house on top of this steep hill, so I knew efficiencies could never be maximized. Had I known the severe angle of that slope, I never would have taken it. The second reason was Berzie's Mastiff dog, named Tramp, who lived at the bottom of that hill. My first time peddling up the hill was tough, having to walk my bike the final third of the way. However, coming down the hill was disastrous. Not only did I not pay attention to Palmer's advice about stacking the papers in my basket with the fold-facing front, but I learned how Tramp loved to chase bicycles. Once the wind caught the loose pages of the papers that were facing forward, they all ballooned up and flew out of my rear saddle baskets. I threw a larger contrail than a jumbo jet, strewing papers all over the place right up till Tramp tackled me at the bottom of the hill. Tramp stood over me licking my wounds as a giggling Mrs. Berzie gathered her paper. I jumped up to collect my scattered news-rags, and couldn't help but think of a few solutions that would keep this incident to a one-time episode. First off, I would always stack my papers with the folds facing forward. Second, I would ride my bicycle up the hill and walk it back down.

Two weeks had finally passed, and it was Friday, time to collect. A bill was delivered with the paper stack that day, and I knew I'd have to start collecting, pronto, in order to pay it. I was given a black-ring binder that was a little larger than a standard checkbook. This book had eighty cardboard pages, one for each customer. When collecting from a customer, I would tear along the perforated edge and remove the little stub containing the current date, handing it to the customer as a receipt.

Ivan Growchon had turned from nemesis to a truly golden customer. I could collect from him behind the counter before I even set out on my route. And, immediately, once Ivan found out that I was his paperboy, the practice of hiding my papers ended abruptly.

I was looking forward to meeting my customers and couldn't wait for my first payday. My first stop was Siepal's Bar. I was feeling bittersweet at this point. I knew I had my guy in there, ready to pay, but since I had never met him, I had no idea who he was or where he was sitting. I walked in sheepishly and started casing the joint. The barstools were crowded with ripened rumps glued to each seat. There wasn't a head without a cap on it.

I went up to the bar and stood there waiting for the bartender to take notice. One by one, the customers turned on their stools, eyeing me up.

"Hey Dorsal, if he's old enough to drink, he's old enough to drink!" a boisterous voice yelled in the background.

Quite profound, I thought, wondering how long that character had been in here. The bartender glanced over at me after being alerted by his astute patron. He approached me with a scowl.

"What 'chew doin here?"

"I'm a paperboy, and I'm collecting from a customer of mine."

"Hey, anybody owe a paperboy?"

The volume in the bar was reduced to a dull roar. The same intoxicated man was noticeably trying to think.

"I owe a paperboy like I owe a paperboy!"

The bartender looked at me with just a hint of pity on his weathered face.

"Who you lookin fer, boy?"

"Lambert Rook, sir. Is he in here?"

The bartender smiled.

"Is he!"

He pointed over to that same obnoxious man in the back sporting a striped train engineer's cap tipped slightly sideways.

"Hey Lambert, I got good news and bad news! Da good news is dat yous don't have ta buy da next round."

"Wit news dat good, what could be bad?"

"Da bad news is dat dis is your paperboy, and ya owe 'em money!"

Just like that, Lambert bolted for the rear door of the thin dingy bar. I just stood there in disbelief, wondering what to do. I had a flashback, thinking that this is one I should have unloaded on Wayne. After recalling the customer swap, I realized that I had been set up. These "stool perchers" were not golden customers after all, as evidenced by Lambert's hasty escape.

"Don't worry kid, he ain't goin' far."

"Emmm, I wonder what I should do?"

"Well, if I were you, I'd just wait over by da cooler. He'll be right back."

"How do you know?"

"Hey, it ain't his turn ta buy dis round, and it's a crap shoot. As soon as he realizes dat he eider collects his beer coming ta him and pays you, or runs and hides, looses his free beer, and den still owes you, he'll come runnin' back."

So I went over and stood behind the cooler waiting for him to return. About two minutes later, Lambert snuck in the back door, looking cautiously around. Once he detected that the coast was clear, he went up and told Dorsal to set him up.

"Yea barkeep, went out to da pickup to grab da checkbook fer dat kid, ya know, and now I come back and he's gone. Go figure. You wanna do right, den day leave ya, spreading rumors."

"Why didn't 'chew pay him out of your pocket?"

"Cause, you know, dats beer drinkin' money. I got ta keep my business books straight and all dat, so you know…"

I heard the conversation and considered that this was my cue. I jumped from behind the cooler and took three steps over to where he was perched.

"Collecting."

"Collecting fer what?"

"I'm your new paperboy, and I'm collecting for the Winona Daily News."

"He's got ya dare, Lam, and besides ya went out ta git your business checkbook, so you may as well settle up."

"Ahh, hell, may as well anti up, I guess. Here son, what do I owe ya?"

"A dollar and a quarter, sir."

I watched as he reached in to his bib overalls and pulled out a wad of rolled up singles along with numerous bar tokens for drink credits. Just then, his daughter Sonja walked in and approached her dad.

"Mom told me to come here after school today to get some money."

"Hey, everybody's hittin' me up fer money. If it ain't you, it's dis kid who claims he's da paperboy. And if it ain't him, din it's da barkeep…."

"I just need a couple of bucks for milk, eggs and bread. There's absolutely nothing left in the house to eat again."

"Here, here's two bucks fer ya and a buck and a quarter fer you. And Sony, while you're dare, grab me some cigarettes and bring 'em right over."

"Hey paperboy, how 'bout a tip?"

"Really?"

"Yea, don't collect from a drunk!"

As I was about to turn and head for the door, he sent a bar chip sailing across the air in my direction. I quickly cupped my hands and caught the shiny chip, noticing that it was a credit for a free tap beer.

"Now don't go spending it all in one place!"

He sat back and exhaled a loud cackle. I pretended to be grateful, thinking that he had really overextended himself on this one, since to him, a beer chip was better than real money.

"Thanks," I said, stuffing the legal tender along with the useless plastic in my front pocket and headed for the door.

Boy, I thought, if it takes this much time and energy to collect from everyone, I'm in for a long night.

I walked my bike over to Stocka's Grocery Store right next door so that I could get a candy bar before my route. I walked up to the counter to find Sonja leaving the register to trade a half-gallon carton of milk for a smaller quart. The proprietor had put her bread and eggs aside, waiting for Sonja to return with a smaller carton to get under her two-dollar quota. I flipped my Snickers Bar along with my quarter on the counter, waiting for Trazor Stocka to give me back my fifteen cents of change. I glanced down quickly, seeing if I could spot the hole in the old hard wood floor that Trazor had supposedly bore out to look up ladies' dresses from the basement. I heard about it from all the guys, but I never found proof that it existed. Trazor returned from the cash register with a dime and a nickel, clicking the money on his side of the tile counter with his left hand while pretending to have the change in his right hand.

"Almost got ya that time."

He performed this money trick for everyone under fifteen, and for whatever dumb reason, my generation always fell for it. Maybe that's why he kept doing it.

"Yup, just about."

Meanwhile, Sonja had just returned.

"I'm gonna need a pack of cigarettes for my dad. He just stopped next door for a minute."

She put down the two dollars of beer-soaked money, and Trazor eyed her up suspiciously.

"All you got?"

"Dad said I could have more, but I just took two dollars."

Sonja was looking down at the floor, unable to look Trazor in the eyes.

"Still ain't enough, especially if you're getting smokes for the old man."

Sonja sighed, seeming to wipe a tear away from under her horn rimed glasses.

"How much am I over now?"

Trazor stood there studying the tape from the cash machine.

"Ninety-five cents."

"Why don't you just get the food, after all, you can't eat cigarettes."

"If I don't come back with cigarettes, I might as well not go home tonight."

My heart went out to her, not only because I could relate to being poor, but I couldn't even imagine living a life like that. I walked back to the counter, performing my best acting job ever.

"Guess what? I know this is absolutely none of my business, but I mistakenly collected from your dad just minutes ago. His invoice isn't due until next week. If I ever told him that, he would probably kill me. Do me a favor. I only have about a buck left, but why don't you take it to cover your bill, and the deal is you cannot tell him about this."

"Hey, that's great."

I flipped the dollar out on the counter and proceeded to walk away, feeling somewhat depressed about parting with so much money. But that only lasted all of ten seconds. Sonja grabbed her bag and headed toward the door. I overheard her saying to herself. "Even I get lucky sometimes."

When I had arrived at the post office, I quickly collected from Ivan, then grabbed my papers. I was beginning to feel a little better because I was now two for two collecting, and the candy bar was kicking in, giving me a bundle of energy. I knew I would probably need it today.

It was great getting out to meet my new customers and establish new relationships. My second challenge, however, took place with the Krumholtz brothers. Both brothers stood on the basement steps of the damp, dingy dwelling, swearing up and down that they had already paid their two-week bill. They were going through the old paper ticket stubs that were loosely laying on a dirty ledge. The smelly brother seemed to be the authoritative one, while the brother who didn't stink quite as much stood in the background.

"I know we already paid, just a little bit ago."

"I never collected from you yet. I have a receipt in my book that has not been torn out yet, because today is the first day that I am collecting."

"I think the other guy was just here a week or so ago."

The point that I was trying to drive home was slightly interrupted as the smelly brother wiped a freshly picked booger onto his work pants.

"Well, that may have been, but that would have been two weeks ago, and we collect every two weeks."

"Well, we'll let it go this time, but we're going to keep an eye on you."

I ripped out the little cardboard square with the applicable dates on it and handed it to the rancid old farmer. I was particularly careful not to let my vision drop to the nasal debris stuck on his trousers.

"Now, please keep this stub right here as proof of payment."

The farmer took the ticket stub and placed it in a pile with the others as I headed for the door. I knew that next time I'd have to go through the same exercise, but it could have been worse. At least they were home, and they paid.

The collection process was actually going pretty well. I was batting about seventy percent. The next house was Romeo Peplinski, and no one appeared to be home. A knock at the door confirmed my suspicion, and I started back to my bike. As soon as I got there, a Chevy Belair came roaring in the driveway, skidding to an abrupt stop and throwing gravel from the crushed rock driveway. A large Yugoslavian-looking woman with a hooked nose struggled to exit the driver's side of the car. The passenger door opened with a younger, skinny woman bounding out, holding a two-foot round, metal pan in her hands.

"Hey kid, grab this thing already, and don't piss in it!"

With a command like that, how could I refuse? I quickly jogged over and grabbed the mammoth steel pan.

"Just be sure that you invite me over for desert after you bake your Angle food cake," I kidded back.

"Romie wanted the son of a bitch to use to change oil, and the damn thing hardly fit in the fuckin' car."

"Change oil, heck, you could use this to store oil after you drill for it."

I then introduced myself and was relieved to be received warmly. Mrs. Peplinski went in to get her purse so that she could settle up.

"Imy, I think I like you because you are funnier than shit."

She then paid me, and we talked just a bit more. She was one of the funniest ladies I had ever met, even though I was somewhat shocked by the vulgarity. Just as I was ready to leave, a big rusty Cadillac went by with a gigantic woman navigating the cruiser. The woman stared at us but did not wave. An anomaly for an Arcadian.

"Know who that load is?"

"No."

"That's Fats McConnon. Is she on your paper route?"

"No, I don't think so."

"Listen, every time she turns a corner, one of her French boobs honks the horn."

"Is McConnon French?"

"Hell, I don't know, but she got 'em from eatin' all that French Bread!"

Seconds later, the Caddy turned right at the T in the road, and sure enough, the horn blasted.

"See, what da hell did I tell you?"

"Hey you learn something every day," I said with a chuckle. "I better get going. See ya next time."

One of my next stops was the new Chief of Police, Lloyd Cotasko, whom the locals called Barney Fife. His personality and stature paralleled Barney Fife from the Andy Griffith Show. This was evident by the strange relationship Lloyd seemed to have with his wife. Rumor had it that she told him that when Snook Surnaw's sewage removal truck was parked in front of the house, he shouldn't come home. Supposedly, Snook and Mrs. Cotasko had a fling going and didn't waste any energy trying to conceal it. Anyway, since the cop car was parked outside of the house, it was a sure bet that I would get a buck and a quarter from the Chief. I did a quick inventory of the parked cars and didn't spot a tanker. I was in luck. I didn't want to walk in on any domestic situation, especially with one of them armed. I proceeded to knock at the door and was told to come in.

"I'm your new paperboy, and I'm collecting for the Winona Daily News."

A tall, slinky lady with a cigarette hanging from her mouth stared me down from head to toe.

"You'll have to get it from Loy."

"Loy, the damn paperboy is here."

"Send him back!"

Because he was the Chief of Police, the most powerful man in Arcadia, I felt an overwhelming command of respect surface in me. As kids, we always made fun of this guy, but now I was going to meet him face to face. I proceeded down the narrow hallway, went around the corner, and headed toward the end of the hall where the command originated. The door at the end was ajar, and I headed for it. It appeared to be an office where I imagined dignitaries came to visit him. I expected to see a decorated public servant sitting at his leather covered roll-top desk, supporting several telephones, one of them red, of course. The walls would be covered with plaques and honors, hanging from dark, wood paneled walls. All of this regalia would be tied together with thick, rich curtains, puddling on a marble floor.

I knocked on the door lightly, with the door widening ever so slightly with each knock.

"Come on in, don't be shy."

I swung the door open, and there sat Chief Cotasko in all his glory. He was on the toilet with his trousers wrapped around his ankles, bending over to reach for the trucker wallet that was suspended from his back pocket. He looked skinnier than ever, with smoke from an idling cigarette hanging from his mouth, defusing the room.

"How much do I owe ya?"

I was flabbergasted, not only by the sight, but by the stench that was starting to set in. While the cigarette smoke was doing its best to mask the putrid odor, it was slowly tiring, admitting defeat.

"A dollar and a quarter."

"Got change for two bucks?"

"Yeah, just a second."

I reached into my money pouch about the same time that he reached back to flush the toilet.

"See ya," he said looking down, making the inference that he wasn't talking to me.

"Here's seventy five cents. Thanks."

I turned around and walked out thinking, man, this world is crazy.

One of my last customers was the Pompous.' The Pompous' had an attached double-car garage with two single car doors separated by a post in the middle. I had noticed in between doorbell rings that the middle post separating the doors was smashed in.

"Hello, who are you?"

"I'm the new paperboy, and I'm collecting for the paper."

"Come on in. Give me a minute. I'm just setting the table."

A nondescript lady in her 50's opened the door for me, and I stepped in, watching her complete her dinner chores.

"Sorry I interrupted you, but since I'm collecting, I'm kinda running behind schedule."

"No problem, I'm just finishing up."

I couldn't help but notice what she was actually doing for dinner preparations. All the plates on the table were sitting upside down, with condiments located in the center of the table. She was inverting the plates right side up. It appeared that they hadn't been washed from the last meal.

I was so appalled that I had forgot my business manners.

"What are you doing?"

"I'm setting the table the easy way. You see, most people, when done eating, wash the dishes. This takes a lot of work and is hard on your plates. So what we do is just take our plates when we're done and flip 'em over. That way the food never dries up and spoils, because it never gets air. It's kind of the same as eating desert off of your dinner plate."

"Wow!"

I stood there too stunned to say anything else. I was usually open-minded toward new things, but this was unreal. Even though this practice could be dubbed as efficient, my stomach became queasy just thinking about the existing bacteria.

"When do you finally wash the plates, I mean, sooner or later you probably rinse them off?"

"Depends. I wash my plate about every three days. Einsal usually puts his in the sink when he can't make out the pheasant wings anymore."

"Ah, OK." I thought this might be a good time to change the subject. "How did the middle post of your garage get banged up?"

"Well, Einsal came home drunk one night, seeing double. So when he approached the garage, he thought he was seeing double again and aimed right down the middle."

"Oh yeah. That's a common mistake around here."

She dug in her coin purse, fishing out five quarters.

"Here you go, and next time maybe you'll stay for dinner."

"There you go, being good to me before I even earned it. That's very nice of you. And on that one, I'd better go!"

I thanked her and exited as fast as I could.

Wow, what an experience, I thought. Just one more customer, and I'm home free. Just as I jumped back on my bike, I heard my name being called out. It was Wayne across the street and down one house.

"Come with me to Minortz's, and then I'll go with you over to the Mileage Station, and we'll grab a pop."

Why not, I thought.

"Sounds good to me!"

We arrived at Minortz's, knocked and were invited in almost immediately. Old lady Minortz was immense, hardly able to waddle around inside her cramped and cluttered house. Knick-knacks were strewn along the edges of the worn carpet, and the walls were adorned with family photos. On the arm of a worn easy chair perched a miniature Chowowa, nervously shaking and barking intently.

"Oh, don't mind him any, he won't hurt you."

She no sooner turned around to find her purse when that rat-like creature lurched airborne and bit Wayne in the crotch, then retreated, all in a blink of an eye. I choked with laughter at the dog's timing and precision, but was muted by Wayne's screams of shock and pain.

Mrs. Minortz whisked around to check out the commotion. By this time the dog was back in attack mode on the armrest of the stuffed recliner.

"Oh, he won't hurt you. He's a lot of bark, but he's more afraid of you than you are of him."

As soon as Mrs. Minortz lumbered out of the room, Wayne took their rolled up newspaper and swatted the spastic pooch right off of the chair. The miniature mutt went flying with about as surprised of a look as Wayne had had a minute ago. Mrs. Minortz waltzed back in the room with her coin purse. The canine was now behind the chair, twitching much more noticeably and barking ferociously.

"See, he's more afraid of you than you are of him." Wayne nodded agreeably as he put the money into his pocket book.

"You can sure bet on that."

Just part of the job, I thought. You've got to be on your toes and always thinking.

We raced over to the Mileage Station, my last customer on the route. Wayne and I had already starting frequenting this place after our routes, mainly because it served as a great meeting place to sit and have a pop. It didn't take long to place names to the characters that walked in on a daily basis.

The lady who ran the store looked just like a man and lived in the back. She was average height, about sixty years old, very slim and had short white hair. She always wore a dark greasy monkey-suit, a one-piece overall sported by most mechanics. Because of the color of her garb, Wayne cleverly named her "Black Widow." Her ten-year-old grandson, Stevie, was staying with her over the summer, and he was a real instigator. "Trained Monkey" and "Mud Sucker" were two locals from the chicken plant next door that made constant appearances, and Wayne had nicknamed them respectively. Trained Monkey was a slightly overweight man in his mid fifties. He would sit on the lone bar stool next to the cash register and spin around as he talked, more times than not ending up addressing the refrigerator more than anything. He usually hung around, waiting for the paper to arrive so that he could read the funnies before he headed for home.

Mud Sucker worked at the chicken plant as well. His primary job was to spray the chicken guts off of the dock and keep the parking lot clean. He walked around wearing hip-waders, always glancing skyward to check out the weather.

Wayne walked in first and went right to the pop machine.

"What kind are you getting?"

"I don't know yet, let me think."

I searched my pocket for the collection ticket for the Mileage Station.

"I'm collecting for the paper, and it will be a dollar and a quarter."

"A dollar and a quarter for this shit? This ain't news, this is crap!"

"Well, now wait a minute, some of dat stuff is pretty darn funny," Trained Monkey piped in.

"Dat's not all dats in dare dough," Mud Sucker chimed. "Da weder is what I read, cause it's always different."

"Yea, but da funnies are funnier!"

Now, I'm getting hungrier by the minute, and I thought it was high time I interrupted these debaters.'

"Well, regardless of what you think of it, you have agreed to pay a dollar and a quarter for two weeks of it."

"Stevie, get my purse in the back."

The grandson soon returned with her purse, and she diligently dug out the money owed.

"There."

She sauntered away with a smirk, as if to recant her dramatic opinion.

I thanked her as she walked to the back of the store to return her purse. Then I scooted to the pop machine to meet Wayne.

Wayne needed change for the machine. He walked over to Stevie who stood guard over the till.

"Here's a buck, and I would like two quarters and five dimes."

As Stevie was doling out the change, Wayne apparently changed his mind.

"Just give me three quarters, two dimes and a nickel."

Stevie appeared confused, so Wayne reached in and took three quarters, two dimes and a nickel, the exact change that he had requested. Wayne stood there with the change exposed in his hand so Stevie could count it to assure that they were even.

"Grandma, they're reaching in the till!"

In a flash, the lady raced out of the back room and grabbed Wayne by the shoulders.

"You reaching in the till, you little bastard?"

"Yea, but he lost count of the change, so I just took it out for him and stood here showing it to him."

"You little shit. Now sit here so I can keep an eye on you."

It would be safe to say that some tension existed at this point. Wayne and I sat in opposite chairs with the lady sitting on a four-legged barstool perched right in front of Wayne's stained over-stuffed chair. The whole thing started to appear funny, and as soon as Wayne started to smile, the lady jumped up as if to slap him.

Suddenly, we heard the bell ring that was connected to the black hose, signaling that a customer had come across the drive and up to the gas pumps. Timing couldn't have been better, I thought. However, a quick glance outside made my heart sink. The bell ringing was the result of our classmate Mike Wineski's bicycle. Mike was a stocky kid who loved to laugh. We really didn't need him here at this point in time. Mike walked in and immediately started laughing as he saw the lady perched over Wayne's chair. My eyes met Mike's, and I knew that I had to release some of the tension.

"Want a pop?" I asked.

"Yea, I'll get one."

Mike returned from the pop machine with a fresh bottle, then sat down with a big grin on his face.

"You know Rummell's with me somewhere....he had to stop and talk to Munch's brother, but he'll be here pretty soon."

157

The scene was degrading fast. Rummell was nothing but a huge goof. Most times, we laughed at him, not because he was funny, but just at him. He was obnoxious, belligerent and slightly crazed, and he was always riding around on his bike waiting for someone to hang with. Mike found a chair, and the three of us sat motionless and quiet for about one minute. Mike took a swig of his pop, then burst out laughing so hard that the pop came bubbling out of his nose. I spewed my fresh mouthful of the carbonated drink all over the floor, and Wayne started to smile. The lady jumped off of her stool as if to slap Wayne again, so he quickly wiped the grin off of his face. The whole scene was so ridiculous that the mood soon went from funny to bizarre. Every time Mike or I would laugh or talk, the lady stared straight ahead at Wayne's face, as if daring him to twitch. I started wondering how we would get out of this one, when my prayer was answered. The hose bell that draped the concrete drive rang again and again. We all sat in our chairs, watching out the window as Rummell's head went by time and time again. Rummell was riding his bike around the gas pumps, jumping up and pushing down as hard as he could to make the bell ring with his bicycle tire. Now the lady wasn't the least bit humored, and a scowl began to dominate her face.

"That one of yours?"

"I think I know who he is, but I don't know him personally."

"Stay here, all of you! He's mine."

The lady lurched in the doorway watching Rummell riding around the pumps while bouncing on the hose.

"Come here, I got some candy for you."

It was as if we were reliving a scene from Hansel and Grethel. She walked out on the drive trying to snag Rummell as he rode by. This was our break. We all put down our pop bottles and headed for the door. As we ran out grabbing our bikes, we noticed she had captured Rummell and was holding on to his bike by the handlebars.

"Come back here you guys, or I'll call your parents!" I couldn't help notice the despondent look on Rummell's face as we tore out of there. I wanted to go back and help him, but, instead, I just prayed that she would show mercy and not torture him too long.

Wayne rode with me through town, to the top of the hill, then continued on home. My first day of collecting was done, and I felt that I had earned every penny that I gathered.

As soon as I got home, I went to my room that I shared with my brother, Tom, and shut the door. I emptied out the contents of my large coin purse on the bed to tally up my collections. After counting it all up, I realized that I had almost enough money collected to pay my paper bill. Eighty dollars would cover my bill, and the rest of the money would be mine to keep. After all of my bookkeeping was complete, I went over to the kitchen to find something to eat. After dinner, I finished my homework and got ready for bed. As I was folding my clothes, I noticed a flat object in my left jean pocket. I quickly dug it out, almost forgetting that I had put money there. As I extracted the contents, a plastic bar chip plopped out on the dresser, dancing briefly before laying motionless. The chip read; "good for 10 cents or 1 tap beer at Siepal's Bar." I just stood there reflecting on Sonja's life. Not only did they not have much, but her dad was spending it as fast as he made it. We never had much either, but at least my dad came home every night after work. My heart went out to her, and a tear ran down my cheek. I immediately brushed it back, recomposed myself and jumped into bed. It was a good day and tough day all rolled up into one, but I was thankful that I had experienced it. Tomorrow would be another day, another adventure and another lesson waiting to find me.

Chapter XVII

Winter had set in, making the paper route a little more challenging. Snow was the prime factor, forcing me to ride my bike more cautiously and stay on the plowed road for better traction. Sometimes I would have to walk my bike if the snow was packed too deep, but I always took it so that I could get across town to the post office to start my route.

It was Christmas Eve, and the papers still had to be delivered. I was in between collection periods and running short on spending money. The silver lining was that there was still one customer to collect from. Mr. and Mrs. Polsnor had been away on a trip to Hawaii, so I had not been able to collect from them yet. Everyone knew that they had gone to Hawaii, mainly because everyone knew where everybody went, especially if it was further than Independence. I was carrying the paper collection stub that proved receipt of payment in my pocket for days now, hoping to catch them as soon as they got home from their trip. The snow on the ground was minimal, but it was flurrying in huge flakes. I took off on my bike a little early, hoping the papers would arrive at the post office ahead of schedule so that I could get home for Christmas Eve dinner on time. Once I arrived at the post office, my hunch was confirmed. I loaded the papers into my damp cloth newspaper bag and slung it over my left shoulder to protect them from the falling snow. Ivan hurried from behind the counter and caught up with me before I got to the door.

"Why don't you just hand me my paper, and I'll take it home."

Ivan had just hid my stack from me yesterday, resulting in the discovery of a box of hard candy hidden behind a sign that read:

"Merry Christmas to the best paperboy on the other side of the Trempealeau River."

It was Christmas Eve, and everyone was being so cheerful. It seemed as though I were living out a Charles Dickens novel. The snow was swirling around in the twilight, and people were wishing me a Merry Christmas. Even the Krumholtz boys invited me in to help them eat up some old leftovers that they didn't want. I declined, but thought that if I had to choose between being a dinner guest of theirs or the Pompous,' I would probably pick the Krumholtz brothers for my dining pleasure. Although the thought of eating at either place turned my stomach, the thought of food did make me hungry. If I only had a little money, I'd stop for a candy bar, or better yet, one of those round pies with the fruit filling and a bottle of pop. The only hope of satiating my stomach was to get lucky and catch the Polsnor's at home.

I had just put Kribecks' paper in their door when I glanced across the street at the small brick home of the Polsnor's. My heart skipped a beat as I noticed the warm glow of a living room lamp illuminating the room. Instead of going to the Woychik's, and over to Whitezal's first, I aborted my usual route pattern and made a beeline for the Polsnor residence. I knew that I had hit paydirt, and I could just taste that fruit-filled pie. I jumped off my bike and ran to the front door. I rang the doorbell, removing my glove to dig out the lone cardboard stub in my pocket. The door opened, and what a sight for sore eyes. Mrs. Polsnor was standing there never looking better. Her red Christmas dress was radiant in the doorway. The broach on her scarf really brought out the sparkle in her eyes.

"Merry Christmas. I'm collecting."

"How much is it?"

"A dollar twenty."

"Oh, what an honest young man you are! You remembered that we had you stop the paper for one day because our son was out of town, as well.

"That's right, Mrs. Polsnor."

"Very well."

She turned to walk down the hall, trying to maneuver her obese body without knocking any of her wooden ducks off of the wall. As she disappeared out of sight, I thought, who would go to the trouble of stopping a paper from delivery for one day? I knew how tight they were with their money. It was rumored that the Mrs. would pinch an Indian Head nickel until the buffalo crapped in her hand. I stopped thinking about it, because, after all, it was Christmas, the season for kindness and sharing. I looked around the foyer of the house. The radio was playing Christmas hymns in the background with the black and white production of "It's A Wonderful Life" displayed on the television set down in the living room. I heard her heavy footsteps approaching the hallway, heading back toward me.

"So, how was your trip?"

"It was great."

She extended a dollar, giving the quarter a ride on top of it.

"Do you have change?"

"Ah, no I don't, since you're the last customer that I had to collect from."

Now I was positive that I had set up the mood, and since it was Christmas Eve, I knew that dollar and a quarter was as good as in my pocket. I was just about ready to give obligatory thanks for the nickel tip when the dollar and quarter combo was snatched from me.

"Now you'll just have to come back when you have change."

That fat, ugly, old hag whirled around so she could close the door.

I reeled out of the house, feeling totally rejected. Out on the sidewalk, I stopped to catch a few snowflakes in my mouth. The wind had picked up a bit, and I pulled my stocking hat a little further down my neck. I had to recount what had just happened back there. Once again, I had depended on human kindness. Maybe that's why Dad is the way he is. He has no expectation from anyone, so he will never be disappointed. I thought about the good lesson that I should've just learned, but I was too disappointed to accept it. I guess you can't put people in one class. Things that seemed fair and righteous to me obviously were not considered righteous to others. Then again, some people are just jerks.

When I got home that evening, I stood on the front porch and looked around the neighborhood. The snow was continuing to fall. From my vantage point, my little town looked like the inside of one of those snow globes. I could smell Christmas dinner cooking in the kitchen. I stood there wondering if Lambert was in the bar, and what Sonja and her family were doing for Christmas Eve. I wondered if Mrs. Polsnor was really that tight or if she actually enjoyed torturing little paperboys. I took one more look around the neighborhood before I responded with a hearty Merry Christmas to a squirrel that had just offered me the very same greeting. Wait a minute, squirrels don't talk, I thought. I did a double take of the squirrel sitting over at our neighbor's house, the Geibels.

"So Imy, think all squirrels just eat nuts?" The chatty gray varmint sat with his lower half concealed behind a cement stair stoop. I stood there shaking my head.

"You're crazy."

The squirrel squatted behind the stoop, talking up a storm, its mouth moving with every word. But the voice began to sound a little too familiar.

"Geibel, you're so weird."

Neebie Geibel jumped out from behind the stoop and held the gutted-squirrel like a hand puppet. Apparently he had been out squirrel hunting and had shot it earlier that day. Neebie had had his hand completely inside of it, working the mouth with his thumb and index finger.

"Pretty neat, huh?"

"Yea, pretty neat and pretty weird. But you know what? I knew since they had written a book about you guys that you must be weird."

"What's the book, smart ass?"

"House of the seven Gables."

"What's a gable?"

"Geibels, Gables, there's seven of ya....hey, I'll explain it to ya when I get a free day. Merry Christmas."

Are people this bazaar, or is this just Arcadia, I asked myself. Since I had nothing to compare life to, I'd just have to wait to find out for myself.

163

Chapter XVIII

Most Catholic churches rely on fundraisers for support, and St. Stan's was no exception. They held church dinners, bake sales and the Fall Festival, of course. But none of these moneymakers could hold a candle to the pinnacle event, Stosh Sikowski's B-ta-dee Bingo. This special event took place only twice a year in the church basement, so people planned for it months in advance. With the weekly pulpit announcements and bold type church bulletin ads, Bingo dates were deeply etched into everyone's brains early in the year. The two dates were usually around St. Patty's Day and the Fall Festival, held sometime in early October. Judging from the size of the crowds, I believed most townspeople considered it a venial sin to miss the Bingo bash.

It was Sunday, March 19, two days after St. Patrick's Day. Bingo didn't start for a good half-hour, but I had arrived at the church basement at 7:30 PM to look for all of my school friends. We always sat together, usually way in back, so all of the goofing around wouldn't be quite as noticeable.

There was Randy Kloneki, his brother Bim, Wayne and the rest of the boys. I didn't need to wait around for an invitation. I quickly headed over to their table and pulled up a steel folding chair.

The rows of card tables were covered with white plastic cloths and crammed end to end in order to accommodate the masses. I looked around at all of the familiar faces sitting in the same places. It's a lot like church, I thought. Once people pick a spot, they always return to it, just so they can remain in their comfort zone.

Mrs. Wilford Breska was already in her favorite place, flanked by the Willard Sobeyuk and the Goober Kabinsa families. A couple of tables over sat old lady Schrepietz along with Pauncho Poohalla who was chewing snuff. Beside Pauncho sat Bill, who everyone called "Apple Ass." I have no idea how he got that name, nor do I know what it meant, but for whatever reason, it seemed to fit. The Bozart boys were sitting with their dad, reminiscent of the Cartwrights on the television show Bonanza. Conrad, the dad, only appeared about ten years older than the eldest son. Like the

Cartwright's, the Bozart's seldom ever left the farm except to run into town for supplies. Everett Skribner and his entire family sat just two tables down from us, and I knew it would probably be a challenge for him to remain conscious through the entire event. But then again, maybe he caught some sleep in church that morning.

Seed corn was used for marking the cards, probably because the common commodity was so readily available. The corn was being distributed by ushers in small equal piles spaced every few feet apart on the tables. The Bingo cards were soon to follow. The number of cards played depended on how many cards each contestant was willing to buy. All of the ushers sported white blazers, and only the heavyweights held this honored position. Aaron Beisik, Penguin Sobotta and Roman Tueshner were on board, just to name a few. The usher who had won the lottery and actually got to spin the number cradle was Ernest Colva, and the announcer who called the numbers out of the cradle was none other than the honorable Stosh Sikowski. Stosh owned this position. Because of his more than apparent guttural Polish accent, some of the numbers were phonetically slaughtered. The worst being when he called out the space for B-3. His B-ta-dee interpretation would send me and my friends into hysteria. As a result, the event simply became known as B-ta-dee Bingo.

It was now ten minutes to eight, and the church hall was filled to capacity. People were spilling out into the isles, and extra card tables were set up to accommodate the overflow. Once everyone got settled, the game was underway. Stosh picked up the microphone and perused the anxious crowd. A shrilling screech pierced the air as Aaron tweaked the amplifier nearby.

"Does anyone wanna play Bingo tonight?" an over amplified Stosh yelled out.

"Yah," was the lukewarm response from the impatient contestants.

"I should ask, does anyone wanna WIN at Bingo tonight?"

"Yah-hey!" was the resounding response.

"Well, let's quit saying, and let's git playing!"

"The first game prize is a donation from da Arcadia Broiler Plant, and dats fer four fryers, and doze of yous dat tink a fryer is a priest, it's not, it's a chicken. And talk about chicken, I tink of Aloyzie Marlolek, who actually won da lotto to be da number cranker tonight but was a little afraid about bein out here in da lime light. Oh well, we got Urine Colva, and he can turn my crank any day."

Leave it to Stosh to skew the meaning of a sentence. Stosh always wanted to be a priest, and since he wasn't, he had to be as close to the church as he could. He was head of the ushers and always had the biggest and most visible positions. He would go on and on about nothing, kind of like a comedian doing a parity of himself. But he was what gave B-ta-dee Bingo its character.

"OK den, yous know da rules, and let's play Bingo. If yous don't like da numbers dat I call out, yous can jest blame old Urine."

"First number...Beee-1. B-1."

When I heard the prolonged B, I thought, what were the odds of hitting B-Ta-dee on the first call?

"OOOOO-74. 0-74."

About eleven numbers later, another one of Stosh's anomalies surfaced again with the calling of; "GGGGG-fifty, five oh."

"BINGO," someone screamed in the front center of the hall.

"Leave da corn on your cards!"

Usher Aaron Bisek clamored over to confirm the winner.

"One," yelled Aaron, projecting his voice so it could be heard above the crowd.

"One," Stosh answered back in confirmation.

"22," Aaron called out again.

"22," Stosh echoed back.

"38"

"38"

"55"

"NO," Stosh signaled, quickly acknowledging that this individual had made a Bingo error and was probably not a native.

"See how important it is ta keep da corn on your cards? Corn is a very valuable ting, but it becomes even more valuable when it's kept on your Bingo card until a winner is officially declared. See, years ago da Indians found corn. Den dey figured out how ta eat it, den before ya know it, dey were growing it. Now corn is all over da world, and here in da Arcadia area, we grow da best of it. Dat's why we'd be considered blessed. Because we have so much corn, we have da privilege of using it fer dis great game of Bingo."

166

The deflated player with the false Bingo claim was sitting slightly red-faced, tricked by the old "O-fifty five O" call. I remembered my first Bingo experience, thinking that Stosh had just called O-55, learning later that he meant O-50. It was just a part of B-ta-dee Bingo.

A couple more rounds were played, and my buddy Bim won a six pack of beer and two pounds of butter donated by the Co-op Creamery and Peanuts Bar of Arcadia. Bim proudly paraded up to the prize table to claim his winnings. Walking past his mother's table he promptly dropped off the butter. No one batted an eye when Bim, a seventh grader, kept the beer for himself.

About a game later, Billy Bert was accused of throwing valuable corn kernels at Randy Kloneki. Mrs. Sovo Klapotic, an intense six-card player, claimed a kernel had bounced on her table, knocking off a kernel from her cards' free-space. Tension surfaced around our table when Stosh dispatched an usher to supervise us. As he was writing down Billy Berts' name, Stosh reprimanded Billy by saying that he was prohibited from winning this game. Everyone was instructed to leave the corn on their cards should Billy Bert call out "Bingo" during this match.

Boredom soon set in across the table of friends, and the king of troublemaking, Mishy Kupietz seemed to sense it. He became unusually quiet, as if his mind was racing, trying to invent the next round of entertainment. Lib, a friend who never would quit talking, was sitting right next to me, chatting up a storm and mimicking everybody that he could. Mishy gave me a look, and I knew exactly what he was up to. All the boys in our immediate area knew precisely what was going to happen. He was to keep Lib occupied while I populated Lib's Bingo card. I had to be strategic and not put too much corn on his card, giving him the impression that he was being set up. I could only give him enough to get Bingo slightly before anyone else. Scrap-Iron Smeetzsak winked, and the gang knew it was his to lead. Scrap-Iron started the diversion by rapping off a loud fart, ricocheting off the steel-folding chair. I was hoping that Scrap-Iron would be inventive and do something a little more original, but it was crunch time, and he had to do what he knew best. Of course, the whole table started giggling, eliciting a chorus of tongue smackings from the old ladies sitting over at the next table. This was my first chance. I slyly slipped a couple of kernels on Lib's Bingo card. Ernie rolled the crank, and another number plopped out for Stosh to broadcast.

"BEEEE-ta-dee, B-ta-dee"

"B-ta-dee, B-ta-dee," we chanted back, with Smono plugging his ears with his fingers so he wouldn't pee his pants from laughing.

Mishy, Scrap-Iron and the boys did a great job of distracting Lib over the next couple of called numbers, and a quick glance at Lib's card assured me that enough corn had been planted. Mishy started to ignore Lib, causing Lib to study his card for the first time. After a pregnant pause, Lib turned and poked my shoulder.

"Imy, I got Bingo!"

"Yea Lib, everyone has Bingo."

"No really, I do. Two places."

"Then call it."

"Bingo, Bingo!"

Lib waved his hand enthusiastically, flagging down the usher that was standing guard over us.

Randy, Bim's brother who wasn't in on the scheme, surveyed Lib's card, comparing it with his own.

"He never called 30!"

Lib's facial expression went from elated to worrisome once he realized that only six numbers had been called.

Stosh seemed a bit perturbed, knowing the odds of landing a Bingo after only six numbers was slim to none.

"We got a Bingo, leave da corn on your cards! Aaron, let's set up da relay system, since dare so far back."

The ushers positioned themselves accordingly, with Penguin Sobotta calling the numbers from the card over to Roman, Roman shouting the numbers down to Aaron, and Aaron announcing the numbers up at the stage to Stosh.

The old ladies were really put out now, especially after all of the commotion from our table. They were veterans and knew how highly unlikely it was to get a valid Bingo after only six numbers. Once the center free space was occupied, four locations needed to be filled. Odds of hitting four out of six numbers were about as high as Stosh pronouncing the words "B-three" correctly.

With the relay system in place, the very first number was sent back for confirmation.

"12"

"12"

"12"

"NO," resounded a scolding voice from Stosh.

"Dat's it. One more goofing around and old Urnie will stop turning my crank! And you'll see how Stellma Wonuk likes dat!"

Stellma Wonuk was one of the cooks in our Catholic School who was one of the most avid Bingo players in town. She would go over the hill to Winona twice a week to play. No one wanted to be on Stellma's bad side, knowing that she shoveled out the main entrée at every school meal. The more Stellma liked you, the more food you got, simple as that. It was quite a spectacle to watch how much tuna casserole could actually be loaded onto a serving spatula. And when she had your number, it was ironic how only a little would fall on your plate, with the rest getting a free ride back to the serving tub.

Heeding Stosh's warning, we cleaned up our act, and I won the second-to-the-last game. I felt a little sheepish walking up to claim my prize, feeling guilty about having so much fun and winning a game to boot. I kept my head low and skirted Stellma's table, just to be on the safe side.

After Bingo was over, Bim, Wayne and I walked over to my house to put the broilers that I had won in the refrigerator.

"We're going over to Schnokie's Road for a couple of beers, want to come along?" Bim asked nonchalantly.

"Eh, I had better not. It's after ten o'clock, and tomorrow's school."

"OK then, see ya tomorrow."

I kind of felt left out, knowing that I had better stay home. My parents were stricter than most, and besides, I thought we were way too young to drink beer anyway.

Chapter XIX

Three miles northeast of Arcadia sat the little town of North Creek. North Creek was comprised of four houses, a red brick Catholic Church and the Hooterville Tavern. North Creek served the predominately Catholic farmers around the area, providing them with church and tavern services. The church had a Saturday night and a Sunday mass. As for the tavern schedule, it always seemed open. North Creek had just gotten a new priest, and the area was abuzz with this Father Zeets. Father Zeets was a man well on his way to retirement. He was described as old and odd and father of the nineteen-minute mass.

Once word circulated about a nineteen-minute mass, Arcadian's flocked in droves to fulfill their Sunday obligation in North Creek. Not only could these devout Catholics satisfy their Sunday obligation on Saturday night before they hit the bar's, but to do it in nineteen minutes was like Christmas come early. Besides, it made sense for logistical reasons. With the bar right next to the church, you could kill two birds with one stone, so to speak. So as soon as one of my friends got the car to go to Saturday night Mass, we took the three-mile ride on the curvy township road out to North Creek Catholic Church.

We pulled up to the rural chapel just minutes before kickoff. The only available parking space was the grass infield of the softball field right next to the church. As we walked away from our car, I noticed other cars streaming on to the grass field, parking directly behind each other, bumper to bumper, prohibiting any early departures. Well, I guess anyone can stay put for nineteen minutes, I thought.

Inside the chapel, we paused before spotting a place about halfway down the short isle. We walked down the center isle, genuflected, then took a seat in the pew. After a quick prayer to the statue of Mother Mary, I scanned the congregation, checking out the crowd. There were so many men with red and black plaid flannel shirts on that you could have held a checker tournament. Others who opted for a sportier look donned nylon windbreakers

170

with their name embroidered on the lapel and bar slogan on the back. In fact, we were fortunate enough to be behind a guy with a nylon windbreaker that had an emblem of a martini glass on the back with the silhouette of a naked woman suspended in it.

As we waited, I noticed Father Zeets playing peek-a-boo with the congregation from the side vestibule doorway. He was a short, bald, slightly built man with huge fish bowl glasses that made his eyes appear twice their normal size. He kept peeking out, using a rolled up missilette as a telescope, as if to get a count of the crowd. He did this until the bell tolled from the bell tower to signal the eight o'clock hour and time for Mass.

After the second toll, Father Zeets rocketed out of the side vestibule as if shot out of a cannon. He was cradling the cruets, chalice and an array of cloths as he streaked to the altar. He plopped down the hardware, then waved his arms as if parting the Red Sea. The congregation interpreted this gesture as the signal to rise and bellowed out a hymn without the support of any musical accompaniment. As usual, they came to a grinding halt after the first verse. The first five stanzas of the hymn resembled a Polish record played backwards. Once the hymn gained momentum, it sounded like an out-of-tune mumble, with just a hint of humming noise. It reminded me of trying to start a lawn mower without the choke set. The motor would spit and sputter, run a couple of seconds, then die. A few parishioners continued on with verse two, however, their voices dwindled and died. During this one verse wonder, Father Zeets had lit the candles with a cigarette lighter and was ready to go.

"Da Lord be which yous."

"And also which yous."

Father Zeets then twirled his arms in a spiraling motion, as if winding up for a fast pitch where he would launch two speeding balls at once. The wind alone created enough gust to snuff out two of the candles on the altar. The entire congregation followed him like a baseball batter studying the third base coach before taking the next pitch. Once the signal was received, the entire congregation sat in unison. He began the First Reading, positioning his gooseneck reading lamp so that he could read from the ancient book. The Bible he was using appeared to be the original one. It was at least twice the size of any I had ever seen, and was bound with some type of animal skin. The Reading amounted to a

171

paragraph from a letter that Paul had written to the Romans. After losing his place virtually after every sentence, Father Zeets finally quit eye contact with the congregation and just followed his finger along each word. At the conclusion, he genuflected, bending his right knee no more than one inch earthward. I didn't know if this was a timesaving measure, or if he had arthritis, or perhaps both. But in any event, it seemed to count as an official genuflection. He elevated his arms vigorously with extended thumbs, looking like a hitchhiker with an emergency. Once again, the congregation studied his gesture and sprang to their feet as Father Zeets turned to the Gospel according to Mark. He leafed through the sturdy book as if it were a car maintenance manual and was looking for a gasket part number. After combing the entire Bible, he finally spotted the book of Mark over in the New Testament. Seconds later, the congregation was again seated, waiting for the sermon to be delivered. Father Zeets glanced at his watch and accelerated the pace. He dug out several sheets of handwritten paper, laid them on the lectern, maneuvering the goose neck lamp around in order to see better through his huge spectacles. After his brief sermon on "thorough worship," he briefly thanked ten families for their hard work, all of them Woletzko's, then gave the "stand" command. A quick prayer was rattled off, and then another hand signal was given, reminiscent of a parking attendant trying to fill a stadium lot. Two ushers, both Woletzko's, hurried foreword with collection baskets attached to long poles. Several ladies had their hats displaced as Delbert and Union whisked their poles past each isle. During the collection, Father Zeets was reciting the offertory as fast as he could. I seemed to have missed a step, because it wasn't until the second hat had been knocked off that I noticed all the people were kneeling. I had no sooner knelt, when the "stand" command was once again given. I stood and noticed parishioners bolting toward the communion line in a speedy gate up the isle. It was as if someone in a bar had hollered out "last call." I decided to get in line for communion, but Gubba Skronsh was sitting between me and the isle, and from the looks of it, he had no intention of going to communion. I stared at his enormous stomach protruding out way past the kneeler, almost resting on the back of the seat in front of him. He looked at me as if to apologize, and I immediately planned an alternative route. I exited the far end of the pew and tried to reenter the communion line through the almost empty pew in front of me. The problem was that both Betsner Boys were sitting there, and chances of getting around them were slim to none. Their dad owned a bakery in Independence, and they must have been taught that it was a sin to waste food. Though they were quite young, they were impressively immense people.

I exited back to the side isle and noticed the pews in front of me were now refilling back up with people returning from communion. I decided to go to the back of the church and enter the line from there. As I started to execute my plan, I could see that I had better put the pedal to the metal because the line was getting noticeably short and moving at a rapid pace. I literally jogged around the back of church and slowed to a speed walk down the center isle heading for Father Zeets. Father Zeets was alone at the altar by this time, motioning me on as if he were my track coach at the finish line. He whispered "about time, body of Christ." I answered with an "Amen," closed my eyes for a split second, then reopened them, finding myself standing alone with Father Zeets, who was already behind the alter, impatiently waiting for me to return to my seat. At my pew, I knelt, only to receive the "stand" command. Father Zeets was working us like an aerobics instructor. He then gathered his cruets, chalice and cloths and poured them into his cassock, which he held suspended with his other hand. Standing proudly with his dishware rolled up in his flowing garment, he waved the final blessing with his free hand. The congregation blurted out one last tune, of course not going beyond the first verse, as Father Zeets blew out the candles on his flight to the vestibule. We took his lead and headed for the door. Outside, it was apparent that everyone was heading over to the bar.

Wayne surveyed the traffic jam, wondering how we would ever be able to exit.

"Man, this ain't good. With all of those cars sitting there, we'll never get out of here."

"I just can't believe people go right from the church to the bar without skipping a beat."

"Hey, we're going to benediction," a worshiper quipped while walking briskly to the bar.

"Yea, and you can bet that benediction will last longer than nineteen minutes!"

Chapter XX

A few years later, the owner of our apartment house decided to sell his property. Dad reacted quickly and found a deserted house for rent down at the bottom of the hill on Main Street. I really couldn't classify this new location, since it was below the hill, but not right below it. Nor was it downtown, and we weren't even close to the river, let alone across from it. At any rate, it was a one-story bungalow, with two bedrooms and an attic converted into a bedroom. The house was owned by a farmer out in Square Bluff named Leonard Woodamacky. Mrs. Woodamacky had bought the house forty years ago hoping to move into town, but she could never entice Leonard off of the farm. So after almost half a century of hope, reality seemed to finally sink in, and Mrs. Woodamacky agreed to lease us the house for $65.00 a month.

The downstairs bedrooms were large, so my parents occupied one, and the three sisters occupied the other. Tom and I were awarded the upstairs attic, which was fine for about four months out of the year. Since we moved in June, we really didn't think about any adverse temperature issues that might surface. The fact that there was no heat or air conditioning in the attic proved rather uncomfortable during the humid Wisconsin summers and frigid winters. The 20 degrees below zero winter cold wasn't quite as bad, because, as a rule, it was warmer in the room than outside of the house. The summer was a different story, since it was insulated, as most attics back there are, it was not unusual to reach 110 – 130 degrees Fahrenheit during the three humid months of summer. There was no electrical wiring to plug in any environmental cooling aid. So there we were, sweating it out through the Wisconsin summer nights.

The older I got, the more I realized how little my family had. Although most of my friends didn't have much more, so I had no other standard to compare to. I guess I assumed that this was all there was. This is how everyone lived.

This period was the beginning of the rebelling time in my life, a time that a lot of teenagers go through. The distance between my father and me was widening, as if that was even possible. He used to at least tolerate me, however he now had a hard time having me around. I had the impressive talent of having anyone I desired to like me, but Dad was the biggest challenge of my life. He wanted to talk about nothing but farming. If you didn't know when the best time was to bale hay, he had no time for you. It was getting so bad that I started to turn into a renegade. Of course, being rebellious in Arcadia was changing barbers in hopes of getting a hair cut that you requested, not one that your parents mandated.

Being a sophomore in high school was great, and my classmate relationships were like being in a fraternity. All of us were being educated, rebelling and having fun at the same time. We were so good at putting on an act for the teachers that it was completely non-apparent to them, since we never showed any visible signs of disrespect.

One of our many victims was Mr. Kaydunk, the English Literary teacher. Mr. Kaydunk was such a cerebral man that he often appeared disconnected from reality. His appearance resembled that of an Ivy League professor outfitted in an oversized tweed suit and outdated bow tie.

During the warmer months when the classroom's tall, vertical, wooden windows were raised to circulate fresh air, we would pass along Kaydunk's classroom handout assignments to Tom Kaldunski. Seated strategically adjacent to the window, Kaldunski would lean over the sill when an unsuspecting Kaydunk turned his back and dump the material out the window. When Mr. Kaydunk would have us reference the work, we would just sit there acting totally dumbfounded, looking just as puzzled as he.

One day Kaydunk located a pamphlet wedged in the tall pine tree that was rooted next to the second-story window. He finally put two and two together. Things became quite tense when Mr. Kaydunk ordered everyone to write down the "problem child" of the classroom.

Since I was popular and a good sport, but hardly the instigator, most of my friends put me down as the troublemaker. A stunned Mr. Kaydunk remarked how surprised he was by the accused perpetrator.

"I would have never suspected you!"

If that was so, I wondered why he so readily accepted the testimony of this band of pranksters.

175

I was promptly assigned to a class guardian who was none other than Wayne Kampa, my newspaper buddy and now best friend. Now, Wayne as my guardian was nothing short of irony. Kaydunk had me whisked up front to a desk next to my new mentor, sentenced to learn under the tutelage of Wayne Kampa.

I now had a bird's eye view of classroom etiquette in action from one of the best. I walked up to the front row and sat down next to Wayne and began to observe.

Mr. Kaydunk stood directly over Wayne's front row corner desk, reading from an open book that he was holding about waist high. Wayne grabbed his Fine Point and reversed the narrow metal clip used to grip the implement to a pocket. With the clip extended past the hollow end of the pen, Wayne leaned forward on his desk. He cradled his chin in his left hand, then took the pen in his right hand and started ever so slowly working the zipper down on Mr. Kaydunk's baggy trousers. With amazing finesse, Wayne worked the zipper about halfway down. The snickers started and Kaydunk soon grew suspicious. A clueless Kaydunk quickly lowered the book that he was reading. He wasn't quite fast enough, however, to catch Wayne's recoil. As Kaydunk continued on, Wayne worked the zipper all the way down, finishing just before the bell. A thunderous round of applause broke out, and a beaming Mr. Kaydunk stood there taking it all in. Certainly, his inspiring reading of "The Fly" enlightened us beyond expectation.

"Maybe I should read aloud more often, and next time I'll pick a brighter subject so I can better appreciate your humor."

A few months down the road, it was time for the dreaded oral book report. Now, most of my classmates were very quick-witted and had lofty life ambitions. Others had their sights set on the family farm and didn't care a whole lot about their high school diploma. The oral book reports were implemented to stimulate some of the underachievers. Monk Sopenski, a popular kid who was one of the few that really didn't fit in either category, was chosen to go first. Since he wasn't much of a reader, he picked up the book "Midnight" from the library and simply read the back cover jacket.

Monk stood nervously, grinning uneasily while standing in front of class.

"This book was about a horse that turned into a racehorse."

Mr. Kaydunk seemed impressed that Monk had the gumption to go up and talk in front of class.

"Would you care to expound on this book?" Kaydunk encouraged.

"What?"

"Please tell us more about this fascinating horse."

"Well, it was a fast horse, obviously, and it could run real fast."

"Well, let's open this up to a question and answer discussion group. We're just dying to hear more about this incredible book."

This interactive forum was fodder for more shenanigans from the class. Bimbo started the nonsense, acting as if he were truly curious.

"How did 'Midnight' get his name?"

"Well, they really didn't say. He was born at night, so I guess that's how he got his name."

Some of the other guys caught on immediately and began the same routine.

"What color was the horse?"

"It was black, I think."

"All black?"

"I think so, but they did say there was a little white spot on his forehead, but no one was really sure about that."

"How fast could the horse run?"

"Once again, they didn't really say, but it was real fast-fast for a horse that is."

"In retrospect, do you think that it would be a safe assumption that since the horse was black and born late at night, that the book may have gotten it's name 'Midnight' from these facts?"

At this point, Monk began to relax and even enjoyed this fictitious dialogue of BS.

"Well, once again, it's so hard to say. I mean, the reader is led to believe that the horse was born between 11:00 PM and 1:00 AM. The reason we know that's fact is because it said that, somewhere. And we know that the horse was black, black as night. So, one could take the approximate time of the birth and compound it with the fact that it was black and make a beautiful argument that it was named Midnight because of that."

Another hand went up, and Monk responded, comfortably pointing to the raised appendage as if he had been a teacher in a past life.

"Monk, I have two questions. First, were the hooves black?"

"They didn't say, perhaps to weave a little mystery into the book. I wouldn't be surprised if they were."

"Second, I know that they never mentioned speed in the book, but how fast do you think this horse could run?"

"Very good question. I know that the horse was fast. The book also let on that the other horses knew how fast he was. When reading between the lines, Midnight himself even knew how fast he was, but when it comes right down to the often asked speed question, I couldn't even venture a guess. I just know that he was fast."

"Next question."

"OK, the horse was born at night, correct?"

"Yes, that's true."

"And the horse was black as night?"

"Yes."

"Well then, how did they see it? How did they actually know that the horse was born at midnight when they couldn't notice it? Do you know what I mean?"

"Terrific point! There was a point in the book where I had to set it down and ask myself that same question. As I read on, the author explained that it was born in a stable where a lantern was glowing. Next question."

The question and answer format went on for six days during the one-hour class. Meaningless question after meaningless question was asked, one feeding into another until Mr. Kaydunk stepped in and closed the session.

"That was good dialogue students, however, we need to work on quality instead of quantity for next time."

We pulled the wool over the eyes of most of our teachers except for a few that had our total fear and respect. These teachers usually were connected to the athletic department in a coaching capacity.

Mr. Schmetzki, "Mad Dog," as he was always referred to, was a leathery old algebra teacher that had been at AHS for over fifty years. He was the head football coach for over thirty years and had the personality to fit. Many of my friend's parents played for or were taught by him, and they warned us kids that nonsense was not tolerated at any level around him. He had a propensity toward the ladies, usually giving them the benefit of the doubt. With the young men, it was a different story. He had his "pet peeve" kid list, and if you had the same last name as a kid on this list, you were in big trouble. If he had a bad experience with an older brother, the rest of the brothers usually couldn't catch a break. If your last name was Goush, Heschki or Cornwallace, it was tough going establishing any kind of personal relationship with this man. Mr. Schmetzki was a well-built man for his middle seventies and still worked out constantly. His arthritic joints looked as if they begged for rest, as he would circle the gym on one of his late afternoon runs. The town of Arcadia named the park next to the swimming pool after him, so rebuking him would not only be risky, but very unpopular.

One day in Algebra class, Mr. Schmetzki was up front trying to prove a point. Usually, the class was fairly quiet, with the students afraid to make too much eye contact with this volatile man. Schmetzki just happened to be in one of his raspy tirades again, his face reddening from elevated blood pressure.

"OK, so A squared times B squared is what? What do I have here, a bunch of idiots?"

He screamed while pacing the room, stopping once to pound on a petrified student's desk.

"Well, what's the answer?"

He was shreiking wildly, as saliva spewed from his gaping mouth. I could smell his breath from my seat that was located toward the back of the room. And a quick dental diagnosis suggested that rotted food had been holding his teeth in position for years.

Everyone sat there motionless, too terrified to offer an answer while pretending to comb through their books for reference. Some just scribbled, giving the illusion that they were trying to figure out the elusive answer. Boots Goush was sitting in the back of class, too unambitious to do either.

"You guys are so stupid, you don't even know what two minus one is!" Schmetzki screamed, as he pointed a crooked arthritic index finger to indicate the number one.

"Seven!" Boots yelled out.

Mr. Schmetzki threw his book like a decathlon athlete throwing a discus and came running through the desks, sending the empty ones flying. With furniture and papers tossed about from a small tornado, Boots needed no further evidence than to get the heck out of there. He ran out the back door with Mad Dog in hot pursuit. Seconds later, the top of Boot's head flashed by the lower section of the window pane, with Mad Dog only twenty feet or so behind. We rushed to the window and watched as both ran about a block until the library blocked our view.

Wow, I thought. I wondered what would have been the right thing to do, stay in your seat and take it or do what Boots did. A few minutes later, Schmetzki entered the classroom as if nothing had happened. I didn't see Boots around school for a couple of days after that, and that was probably best.

Chapter XXI

Every autumn, three things in Wisconsin were a sure bet. Autumn brought the end of road construction. The hardwoods were ignited with splendid bursts of color, and the fall season brought on the start of Green Bay Packer Football. Football was bred into an Arcadian from birth, and football in Wisconsin meant "da Packers." People from Wisconsin lived and died for the Packers, and I was one of them.

The Pack was followed so closely that an occasional Thursday night televised game would cause Dad's bowling league to cancel. About once a month during the school lunch hour, Happy Brown, the science teacher, would play old footage from the championship game against the NY Giants that the Packers had won in the early '60's. Of course, we wanted to watch the first two Super Bowl victories that the Pack had won five years later, but since those victories were so recent, we were told that the school couldn't yet afford the films.

Far removed from their glory years, the Packers were now a hurting team. So like typical Packer fans, we lived in the past. People still rambled on and on about the infamous "Ice Bowl" against Dallas. The temperature was around 50 below zero, or so they would say. It was fourth down and goal from the one-yard line with virtually no time left on the clock. Vince Lombardi called time-out, then called the play of the century, a run off of right tackle. That was the day that time stood still for all Arcadians. Almost everyone in town could tell you what they were doing that day. Even more so than when President Kennedy was shot.

But that was the sixties. It was now the early seventies, and the Packers hadn't had a winning record for years. Every Sunday was another big disappointment. Bart Starr, the Hall of Fame quarterback, couldn't throw a ball over 20 yards. The play calling became so predictable that the opponent would call it out when the Packers broke the huddle. The Packer's punter would have ice on his leg by halftime, and the opponent usually seemed bored.

But the fans continued to watch and cheer for their Packers. And talk about how close we were to winning one. Every loss got harder and harder to take, some of them so heartbreaking that it would take up until the following Thursday to recover. The gut wrenching heartbreaks would continue right up to the most hated division rivals, the Minnesota Vikings.

Not everyone was a Green Bay Packer's fan. Although every child raised in the tri-county area was taught morals, ethics and Green Bay Packers, every once in a while a troubled youth would break out and rebel. These hooligan's secretly rooted for the Vikings, the most hated opponent of a Packer fan.

Packers' headquarters was unofficially located right in downtown Arcadia on Main Street. It was an old hotel upstairs, but downstairs was set up as a grand bar, owned and operated by none other than Iggy Sikowski. Iggy talked and lived for the Packers and would sponsor a bus to Minneapolis once a year to the Viking's game. After a Packer victory against their most hated rivals, Iggy would drive up and down Main Street with his vintage eight-door, stretch green Cadillac. He would drive through town blowing the horn with a polka band resonating from the back speakers playing the unofficial fight song, which no one could understand. The commotion was enhanced by dragging an array of empty beer cans tied to the bumper with rope.

Now, Iggy's nemesis was Klaus Progburg, one of the few pure Germans living in the area. He was a farmer who was obviously one of these troubled youths years ago. According to some folks, Klaus rooted for the Vikings just to piss off Iggy. Every time the Vikings would beat the Packers, Klaus would shoot off purple fireworks from on top of the hill over town. Then he would drive through town in his pickup, announcing the score repeatedly with a hand-held bullhorn.

This spirit lived on for years as Klaus groomed other individuals to carry the baton.

Chapter XXII

It was the summer between my sophomore and junior year in high school, and I had another summer of work waiting for me down at the feed mill. I didn't feel too badly because most of my school buddies finally had to go out and get summer jobs.

The three best, and pretty much only, jobs in Arcadia were working for the city, working for the furniture factory or working in the chicken plant. Working for the city was the most coveted position, and high school kids would practice leaning on a shovel for weeks before the formal interview. For the actual interview, the city wanted to see how applicants could work with the appropriate tools, such as a shovel, pick and gasoline-powered lawn mowers. It was rumored that in between the actual interview, points were issued on how well an applicant leaned on an implement in order to conform to proper posture. There seemed to be truth to the rumor, since I would always see city workers standing around leaning on their shovels as they watched another person work.

Arcadia's lone garbage truck was the only exception to the city worker's reputation. The two-man crew of Axey Smoltz and Sutter Toly was work in progress. Their fifty years of combined experience afforded them plenty of time to hone their skills. Axey was a tall, rail of a man, with long arms resembling buggy whips. Axey would ride on the back ledge of the truck, hanging on with one arm, freeing the other for grabbing garbage cans and waving. Sutter would drive the truck, getting so close to the cans that he oftentimes bumped them. Getting as close to the can as possible was paramount for Axey to do his thing. Sutter would slow the truck to a crawl, then Axey would lean over, grab the can and empty it in the back of the truck in one fell swoop. This two-man crew was the most efficient operation in town. But as far as the other city and county employees, it was another story. Their blatant sloughing off on the job would be the brunt of jokes around the area.

"What's orange and sleeps three?"

"A city truck."

"What's the slowest death in the world?"

"Being run over by a city truck."

Working at the furniture factory wasn't a bad way to make an honest living, but working at the chicken plant was darn near abusive. The "chicken line," where an employee actually grabbed the chickens and hung them by their necks while they went through an automated guillotine was nothing short of gross. Workers performed different functions while the chickens went around on this assembly line carousel, dangling from their necks. I don't think this is what Henry Ford had in mind. I know for a fact that my pal, Basil, didn't eat chicken for a year after working there that summer.

Since Dad needed my help again, and this time agreed to pay me, I had no choice but to partner up with him for another summer at the feed mill. I knew the pay scale would be pretty much like last year where he agreed to pay me $50.00 per week. After the first week of that summer, I was $50.00 richer and put the money into the bank to use for college. Three hot months later, I still had $50.00 in the bank. I knew that sometime soon I had to start making some money. Dad had great intentions, but intentions wouldn't pay my college tuition. I knew there were ways of getting to college on grants, student loans or the armed forces. Since I had to work anyway, it sure would come in handy to be paid for it. So here was the start of summer vacation again, and Dad had plenty of work but no money.

A few weeks later, I received my driver's license and was waiting for any excuse to drive. I had just completed the driver's education course offered by the school with Irv Ganshaw. Since the novelty hadn't worn off yet, I would jump in any farmer's pickup and back it up to the conveyor just to gain a little more experience. Finally, one day my ship came in.

It all started with Alphonse Kokett coming to the mill one morning. There were four trucks in front of him, and Alphonse had to get back and bail hay.

"Arno, how 'bout I jist leave da pigup here and take yer car home? Den when you've ground me out, call da house, and da old lady will bring yer car back and git da pigup."

"Sounds okay, Alphonse. We'll give ya a holler later."

About two hours later, we were done grinding everybody's grain, so we headed into the office to get a cold drink of water from the jug that we kept in the old refrigerator. Dad studied his watch, thinking intently.

"Well, that was a good piece of business. Norbie, even though we're running way behind schedule, why don't you go home and catch a quick bite. Imy, why don't you run Alphonse's truck back to him, and we'll meet back here inside of an hour. Then you and I'll head to lunch."

"Sounds good to me," Norbie said while making his way out of the office en route to his car.

I was so excited at the chance of driving Alphonse's pickup that I visibly started to shake.

"Sounds good to me, too!"

"Now, you know where Alphonse lives?"

"Yea, North Creek."

I headed for his truck at a dead run. I opened the door of his faded green pickup to the sour smell of wet burlap and hopped inside the cab. I wondered what the gearshift pattern on the floor shifter was as I held in the clutch and turned the key on the old '53 Chevy. As I held my right foot on the foot starter, the pickup came to life. I found first gear and slowly ascended the mill hill. I shifted to second, then depressed the clutch and brake in order to slow up for the stop sign at the top of the hill. This is great, I thought. Total freedom.

On the road to North Creek, I observed farmers out in the fields raking and baling hay. What a free life these guys have, I thought. Absolutely no one to answer to but themselves and getting to be outside most of the time seemed to be two of the biggest perks. As I rolled along, I took the County J turnoff, and, in no time at all, I was going past the North Creek Catholic Church. This had all been familiar territory until now, since I had only been past the church one time previously. I proceeded to climb a hill on the skinny blacktop township road. Several farms went by, none looking the least bit familiar. A couple of miles farther, the obvious was starting to sink in. I was lost, however, I knew that if I just turned around, I would at least get back to where I had come from. I started to slow down to look for a driveway to back into when I noticed a farmer out in a field nearby crimping some hay.

185

After riding with Dolf, I remembered how much farmers seemed to appreciate visitors, so I pulled over and waited for him to get closer to the road. A few minutes later, he came over to the edge of his field, slowed down and reduced the throttle of his tractor to a quiet idle to engage in conversation.

He was a short heavyset man with forearms twice the size of mine. I couldn't help notice the bead of sweat working its way down through his wrinkled face like a ball following a vertical obstacle course. I watched, wondering how long it would take before the drop of perspiration would reach the edge of his chin and plop down on his lap.

"Git yer ass on da Alice, and pull dis hay rack ober to da barn!"

"Pardon me?"

"Why, 'chew fart?"

"No, excuse me, but I don't work for you. I just stopped with a question."

"So now school kids come all da way out here jis ta ask me questions like I'm Alfred Einstein."

"That's Albert Einstein."

"Whatever. Yous, Motezko's boy?"

"No, Arnie Lecheler's boy."

"And your mom?"

"Ahh, Louise."

"Well, who was she from home?" a vernacular for inquiring about her maiden name.

"OK, I just want to ask you if you know where Alphonse Kokett lives. I came out here to return his pickup, and I think I've gone too far."

"I not only know where Ali lives, I know where his udder place is, I know where da upper place is, I've driven two of his tractors, know what kind of baler he's got, know......"

"Well, I'm looking for Ali's home place. Would you know where I may find that?"

"Dats easy. Know where Ole Woyzney was tinking 'bout building dat new pole shed?"

"Ah, no."

"OK, you know where Berbage Gimeaza bought dat piece of land dat used to be Sigman Walski's, den found out later dat it was really Apollinary Shucks?"

"Emmm, not really."

"OK, don't eben tell me dat yous don't know Rufus Kleimik."

"Yea, I think I might know Rufus."

"OK, now we're gittin somewhere. You know where Chink Chewsna's place is?"

Now everyone knew where Chink Chewsna lived. He had the most dilapidated farm in the valley. You couldn't even count the number of rusted farm implements resting in tall weeds stashed around the farm buildings. One couldn't tell where the farm ended and the yard began because it all looked the same. There was usually a sparse corn crop growing right up to the back door of the house. The last time that Dad and I drove past his place, there was a mammoth Holstein cow lying on the front porch, as if waiting to be invited in for dinner. Anyway, finally a connection, I thought.

"Yea, I know where Chink lives."

"OK, if ya go on County M past Chink's to da north, dat field where Rufus always lets Chink's cows go on, right dare, go up da hill, den cut ober as if yous was going to Emil's. As soon as you git ta da top of da hill, look west, cause dares a barn dare dat you'll never forgit. Dat barn, some say, is one of da longest barns in da county. Anyway, go ohhh, 'bout ten maybe twelve acres down dare…

"OK, now who's Emil?"

"Emil Stelmach. Actually Emil lives in Travis Valley, but his udder place is up dare in Square Bluff."

"Oh, so just go up the hill, sure I know right where it is."

I acted as if I was in total synchronization with this directional consultant. I could see the enthusiasm radiating through his face now that he could tell that I was totally enlightened.

"Thank you. You've been a huge help."

"You betcha."

The bead of sweat was now making its way under his chin, following the curvy route of his neck wrinkles. This short stocky man increased the fuel to his tractor while putting it in gear and slowly rolled away.

I jumped back in the pickup, knowing that I had to turn around and try to find this farm on my own. I thought, you know, the only thing that separates this farmer from an executive in New York is the type of data they hold. They are both storehouses of knowledge, each an expert in their own subject matter. Neither could do the other's job. It seemed to make perfect sense, but I

187

thought that I would reserve an opinion on the comparison until I had actually met an executive, in person.

After lunch, I was back at the mill, ready to get started on the afternoon. Since most farmers were out in their fields baling hay, I decided to fire up the lawn mower and cut the grass. There wasn't a whole lot of grass to cut, but with all the junk to mow around, it still took about an hour to complete. I had just finished mowing around Dad's two Buick's dubbed White Lightning and Blue Streak. They were four-door sedans rusted up to the door handles. Once I was done, I sat down on the front porch with the new hired hand Norbie and listened to Stu Ensta's one-hour radio show on the AM dial.

Stu's weekday one o'clock show was broadcast out of a bigger town, located two counties over. The format consisted of nothing more than a series of polka music played in between advertisements sponsored by Arcadia businesses. Dad was trying to get his sponsored polka song in the second segment of the show, allowing old Stu a little more time to "hit the coffee." I didn't really know what that meant, but I could tell that his words were not as slurred in the second half of the radio program. Regardless, Dad's ad pretty much sounded the same and was read with a Polish accent.

"OOO-key, OOO-key, anoder classic brought to yous by East Arcadia Feet Mill. So go see Arnie Lecheler for all your feets and seets neets."

From the sound of the ad, you'd think we owned a shoe and furniture store, specializing in recliners. Another Polka song had just gotten underway when we spied the gas delivery truck at the top of the hill heading our way.

"Looks like Grunuit's a little early this month," Norbie stated while watching the tank truck descend the hill. The tanker pulled up to the two one-hundred-gallon rusty fuel tanks standing between the corncrib and mailbox. Norbie waltzed over to the truck with me in tow.

"Hey, Grunuits!" Norbie shouted while the petroleum truck ground to a halt.

"What's Grunuits?"

"That's his nickname."

"What's his real name?"

"Ron."

"Why with a name like Ron…. Ah never mind."

"Need a little gas, Norbie?" Grunuits asked.

"No, had beans last night, got plenty of that."

Grunuits exited the truck and tapped on the side of the fuel tanks with his knuckles to determine the hollowness inside.

"Well, looks like you need a little."

Norbie stood there, disgustingly shaking his head.

"I don't know why we need some. We hardly used any at all this week. I guess it's time to do the old switch-er-ou again."

Grunuits nodded, understanding exactly what Norbie was telling him.

"What's the old 'switch-er-ou,' anyway?" I asked.

"We have to do it when old George Guentrig's kid runs out of money at the end of the month. Seems he found a self-service pump with a great price to boot. So to discourage him, we put diesel fuel in the gas tank and put gas in the diesel fuel tank."

"How do you know it's that same guy stealing gas?"

"Since we started the old switch-er-ou, he's had to work on that old Skylark quite a bit."

"Well Norbie, seems to be quite a bit of petty crime stuff goin' 'round. Ya know, Donnie Zagoonski, who just works over here at da concrete plant, had someone break into his garage and swipe his new chrome rims dat he was fixin' ta put on his El Camino."

"Keystones or Kregors?"

I felt pretty prideful asking that question, making it evident that I knew the difference between brand name wheels. Old Norbie picked up on my boasting and quickly defused it.

"I guess they were the round ones."

"Well, at any rate, just remember ta tell Arnie dat da tanks are reversed. I want ta make sure dat he doesn't get da tanks cornfused."

After Grunuits was done filling the fuel tanks, he handed an invoice to Norbie and jumped into his truck.

"Life is gettin' so confusing, fellas. It's come ta da point where many of my customers are doing da old switch-er-ou. Da problem is dat because of frequent theft of fuel out of my truck, I got ta do da old switch-er-ou too. So now, half da time I don't know if I'm puttin diesel or gas inta a gas or diesel fuel tank. Cornfusing, huh?"

Norbie nodded his head, thinking of a comeback line.

189

"Look at the positive side. After all of the mixing up, you've still got a fifty-fifty chance that you're right!"

"Hey Norbie, dat makes me feel better. But do you know what makes me feel even better dan dat? Knowin dare is a one hundred percent chance dat I'm goin' ta have a beer tonight!"

Grunuits chuckled after that one, humored by his own quick wit. He put the truck in gear and headed up the hill.

No sooner was Grunuits out of sight than Dad came out from the office.

"That was Frankie Wojomuskie on the phone. He wants to know if you would be interested in working part-time for him baling hay in the afternoons. I told him since the feed mill is slow in the afternoons anyway, the decision was yours to make."

"Dad, sure you won't mind? I'd really like the extra money."

"Well, he first wants to talk to you to see if you will work out. Here's his number. Why don't you go and give him a call."

"Thanks. I will."

I jumped off the mill porch to head for the office, so I could make my first official call to a prospective employer. My nerves started to twitch, so I stopped to compose myself for the big interview.

I dialed the number and listened to the ringing on the other side, thinking about what I was going to say to this land baron who actually had employees under him. My thoughts were soon interrupted as the telephone was answered by a crackly voice resembling an elderly lady.

"Yello."

"Hi, uh, this is Imy. Is Frank there?"

"Which one, Frank or Frankie?"

"Frankie, I guess."

"Who are you?"

"Dad told me that Frankie just called, looking for some hay baling help."

Total silence greeted me after that statement, and I waited for a response, but never received one.

"Uh, so I thought I'd give him a call right back."

"Well, Dad's standin' right here cause his hemorrhoids hurt too damn bad to sit down, and he don't even know how ta dial da damn phone, so how da hell did he call you?"

"Uh, my dad, Arnold Lecheler, told me to call you."

"Son, I don't even know your dad, so why would he tell you to call me?"

"OK, my dad, who is Arnold Lecheler, whom you've never met, told me to call Frankie Wojomuskie. He said, here's the number. I called it, and you answered. If I could just talk to Frankie, this could probably be settled."

"Well, why didn't you just come out and say dat? Hold on, he's down by da barn. I'll run and fetch him fer ya."

"Frankie," she shouted as she headed for the door.

"Whaaat," came a dreadful voice that sounded like it was awakened from the dead.

"Not you... Frankie, your son. Go over dare and sit your ass down."

A wretched scream erupted in the background.

"No, I mean......Just stand dare."

I heard a screen door bang in the background as her voice got fainter. Boy, this was truly interesting. Can't wait to finish this one. It should be a doosey, I thought.

About a minute later, I heard the screen-door pop.

"Yep."

"Hi, this is Arnold Lecheler's boy, Imy, calling about your needing help baling hay."

"Yep."

"So, I thought I'd give you a call for an interview."

"Yep."

"So, here I am. On the telephone with you."

"Yep. You can start tomorrow afternoon. Bye."

A loud click sounded in my ear, this time greeting me with a dial tone. I guess I had just been offered a job. I wasn't sure, but I was going to take it as an offer and head over the hill to his place tomorrow. Wait a minute, I thought. I don't even know where this guy lives. Odds are, it's over a hill. I hung up the phone and ran outside to tell Dad and Norbie of my new opportunity.

Dad congratulated me on my new endeavor, seeming relieved that finally someone would give me some money. Norbie proceeded to tell me that Frankie was in deep trouble with the law.

"Why is he in trouble with the law?"

Norbie acted as if he was in a deep trance, as if under oath and trying to recall all of the facts correctly.

191

"Well, I don't know for sure, but Frankie could be baling round bales over there."

"Why round? Why not square like most farmers? Besides, what does that have to do with anything?"

"Well, I know for a fact that he got ticketed last week, and they said he may get arrested if he continues baling the round bales."

"And why might that be?" I asked.

"The reason being that the cows aren't getting a square meal!"

"Now that's a good one," Dad said, chuckling.

Oh my gosh, I thought, Dad actually laughed. Maybe he'll come around sooner or later.

Dad glanced at his watch.

"Norbie, Imy, let's lock her up and head for the hills."

Neither Norbie nor I needed to be told again as I ran for the salt shed and Norbie strolled over to push in the bag conveyor. After everything was secured, Norbie meandered to his car that was parked in the weeds, looking over his shoulder to bid us his usual farewell.

Dad and I jumped in "Blue Streak." Another day in the books, but tomorrow would be different. I had a new experience to look forward to on both sides of the spectrum. Not only did I have a new job, but I'd actually get paid for doing it. Now how exciting is that, I thought.

Chapter XXIII

The following morning was a beautiful one, with plenty of dew sparkling off of the grass by the mailbox. Dad and I parked the Buick and opened up the office. I grabbed the key chain and headed over to unlock the doors for business. As I reached the salt shed, I noticed a nondescript Buick sitting on the other side of the rusty one-lane bridge. The automobile was deep burgundy in color and appeared to have been painted with a paintbrush. There were reddish streaks throughout the paint along with incriminating dark brush marks. There was also paint along the window edges, indicating that the art of masking had been overlooked. The only thing worth appreciating were the four brand new Kregor chrome rims attached to the well-traveled tires.

"Looks like our friend bit early and hard."

I jumped as I turned around to see Norbie walking up beside me.

"Is that Guentrig's car?" I asked.

"Yep. Different color, though. Used to be black. Looks like he painted it with a paint brush."

"Why would someone do that?"

"Why would someone keep stealing gas from the same place all the time, especially when they live just across the way, and they know we do the old switch-er-roo?"

"Well, I guess you just answered a question with a question."

"Did I, now?"

"What?"

We were both interrupted by the sound of a green Dodge pickup with booming pipes coming down the hill. Norbie glanced at his watch.

"Donnie's early."

"What?"

"I said, Donnie's early!"

"Why does his truck make so much noise?"

"He's running straight pipes on her, and he drives around in low gear just so he can make all of that racket. Guess he thinks it's what the ladies like."

The Dodge pulled up and parked next to the corncrib. Donnie bounded out, heading toward us. Donnie Zagoonski was a thin guy in his late forties with long dark sideburns running down to his jaw line. When he spoke, he sounded like a radio with a bad speaker. His voice was low and raspy, and for whatever reason, he would fade in and out while he spoke.

"Imy wants to know if your ears hurt from riding in that loud truck of yours."

Feeling embarrassed, I quickly tried to recover, knowing always to respect all people no matter how odd they appeared.

"Well, really, what I was asking Norbie was, with that cool noise going on while you are driving that bad boy, does the sound ever get to your ears?"

"No, dat part dud bodder me so much. I mainly git headaches from playing da radio loud."

"Oh, that explains it."

It took but a second for Donnie to adjust his gaze on the car parked across the bridge.

"Norbie, what's wit da paint job on dat car? Looks like he painted da damn ting wit a brush."

"Donnie, I think that's old Guentrig's kid's car, and I have a hunch why it's parked there."

"He steal gas agin?"

"I bet he did. Let's go check it out."

The three of us walked across the bridge up to the stalled vehicle.

"Yous guys gotta start lockin' down dose tanks better. I got gas up da ass at da house, and nobody monkeys wit it cause I got her all locked down good, hey."

"You also have your tanks sitting right next to your house in town where you can keep a close eye on them, Donnie."

"Ya Norbie, but yous know what? Of all dat stuff I got, no one monkeys. And da big reason fer dat is ..."

"What about your chrome wheels that you were pining about that showed up missing yesterday?"

"Now dat was a fluke."

"Do you think it's a fluke that this car has new chrome rims on it that probably resemble yours?"

"Hey, da guy dat stole my wheels had a black car."

"Maybe this car used to be black, ever think of that?"

"Shit, dos ARE my wheels!"

Donnie jogged over to the salt shed, grabbed a big piece of stained cardboard that was resting up against it, and proceeded to make a sign.

"Guentrig, you got 24 hours to return the wheels and fix my garage door, or I call the cops. PS. The back yard needs mowing, and you know where the mower is."

"Why don't you just call the cops now?"

"Because if I do dat, den dey arrest him, and I gotta do all da work. Wit pullin' da tires off, pickin' 'em up and all dat. Dis way, he does da work. Besides, my lawn needs cuttin.'"

"Good point."

We walked back over to the mill to get ready for the business day. I was more excited than usual, mainly because of my new job that would start this afternoon. I couldn't wait to go for a drive over the hill and explore new territory.

After a slight flurry of business, I walked out of the mill toward the office. I noticed the black pickup parked in front of the mailbox, and again, wondered who it was. This person would always go in and talk to Dad, sometimes for over an hour.

"Who is that guy, Norbie?"

"I don't know who that is. But I do know that the cat took a picture of his truck the other day."

Well, I knew Norbie wasn't going to be any help, and I would have to ask Dad to get to the bottom of that one.

After a big lunch, it was getting to be time for me to head over the hill to Frankie's farm to start my new job. Dad let me take "White Lightning," cautioning me to be extra careful around the curves, since the shock absorbers were non-existent, and the coil springs were shot. The car would swerve back and forth after each curve as if it were half full of water. A few minutes later, I was driving up the hill to Tamerak. Now how many people get to do this, I thought, as I hung my arm out of the open window and waved to every truck and tractor that I met on the county highway.

Norbie had given me explicit instructions, explaining that once I got over the hill, I should go past the old Addleman place just on the other side of Roy's Store. Two farms later, just before Sigman's, I would spot a dirt driveway on the east side of the road that would take me right into Frankie's place. After heeding Norbie's directions and finding all of the markers, I made the left turn into the dirt driveway and followed it for about a half-mile through a shallow valley, terminating into Frankie's farmyard.

The farm was completely hidden from the main road, offering a panoramic view of lush crops growing up in the hills in all directions. The buildings and farmhouse on the property were dilapidated but the scenic view of the hills was breathtaking. I rolled into the yard and drove around a huge tree, avoiding the exposed roots while attempting to remain on the dirt driveway. I parked and started to exit the old cruiser.

As I turned my head to grab for the door handle, I noticed out of the corner of my eye a large goat staring me down as if daring me to set foot on his turf. I waited a few minutes, hoping he would get bored and wonder off. It took nearly five minutes until he finally strolled away. I got out of the car and walked briskly up to the porch. About half way there, I heard a woman's voice scream, "run!" followed by hysterical laughter. I turned around, and, to my horror, the goat was approximately sixty feet away, running full boar toward me in a "heads down" position. I sprinted to the farmhouse. The old lady continued laughing while holding the wooden screen open for me. As I darted past her she promptly slammed the door behind me. The goat flew up the porch step and rammed its head into the door, drawing more laughter from the lady.

"Dat's Eli. He got out of da pen about a year ago, and we can't git da bastard back in."

"Is he ever friendly?"

"No, he chases us all around. Frankie always has ta go out and distract him while Dad and me find da car fer church. Otherwise, we don't go nowhere's anyway, so he really doesn't bodder us dat much."

"Well, I'm Imy, and I'm here to bale some hay."

"Well, I'm Frankie's mom, and I got meatloaf in da oven, so hold on a minute. I don't wanna burn da shit out ta it. I'll be right back."

As I stood there in the doorway, I saw a silhouette of a man slumped over, leaning against the archway of a windowless room. He stared at me with blank eyes, as if he was being held prisoner in his own house.

"She's lying," he whispered.

"Pardon me?"

"She lies constantly. It's all lies. She stopped telling the truth years ago, and it gits worse and worse every day. Why jist da utter day, she said we were having chicken, and it turned out being hamburger."

"Hmmmm."

The lady interrupted this bizarre one-way conversation with the stomping of her heels on the old tile floor. The old man slipped back into the shadows.

"Now Frankie is up on da olt Surmoulski place, so why don't you jist drive ober dare."

"OK, now where is the old Surmoulski place?"

"Well, it's actually da old Brown place. But Dad had a tough time pronouncing dat name, so we refer to it as da old Surmoulski place."

"Ah, OK."

"You know where Hollywood Hal's place is?"

Now everyone knew about Hollywood Hal. Hal Grotchon was from Milwaukee and had married a girl who had relocated there from Arcadia. He ended up moving to Arcadia and taking over the in-law's farm, something people wondered if he knew anything about. Hal seemed a little unusual, mainly because he constantly wore a white shirt and tie, complete with suit coat, when working around the farm and milking cows. His formal attire landed him the name "Hollywood Hal."

"Yea."

"Well, don't go by his place. Go da udder way past Kamarawski's, den go past da Laverne Bodang old place. Just turn right dare and go up about a mile, and dare it is."

"OK."

I walked out on the drooping porch, calculating if I could get a bead on the goat before I made a run for the car. Safely inside, I started up the engine only to be stopped by the old man leaning up against the front hood of my car. I leaned out of the window and said hello as he made his way over to my open window.

"She was doing good till she got you up ta Hollywood's place. The Surmoulski place is right next to Hollywood's place. Just another one of those lies again."

"OK, thanks."

As I slowly snaked around the big tree in the farmyard, I couldn't help but notice the curtain flutter in the dining room of the old farmhouse. I felt like I was starring in a horror film and started to laugh at the humor in all of this. Suddenly, a face appeared out of the screen door with a look that would stop a train. I immediately turned away from the angry scowl of this supposedly sweet lady into another just like it in my rear view mirror. To my horror, the old man had grabbed on to my back bumper and was hanging on for the ride. I noticed a small wake of dirt being kicked up by the heels of his worn work boots while I glanced back in my side door mirror. Panic caused me to press on the accelerator, which caused him to lose his balance and let go. With my heart pounding in my chest, I headed to the end of the dirt road, stopping to check for traffic. I turned my head to status traffic and looked straight into the eyes of that mangy goat. He stared back at me as if he had an agenda. I hit the accelerator and headed down the highway.

I headed in the direction of Hollywood Hal's house. A few miles later, I noticed a manure spreader being pulled with a John Deere 3020 tractor. As I passed this rig, I couldn't help notice the necktie waving wildly in the wind. I gave the obligatory courtesy wave and turned on County Road H right on the other side of Hollywood's barn. A few miles down the road, I came upon an abandoned farm, flanked by acreage of hay fields. Up on the side of a hill, not far from the dilapidated buildings, was a farmer pulling a hay baler and rack. The bales simply flopped onto the hayrack, many of them falling off back onto the field. I pulled in the driveway, grabbed my Nutrena Feed cap and jogged up to this agricultural entrepreneur.

"Hi, I'm Imy."

"Yah."

"Well, we spoke yesterday, and I am here to help you bale some hay."

"Well, I tought dat da last guy dat come strollin' up here was to help me make hay. Dare I was standing in da barn den, and he came out of da haymow. Turned out he was drunk, missed dat curve right on da udder side of the barn on da home place and ended up with his car in my haymow."

"Wow."

"Wow is what I said, too, you know hey. And da guy said 'shit,' I tink."

"Who was it?"

"Rufus Ruskus."

"With his Mustang?"

"Yea, I guess it makes sense, a mustang belongs in a barn."

"Hey, that's actually pretty funny."

"Eh?"

"You know, the comment a 'mustang belongs in a barn,' and he had a Mustang, a Ford Mustang, you know, a car....ah horse...barn..."

"Yea?"

"Yea."

"Yea, hey."

OK, I'm thinking, what an odd conversation this is with a person that I am meeting for the first time. If they say that first impressions last a lifetime, then that's what he accomplished, because I never forgot it. Anyway, I thought it was probably up to me to steer the dialogue, so I took the bull by the horns.

"Well, anyway, what do you want me to do?"

"Well, first stack da rack, den I'll pull da works till da side hill's done, den you kin fetch er back and auger her up."

"Sounds easy enough."

Meanwhile, I had absolutely no idea what he said, or had any clue what he meant and not the foggiest idea of what he wanted done.

"Well, let's get to it," I said enthusiastically.

It was now early evening, and four loads of hay had been loaded in the haymow. I followed his lead, occasionally asking questions as we went along. It seemed as if he enjoyed the company and even started relating to me. The more we talked, the more he wanted to talk. We talked about everything except farming, unlike my Dad. The sun was starting to drop slightly in the west, and all of the hard work was making me ravenous.

"Let's go back to da home place fer some supper, den I gotta go milk."

199

Now, I wasn't looking forward to going back to the house, mainly because of the spooky trio that resided there. Nevertheless, food is food, and I was hungry, so I agreed to follow him over there for supper.

Once we got to the old farmhouse, I gingerly walked in and was told to take my seat at the kitchen table. The outdated kitchen had an old wood cook stove along the wall next to a one hundred gallon round, steel tub filled to the brim with water. Pieces of baler twine were tied to the edge that disappeared into the murky depths. I sat down to a distressed farm table covered by a red and white checkered tablecloth. As I took a sip of lemonade from my oversized yellow plastic cup, I noticed the old man sitting in the windowless room off to the side of the kitchen. He appeared to be sitting in front of an industrial fan that was propped up in a chair right in front of him. The fan was operating at such a high rate of speed that I thought there was no way for that old soul to get out of that chair even if he wanted to. Frankie noticed my gaze in his father's direction.

"We pulled dat fan out of da chicken coop. Hell, dats all we had to do was clean it up a bit. Besides smelling a little like chicken shit, it sure beats buying a new one!"

"Yea, I suppose."

Wow, that's what that smell was, I thought. I had smelled that semi-familiar scent before, but just couldn't quite put my finger on it, especially in a house.

"Frankie, go git Dad, and let's eat."

Once the old man was seated, dishes filled with food were passed around, and I loaded my plate to the top. Frankie's dad put everything on the tablecloth right next to his plate, and I couldn't tell if that's the way he liked to eat his meal, or if he was suffering from bad aim. I chose the latter, right up until he poured the gravy about as accurately as one can, right over the mashed potatoes. He put a little on the roast beef, totally missing the vegetables, with absolutely no over-spray on the cranberry sauce. With such incredible precision, he must just choose to eat directly off of the table, I concluded. But then again, who cares I thought. This is the farm, and you can eat however you want.

"Oh, I'm sorry boys. I forgot the butter."

Frankie's mom got up and dashed for the large steel tub. She pulled on one of the thick strands of baler twine and fished out a plastic container that housed the butter.

"Interesting. Is that how you keep your food cold?"

"Ya."

Frankie watched as his mom pulled the butter out of the container.

"We jist couldn't see buying a refrigerator, especially when dis old tub was jist sittin' in da milk house, just off da barn."

"Kind of like the fan?"

"Ya hey."

"Excuse me?"

"Ya hey."

After three helpings, two pieces of pie and at least twenty "ya heys" later, I got in the old cruiser and headed for the hill. Life was good. I was able to be in the sun all afternoon and got served like a king at supper. Not to mention the dollar seventy-five an hour that I had just earned. The only thing that could have topped it all off would have been a working car radio on the drive home. Oh well, maybe someday.

Chapter XXIV

Another year had come and gone, and I could finally relate to what my Grandma now meant when she said that the older you get, the faster time goes. Boots Goush had another old saying "the older you get, the older you get." I guess both were accurate.

It was early fall in my senior year of high school, and all of my friends could feel that it would be our last time together. Most everyone was going to be headed out of town next year to college, and I knew that I would follow suit, although I had not made the official decision yet. Everyone had worked a job throughout the summer, and I had worked at the feed mill in the mornings while baling hay in the afternoons.

Dad had just hired another hand at the mill, Skrofty Halsner. Skrofty had landed here from Texas to be with his brother, who had a job out on the Giemza farm. Although Skrofty weighed all of one hundred pounds, he eclipsed his tiny stringy-haired wife. They lived with his brother out in Nuecome Valley in a modular home.

Pound for pound, Skrofty was the most efficient transmitter of "BS" this side of the Mississippi. Either it was his slow southern accent or his incredible gift of yarn spinning, but his stories seemed so believable. Apparently, he had worked his way up to a lofty corporate level while living in Dallas. His good fortune ended when he was arrested for breaking and entering into his own house. This was a charge that Skrofty could never beat because, even though he had concrete evidence that the house was his, the courts never quite saw it that way. Seems the fact that he had sold the house some years ago maybe had something to do with it. So, Skrofty ended up as many colorful characters end up, working at the East Arcadia Feed Mill.

Skrofty was actually a good addition to the company work force, which, at this time, was Dad and me. He had a different way of doing most things, and word got out around the area about his peculiar method of executing normal work tasks. The first time he had to move bulk feed from one side of a bin to the other, he jumped in and proceeded to sweep the bulk feed with his hands while laying in a crouched position, as if doing the dog paddle in a swimming pool.

"Skrofty, don't you want to use a shovel?"

"Na, actually this works better. This is how dogs have done it for years. And we can learn from them."

"Ahh, OK."

Now we had a dog, and he was a good dog. The only talent that Prince had was covering up his poop with grass, and that's nothing that I needed to know. I never got any tips from him, except finding a cool spot in the shade to sit during a hot summer day. But I already had that one all figured out.

I figured that Skrofty was either incredibly odd, mentally challenged or did massive amounts of narcotics in his day. Another bizarre occurrence came one morning a few months after he started working for Dad. It was an early morning, and someone was at the front door of our house. I ran downstairs after glancing at the clock which read 5:20 AM. When I got to the door, who was standing there but Skrofty and his scrawny wife.

"Mornin.'"

"Ahh, good morning."

"Well, mind if I get a ride to work this morning?"

"Ah, not at all. It's a little early though, isn't it? Nobody's up yet, and the mill doesn't open for another, oh, two hours or so. What are you doing here, anyway?"

"Well, we had a flat tire, so we just thought we'd come over and get a ride in."

"A flat tire? Don't you have a spare?"

"Well ..."

I knew what the answer was, so I thought I would interrupt him to expedite our conversation.

"But that's flat too, right?"

"Yea."

"Let's go take a look at it. Just give me a minute to throw something warm on."

After donning a flannel jacket, I followed them across the street and over one block. To my astonishment, there sat his rusty green Pontiac sedan, leaning so heavily on it's left side that I thought he had parked halfway in a ditch. Further inspection revealed that the car had lost both tires on the left side, along with the rims. The car seemed to be supporting its entire weight on the brake rotors, which were, at this point, worn down to the size of bottle caps. The chassis underneath the doors and the fenders had been ground off, as if someone had taken a blowtorch to them. I looked over at the waft couple, unable to conceal my grin.

"What happened here? Why, I can't even get a tire jack low enough to hook into!"

I couldn't keep my eyes off of the spectacle as Skrofty continued on.

"Well, about nine o'clock last night, the old lady asked if I wanted to go for a ride, and we did. We headed up towards Fountain City, and when we were almost there, we blew out a tire. I decided to turn around, since the spare was flat and all, and then we popped the second."

"Look, there's twine and crap all wound around your brake rotor here."

"Anyway, we tried to make it home and got here about midnight, so we just slept in the car, running the engine for heat. We just ran out of gas, so that's why I had to wake you up, cause it's cold out."

"Wow."

Skrofty's oddities soon became somewhat of a marketing tactic. I don't know how it happened, but someone at the repair shop or the junkyard got a hold of those brake rotors and hung them up in the creamery. It wasn't long after that that everyone knew the story. Every farmer in the area wanted to meet this guy, which was apparent by the increased traffic around the feed mill over the next couple of months.

Customers soon came in from all around the area to pick up a sack of dog food or a bag of fertilizer just to meet this "Skrofty fellow." One of his many attractions was his overdone southern drawl. Not many Arcadians had ever heard a live person talk this way, except maybe on television. Nevertheless, business was good, mainly because of this hired hand who was just a little different than everybody else.

Delbert Pajeanna had just pulled in to pick up a few bags of barn lime. He had heard about Skrofty from his neighbor up in Travis Valley and wanted to come in and take a look for himself.

"Hey Skrofty, bet you can't jump on the feed scale and make the arm go up."

Skrofty eyeballed the wooden, inset floor scale, fixing to take him up on it.

"How much?"

"Got a bottle of pop right here."

Skrofty went over and surveyed the three-foot square piece of oak where he would have to land. After setting the weight hammer in the 100-pound notch, he squatted to study the scale's properties while stretching, as if this was an Olympic event.

"I'll be right back."

Skrofty shot out of the mill, only to return seconds later.

"I loaded up with water."

Skrofty turned his head slightly to the side as he let out a belch.

"Now that I've got a little more weight in me, do ya wanta still go for it?"

"Hell, I feel lucky, why not?"

On that note, Skrofty took two steps and leaped high into the air. His jeans came up over the tops of his cowboy boots, exposing the shelled corn that he had tucked in his boots to gain better weight advantage. As he hit the feed scale, the weight arm remained motionless, producing the same result as if a fly had landed on it.

"Pay up, baby! Pay up!"

A disappointed Skrofty took a chuckling Delbert into the office and borrowed a dime from Dad so that he could pay his debt.

Skrofty walked out of the office with a bothered look of defeat on his face. I couldn't help but feel sorry for him.

"Next time, repeat the bet using literal terms," I said.

"What do ya mean?"

"Well, next time someone tells you that he bets that you can't move the arm on the scale, repeat the bet, then go over and move the arm. You have won the bet by moving the arm, which was the goal of the bet. Even though he may have had a different idea of how the goal was to be achieved, it was never communicated. The goal gets accomplished, and you get your money."

"Huh."

Skrofty's stories got bigger and bigger until even Dad had enough of the fish tales. One day, the three of us were sitting in the office after grinding a batch of cow feed for Johnny Potzner. Dad was on the telephone with Mom, mentioning that he had to go

205

bowling that night. As soon as Dad hung up the telephone, Skrofty was all over it.

"Arnie, so you bowl too?"

"Well, I try to every week. I think I have my hook working again, so I'll try that tonight."

"Well, I have a two-hundred-eighty average."

Dad was noticeably aggravated.

"If you have a two-hundred-eighty average, then what the hell are you doing here?"

"Well, I used to bowl three hundred so many times that the State Commissioner of Texas wanted to make the game harder by making the lanes longer or the pins smaller. Since he was overruled in his request, I became kind of depressed. I quit bowling, since there was no challenge to me anymore."

Dad never looked up, except to reach over and dial the telephone, as if he hadn't heard a word Skrofty said. I exited the office to find a more peaceful place, walking over to the bridge and right next to the cat who was taking a picture of the mill.

It was getting close to lunchtime when Carp Klopotic came in to pick up some baler twine. I was out front sweeping off the mill porch.

"Where is he?"

"Skrofty?"

"Dare he is!"

Carp had eyed Skrofty over by the grinder pit. He went running over to him.

"Betch ya a pop you can't move da arm on da feed scale."

Skrofty looked him in the eye, deep in thought.

"You want to bet me that I can't move the arm on the feed mill scale?"

"Wit jist sheer weight, I bet you can't stand on da scale wit nobody else on it and move da arm."

"You're on."

Skrofty disappeared for a minute, returning with a fifty-pound bag of "Pig Starter."

Skrofty wrestled the bag on the scale, then simply stepped on, watching as the arm came up and rested on the steel bar above it.

"I'll take an Orange Crush, Carp."

"No fair. You cheated."

"Your bet was that I couldn't make the hammer move with anybody else on the scale. There was no one else but me on that scale, so pay up."

As quickly as the low-level argument started, it subsided with the three of us sitting on the front porch drinking our soda. I had called off the bet and used Dad's money to buy us all a pop. I could see that this little sideshow was becoming a double-edged sword. On the one hand, more people would come in to patronize us, but in the long run, Skrofty's antics started aggravating the customers as well. I knew deep down that this circus show was becoming more of a liability than an asset.

Chapter XXV

It was a beautiful, crisp Saturday morning, and I was, as usual, working down at the mill. Dad had just walked in the mill from the office to inform me that I had a phone call. I ran over to the phone extension.

"Hello."

"Ya hey."

"Oh, hi Frankie. What's going on?"

"Well, da old baler broke, and I fixed er up, but den da auger scheered a cotter key, got dat ting up to da machine shop…"

"Uh, I mean, what are you up to?"

"I'm up to my waist in water in da kitchen, cause da steel tub rusted through, ain't got no cold milk no more…"

"Frank, uh, what do you want?"

"I was wonderin' if you wanted to come ober da hill today to help shock some oats."

"Hey, why not. Beautiful day out there. But I've never done it before."

"Piece of cake, well not quite, cause if it was, my mum would be here helping me."

"I'll be there at one o'clock. Where do you want me to meet you?"

"Come ober ta da upper place, dats where we'll be."

"OK. See ya at one."

"Ya hey."

"Bye."

"Ya hey."

I hung up the phone thinking, boy, I can't be any more ambivalent about this. I love to work, but around this guy, it could really be a challenge. But then again, it was always an experience. And besides, the weather was beautiful, and what else was I going to do with the rest of my day but come back here with Dad and wrench on something. Anyway, I needed the money, and it was good to get away for awhile.

Four helpings of creamed chicked beef over toast later, I was in the car and heading for Frankie's. I turned onto County H, heading toward the back way to Pine Creek. Soon after, I came upon what I referred to as "Board Henge." This was a series of old slat boards plastered in the earth pointing skyward, partial remnants of an old farm. What happened to the farm was anybody's guess, and why the remaining few stands were never demolished was also a mystery.

I got out of the car and headed to the top of the side hill where I spotted Frankie with another man standing next to a colossal, rusty contraption. This piece of equipment had pulleys, augers, belts, gears and spouts. I was amazed that someone could design a machine that had a use for this many obscure devices. I walked over and inspected the thing while tapping on one of the four pulleys with my knuckles, verifying that it was steel.

"What the heck is this?"

"It's a threshing machine."

"How does it work?"

The other man stared me down, as if threshing is the first thing all men learn after coming out of the womb.

"Son, you don't know how ta thresh?"

"No, not really."

"Den how da hell are you gonna help? I bet you don't even know how many grease zirts are on a threshing machine."

"Now Edgar, he don't have ta know eberyting to be a big help. Now, dis is how it works. You put da bundles in here, and it poops out ober dar."

"Bundles of oats?"

"Yah."

"I thought farmers combined oats."

"Yah, if yous got a combine."

Frankie noticed the confused look on my face.

"OK, let's start from da beginnin.' Yous plant da oats. Den yous cut 'em with da hay knife. Den ya go ober wit da binder, which crimps it and ties it into bundles. Wit me?"

"Yes."

"Now, what we're gonna do today is ta take da bundles of oats dat are still connected to da stems and build grain shocks."

"You mean the shocks you see in the Halloween pictures, with a big orange moon?"

209

"Yah."

"How many bundles to a shock?"

"Seven. Six of 'em get stacked tagedder in a group, den da seventh is da cap, which gits bent and draped ober da top."

Frankie picked up two bundles, one in each hand, and stood them up side by side resting on each other. Then he took two more and leaned them in on one of the two center bundles. He grabbed two more and repeated the process on the other side of the shock. Then he took one bundle, pressed and bent the long stems slightly over his knee and placed it on the shock horizontally.

"You should be able ta stand on a good shock if it's done right dare."

A confidant Frankie stood with his hands on his hips examining his latest piece of work.

Then I tried it, repeating the process that had just been demonstrated. When I put the cap on, my shock toppled over.

"Ha!" yelped the elder farmer, slapping his knee while letting out a rather loud and long gush of gas.

"Hey Frankie, don't let your dog piss on it, or it'll fall over!"

"He'll be fine. Imy, why don't you come wit me up to da top of da hill, and we'll start dare."

About three hours and one hundred shocks later, Frankie grabbed his pocket watch out of his bibbers.

"Imy."

"Yes sir?"

"I almost forgot. Jump on da Allis and swing down to da pickup. I got a jug of water dat you got ta git ober to da Lesmen Boys. Dey been on da uder side of da field fer hours wid out water, and I almost forgot about 'em."

"Who are the Lesman Boys?"

"Two guys dat went to California to check it out and just got back ta town. Day are kind of doing some odd jobs jist till dey know what dey want ta do wit dare life."

"OK. Now where are they?"

"Go ober to da uder side of da field, den follow da trail in da oats down by da road. You can't miss 'em. You'll see dare car down dare by da road."

"OK."

I was happy to get away from this job that, for some reason, I couldn't do very well. I jumped on the Allis, circled down to the truck to grab the water jug and took off in high gear to the other side of the field, which was a mile and a half away. Once I got to the other side of the field, I found the trail that Frankie was talking about and wound myself around down by the road. Off to the side was a parked, four-door Chevy Belair, about fifteen years old with California plates. About a mile later, I saw two figures off in the distance. I pointed the tractor toward them and continued my journey. The closer that I got to them, the older they appeared. And to my surprise, they made the "old fart" back at threshing headquarters look like a preschool kid.

I jumped off the tractor with jug in hand and gave it to the one that looked more likely to faint. Each was donned in bib overalls, sporting a wide-brimmed hat. After both men appeared more revived, I offered them a ride down to their car.

"Na, we got too much shocking ta do. Besides, wit dat shot of water, we're good till sundown."

After a few more pleasantries, I jumped back on the tractor and headed back to the upper place. Frankie asked if I wouldn't mind cleaning out the barn, the only complete building that was still standing. I could tell that while I had been away, my credibility of building a good and healthy shock had been challenged, and Frankie bought into it.

At the barn, I grabbed a pitchfork in the doorway and walked into the dank, dreary structure. Cow manure was piled up almost knee deep, so I slipped on some old barn boots to insulate myself from the valuable fertilizer. There was a manure spreader backed up to the side door, so I followed common sense and started shoveling. It was blistering hot in this unventilated structure, and the sweat soon started to pour down my forehead and sting my eyes. I felt as though I were doing an exorcism on this building, with thousands of flies buzzing around my sopping head. I stopped to dry my forehead, then noticed an old thermometer leaning against a beam. I walked over and wiped the pigeon poop off of the thing so that I could get a read on the temperature. One hundred thirteen degrees, I estimated. I had shoveled feed in the upstairs bin at this temperature before, and for sure had unloaded hay in the haymow at this range, if not higher. But when you combine the irrefutable intangibles of the slooping noise of moist manure oozing under my feet, flies beleaguering my head and the staggering stench, this was by far the most undesirable job that I had ever encountered. Had I not needed the money, I may have left. However, that wasn't my style, and I did need the money. After all, this was character development, or so I told myself. Something that I always could look back on when the going got tough.

A couple of hours later, I was in the car and driving back over the hill toward home. At least I enjoyed part of the afternoon and learned something very valuable that day. I learned that nothing is more important than a good education. From the Lesman Boys right down to the barn-cleaning job, without an education, this is the life you'd learn to get accustomed to. I was satisfied that I had experienced a lesson that probably couldn't be duplicated. However, I was still miffed about not being able to build a sturdy shock. I guess that's just one talent that I'd have to admit I didn't possess.

Chapter XXVI

School had begun, and this would be the last year of my education in Arcadia. If I wanted to further my academics, I would have to leave town, as well as all of my friends. Independence offered a meat cutting course, but I had aspirations slightly higher than that.

Football practice was in full swing, and for those of us enrolled in the senior class, this would be the last season. I had stayed in great shape through the summer and couldn't wait for a chance to fully participate. Through most of my high school sports, I had suffered severe shin splints, torn muscles and a broken nose. Finally, my muscles were healed, and I couldn't wait for the season to start.

Our first game of the year was on Friday night. We already had a pre-season game under our belt, which we easily won 70-0. We were a powerhouse this year, and it was going to be a great season. Our football team held a lofty position in the power polls for the state of Wisconsin, and everyone could feel it. It had been over fifty years since Arcadia went undefeated, a goal for which we were all aspiring.

My position on the team was defensive halfback. I was a sprinter in track and possessed great speed. I was long and lean, and didn't make a good tackler or blocker. But because of my speed, I returned kickoffs, punts and played in the defensive backfield.

As long as we were winning big, the pressure was off, and the team could really enjoy playing. Right down to bus driver Boozie Benusa, it was constant shenanigans after the game.

John Gamoke, the high school prankster and captain of the football team would usually get the chant going.

"Who's our bus driver?"

"Boozie!!!"

"Who's he?"

"Boozie!!!"

Well, you'd have to have been there, but life was just incredible living in this small community, having so many close-knit friends.

I was kind of dating a few girls, and everything was coming together. I loved life and learned immensely from every little lesson. I had tons of friends and knew that soon I would be able to support myself mentally without the negative and domineering comments of my parents affecting me.

It was a perfect Friday evening, and you could smell Autumn in the air. The pre-season games were over, and it was time for the real thing. Most of the entire town of Arcadia was there, as they were for every home football game. One of the most amazing things was that my parents finally came to see me participate in an athletic competition. The rest of my family was about doing their own thing, so it was wonderful to have some sort of family support since I didn't have a next of kin in town.

West-Salem, one of many consolidated schools in our area, had won the coin-toss and elected to receive. I was on the kickoff team and sprinted down field to make the tackle as soon as the ball was kicked. I planted my leg to make a cut and was immediately hit directly in my lower left leg by two defenders. I ended up on my back and knew I hurt a little more than usual after a hit like that. As I lay on the turf, staring up at the lights, I looked up at the face of Basil Arnold.

"Imy, get up, we got to play defense."

"I think I'm hurt."

"Well, I don't want to waste a time out."

At first a wave of panic went through me, and I had this vision of lying there helplessly while the game continued on around me. I let out a small sigh of relief once I heard the referee's whistle blow and heard a booming voice over the PA system say that a player was down on the field. As I laid on my back and continued to stare at the lights, various faces came in and out of view.

Steve LaLiberty, one of the trainers who was a classmate and good friend of mine, arrived at my side. I knew that help would be on the way. Steve was a basketball player and the closest thing to a doctor that we had there that night. He was going to go to college next year to study pre-med.

"Oh my God, look at his leg! Get the stretcher over here for this one."

214

A few more trainers appeared to view the carnage.

In a matter of minutes, an adjustable stretcher, a new addition to the ambulance service, was wheeled out on the field. A few brackets were adjusted, and the high-wheeled body carrier dipped low enough for me to be rolled onto it. On the count of three, I was raised up to the chest level of the two obese medics representing the ambulance crew. I was rolled across the field absorbing every gopher hole and nonconformity into my pain-stricken body for the entire length of this divoted football field. The trip seemed to last an eternity, with every clump of dirt causing my compound fracture to rub back and forth inside of my skin. The crowd was giving me a standing ovation, which gave me a little something to feel swell about for awhile. But this heroic salute was abruptly halted when we got to the waist-high wire fence that surrounded the parameter of the football field. My chariot stopped there as these two medical professionals stopped to catch their breath and plan how to get the tall stretcher under the one strand of wire fence.

"We could take out a few stakes, maybe den we can lift dat wire up jist enough to git 'em undernead it."

"Yea, but what if we can't git da stakes back in, and someone runs out in da field and gits hurt when dare ain't no ambulance cause we're takin dis guy to da hospital?"

"Good point. Let's jist put 'er down, go undernead, den go back up with 'er."

Now this was one of those times that I wished I was coherent enough to respond so I could give these guys a hand. Being delirious with pain, I knew that my well being was in their hands. Before another thought could pass through my brain, I dropped four feet faster than I ever had before in my life. I dropped so fast that the wind was knocked out of me, and I laid there on my back gasping for air. I heard the crowd gasp in unison, as I struggled to take in another breath. Obviously, they had found the release bracket, and now I was about as close to the ground as I could get. A couple of seconds later, I was raised back up to beer gut level, so the boys could finish this harrowing excursion to the awaiting ambulance. At least one of my daft caretakers had the gumption to apologize for the less-than-smooth stretcher ride, mainly because he didn't have time to read the apparatus instructions.

Moments later, I was in the emergency room of St. Joseph's Hospital just on the edge of town next to Shnokie's Road. I was placed on the X-ray table, and a nun proceeded to pull off the first of four pairs of socks that I was wearing that evening.

"Why so many socks?"

"Because they didn't have size eleven shoes, so I had to wear enough so that my cleats would fit."

As she pulled each sock, I grimaced with pain and implored her to cut them off instead.

"Why would I want to ruin a new pair of socks? Why, there are some poor children in this world that have no socks."

Now what good would my tarnished and blood stained socks do for them, I thought?

As Mother Nazi continued to yank my skin-tight socks off, one by one, I couldn't help but notice that my left foot was actually being stretched beyond my right one, even though I was still wearing my right football cleat.

Following my X-ray, Dad and Mom walked in with Doctor Moscana in tow. Arcadia had a hard time getting doctors to work and stay in the community. St. Joe's had finally found a couple of doctors from the Philippines. Dr. Moscana and Dr. Eray not only appeared inexperienced, but they were very hard to understand, especially when you're used to hearing a Polish hybrid lingo that was so prevalent in Arcadia.

"I just lit a cigar, had only one puff, and then had to come up here," Dad said, sounding more disappointed then sympathetic.

"Well, sorry Dad, I wasn't trying to break my leg."

I laid there viewing the milky white membranes on each end of my leg that didn't even come close to touching each other. This X-ray was a no brainier, I thought. Even these doctors should be able to figure this one out.

"Well doc, is it broke?" I jokingly asked.

"I'm not sure. We'll have to send these E-rays to Dr. Tester in Winona, and he reads them."

"Even I can see that it's broken."

"Yes, but I am not licensed to read E-rays."

I laughed, trying to find humor with his broken English, mainly because I couldn't find anything else to laugh about.

"Read E-ray's what?"

"Imy, that's enough. Mom and I will be back tomorrow. Try to get some sleep."

With that, they wheeled me into a hospital room and gave me something to help ease the pain. A few minutes later, as I lay there getting sleepy, I wondered how I was going to get out of this one. What an ending to my first play of the first conference football game of the season.

One week later, after being prescribed bed rest for the week, I was taken down to LaCrosse, the large town that actually had a medical staff that had been to medical school.

"When did this accident happen?" the doctor casually asked Dad.

"A week ago Friday."

"A week ago what?"

"Nine days ago."

"Why didn't you bring him in here earlier?"

"We were told to go home and have him rest in bed for a week."

"Who told you that, your plumber?"

"The doctor in Arcadia."

"That's ludicrous. This kid should be in school walking around with a pair of sticks. Well, we may need to do surgery on his leg, so we'll need to put him under. When's the last time he ate?"

"We had him back up at the hospital this morning, and they fed him a big lunch."

"Well, we'll schedule it tomorrow morning. I need to get more information from the medical staff there."

I ended up having surgery on my leg and was back in school a week later. It was awkward getting around with my leg in a cast. And I struggled with my new role as a football fan and spectator. I wasn't one to sit around and just watch all of the time. The only good things about hobbling around like this were having the girls feel sorry for me and not having to go to the mill every Saturday.

One Saturday late in the fall, I went down to the feed mill just to get out of the house and see some people. Skrofty was down there still putting on a show, this time for Mugsy Gandera. Skrofty saw me and walked over to greet me, helping me out of the car.

"Bowled another three hundred last night."

217

"Really?"

I got out and made my way over to the mill where Mugsy was standing.

"So Imy, no deer huntin' dis year?"

"No, I guess not. Not with this thing."

"Da hell."

"Yea."

"Ya, hey."

"Excuse me, I'll be right back."

I made my way over to the office. Several farmers were just leaving the office, congregating on the front porch to strategize where to go deer hunting this year.

Hunting was the national duty and civic obsession of every red-blooded Arcadian. Regardless of age, everyone participated in the sport. In fact most children received their first rifle by the time they were ten. The target was almost everything from squirrels to turkeys. But the season that every hunter lived for was definitely deer hunting.

My brother-in-law's dad, Ray, had his funeral on an opening Saturday, and we literally had to search for six people to carry the casket. I still remember the comment that Ollie Lugginski made to my brother-in-law, Bob, at the wake.

"Bob, I'd be dare, you know dat, but he'd understand. It's opening day, and you know, if we don't go out and get our deer, someone else will."

For ten days, the town would be empty until dusk. Then all of the hunters would drive up and down Main Street sporting their kill on the hoods of their cars. The taverns would be packed from the late afternoon on, with hunters dressed in their red wool coats, a paper license stapled to the backs. Each story seemed to top the last, and the more the beer flowed, the more incredible these tales became. Unintended livestock shootings were always blamed on the "big city" guys who came up here to hunt, but the size of the flasks that some of these guys carried told a different story.

I personally never hunted but would chuckle to myself remembering the time when I was driving just outside of Independence. Dusk was approaching, and I saw a pickup truck parked off the road in a field. The hunter was leaning over an open drivers-side door with a set of binoculars. Up against the bed of the pickup leaned a rifle. The hunter was scanning the horizon through his field glasses while two deer grazed one hundred feet behind him. A honk from my horn later, the hunter waved while the two bucks scurried away.

"You know, if Benny drives and Clarence and Clifford post, den dose deer will come right by dat stand, and it'll be like target practice."

"Another ting…"

Apolinary stopped short, rotated and stepped out on the stoop to spit out some tobacco juice. The black pile of gunk landed right on my cast as I was working my way onto the rickety front porch.

"Now, if I can be lucky and hit a deer dat good, I'll be doin OK," Apolinary heckled.

"Thanks, Pauly."

Apolinary followed me back into the office as if nothing happened.

"Another ting, what if one of doz big city democrats come to my farm carrying a rifle, and lets say starts shootin' at my hay baler, den what da hell should I do, Arno?"

Dad stared at Pauly in total bewilderment, then smiled as I walked in the office.

"Well Pauly, let's cross that bridge when we get to it."

"Ya know Arno, dat reminds me of a story dare dat happened jist a couple of years back. Dare was dis city slicker huntin' up dare by Ederd's udder place, and da nin-ka-poop witnessed a calf being born out in da field. Since he didn't understand what had jist happened, he ran ober to da calf, grabbed da hind legs, and helped pull it out of da cow. Da feller den looked at da calf and said, 'Now watch where you're goin' next time!'"

"OK, Pauly, after that one, I've gotta run. Dad, I can't stay long. I just wanted to get out of the house and say hi. I can't wait until I can come back down here to work. I'm getting so bored."

Dad looked away and continued to engage Pauly in a serious tone of voice. I listened politely, pretending to be interested. A few minutes later I turned around and exited, leaving an involved farm discussion. Some things just don't change. Same Dad and same cast of characters, I thought.

I thought how different the world must be in other places, or even just on the other side of Independence, for that matter. I wondered why I saw the culture in which I was raised to be so humorous,

219

while others obviously bought into it. I don't know why my immediate friends and I were so different from the rest of this town. But we were. For whatever reason, we just hadn't assimilated. What a place to be from! I knew after graduation, I'd finally experience the independence to see what else the world had to offer.

A half-year later, our senior class sat in folding chairs on the gymnasium floor, staring up at the stage as graduation exercises dragged on. Everyone knew that this was the beginning of the end. All of the fun and shenanigans that were the staple of our lives were drawing to a close. For most kids, graduation was a stamp of achievement and marked the beginning of a new and prosperous life. I on the other hand, had mixed emotions. My home life was anything but good, so having the camaraderie of my school friends served as having the best family possible. We all loved each other and laughed each day away as if we were on some sort of drug, although none of us had ever used any. Even though the people of the area fell prey to our humor and were the brunt of our jokes, it was all because of the way they acted, not because of who they were as people. We respected everyone, no matter how bizarre that person seemed to behave.

As the valedictorian droned on with his monotone address, I began to look around the gym and flash back to some of the signature events that took place here over the years. The first memory that surfaced had happened just a couple of months ago. I was rehabilitating my leg, trying to run track one last year. I was given a sweat suit, along with the rest of the guys who had lettered the previous year. The team was about to assemble in the gymnasium for calisthenics when the track coach came into the locker room.

"Listen up. The high school girls are having cheerleader tryouts for the upcoming year, and the gymnasium is closed. I want all you guys outside, and if I see anyone inside near this gym or locker room area in the next two hours, I'll' kill ya. That especially means you, Kaldunski."

After a moment of silence with the dead stare of Coach eyeballing every last one of us, he walked out of the room, returning to the coach's den.

220

Now, Kaldunski really wasn't the culprit, he just hung around bad influences, like Steve LaLiberty and John Gamoke. In fact, Kaldunski was Arcadia's premier heavyweight wrestler with a very laid-back personality. So much so that he occasionally had to be awakened from a deep sleep while he waited his turn to wrestle, since the heavyweight was always last on the docket. Steve was constantly crossing the line, and John was a born actor who could talk the habit off of an eighty-year-old nun. But Kaldunski was big and noticeable and not very smooth, so he got blamed for more than he really deserved.

It didn't take long at all for John to talk us into checking out the cheerleaders, with Steve immediately devising a plan to do so. Once the contests started, Steve, John, Billy-Burt, Kaldunski and I ascended the back staircase and entered the stage from the rear. The long thick curtains were pulled completely closed, muffling the sound emanating from the cheering enthusiasts down on the gym floor. When a cheerleader was done with her competition, total silence dominated while judges from the big town of Winona, Minnesota marked their score cards.

We snaked to the front of the concealed stage, edging the weighty curtain ever so slightly to create a peephole from our secret vantage point. As soon as Billy-Burt and I peered out of the curtain, Steve grabbed Billy-Burt's knee and applied pressure. Billy Burt yelped, forcing us to scramble from the stage and run out of the building. Recomposed, we decided to go back in for more, since our previous exploit was so short-lived. We were back on stage some twenty minutes later, only to repeat the entire scene again. Steve grabbed Billy-Burt's knee, and once again, Billy-Burt howled. We did the same mad scramble to exit the stage. Since I was at the front of the stage, my trek was longer, and to my dismay, the rest of the crew had ran out of the back stage door with Kaldunski acting as a human door lock, assuring that I stayed put. This was the one time in my life where center stage was anything but appealing. A few panic-stricken pushes on the steel stage door netted no effect, other than the muffled giggling of my buddies on the other side. I knew I was under pressure to think fast. A quick glance around the stage confirmed the obvious. There was just no place to go. A rolled up wrestling mat leaned up against the wall. The only other noticeable item was the cabled stage rope that suspended down to the floor from the ceiling right next to the stage curtain. The competition had stopped, and all that was heard was the clacking of heels making their way across the waxed hardwood gymnasium surface.

OK, Imy, just stop and think. Think of the situation, think how you're dressed, and think what you're supposed to be doing. A myriad of thoughts raced through my head as the footsteps increased in volume right up to the front of the soon-to-be-exposed stage.

Dead silence prevailed, only to be interrupted by the whoosh of the pulleys that supported the massive curtain. Slowly, the thick drape started to dance, then they began to open, revealing the stage. There I laid doing pushups diligently on the unrolled wrestling mat in my track uniform, pausing for a moment as if I had been interrupted. No less than 50 girls in cheerleading uniforms along with coaches, teachers and other school dignitaries stared at me in utter silence. I looked over at my red-faced track coach, Coach Fredrickson.

"If you want to see the practice so damn bad, just get in here, sit in the bleachers and watch!"

With permission granted, the enticement became no big deal, so I declined the invitation.

The commencement speaker continued to ramble, and again I was swept into another scene from memory lane.

We were all assembled outside of the gym for a Veteran's Day celebration, culminating in the American Legion's 21-gun salute. When the command was given by the drill sergeant, the Color Guard raised their weapons, then fired in unison, all except for Burzy Conzar. Burzy was always a late shooter, so the one-second delayed "pop" from his gun wasn't necessarily that funny, since we had all come to expect it. What was funny was how he reacted from the uncontrolled recoil. The rifle would end up facing a whole different direction than intended. On the third round, he accidentally shot a squirrel on a high voltage line over the dike road. We just about died with laughter. It got even funnier when "Taps" immediately followed, as if it were for the poor varmit. Our laughter soon subsided, and an uneasy feeling set in when the audience realized that live ammunition was used for these events.

The graduation speaker kept on babbling, stopping intermittently to collect applause. I was thankful that our valedictorian and salutatorian promised only five-minute speeches.

My attention wavered again, and I looked around at some more familiar faces seated in front of us. Just up in front of me was Gopher Zelna, one of the school's history teachers and assistant football coaches. Every time someone was hit hard on a play, Gopher would run out to the field to assess the damage. If the player appeared to be hit in the head, Gopher would put his hand over the top of their helmet and ask:

"How many fingers?"

Since he held his hand toward the top of the helmet, his hand would always end out of the field of vision when viewed through the facemask.

"Son, how many fingers am I holding up?"

"I can't see."

"That bad, huh. Son, you better take the bench."

We all got accustomed to this routine, so we would start guessing how many fingers he was holding up, knowing at least we had a 25% chance of getting it right.

Sitting next to Gopher was Roust Soppaski. Roust was about thirty years old and would show up for anything as long as he thought there might be free food. He was an avid trick-or-treater, mainly because he figured that as long as he was incognito, no one would ever know. He may have gotten away with it had he invested in a costume change over the years. Besides, he was easily identified either from a front or rear angle due to his distinctive bowed legs. His lower torso resembled a doughnut with a bite chomped out of it.

Right behind Roust sat Leroy Schnuk, who never came to school when he was supposed to but had enough guts to sneak in to witness his little brother's unlikely graduation. The last time I had seen Leroy was at the Buffalo City Days demolition derby. He had taken first place in the cow chip throwing competition the previous evening and had been drinking heavily since. Leroy had recently purchased a new Plymouth and appeared more than eager to answer the amateur demolition derby competition call that took place before the championship heat. Leroy sprang to attention, then tumbled down the bleachers and was helped into his brand new Plymouth. His car was obviously easy to spot, since it was the only one out there without a scratch or dent. Within minutes, his pristine ride resembled the rest of the competitors, except for the easily identified temporary license tag taped to the rear window. Ten minutes later, the only piece of car that was salvageable was his radio antenna.

Over a couple of rows sat Verba Lanquest. Verba was an occasional attendee who dropped out after our junior year. Verba was a born farmer who seemed to attend classes only during fence-mending season. I'll never forget the time when Verba was asked a question regarding the "Declaration of Independence."

"Isn't dat when day put up da fancy street lights an all during Christmas time ober dare in Indy?"

Behind Leroy and two seats over sat Stri Vaugh. You couldn't help but notice Stri. He took up two folding chairs. It wasn't that long ago, oh maybe about ten years or so, when Stri used to fit inside and drive around in a sedan. Even though his spacious Lincoln could have been classified as a boat, it was still a car. Many smorgasbords and kegs of beer later, Stri graduated to a pickup truck. He then moved on to a tractor to get himself around the area. I have no idea where he bought his bib overalls, but they were monstrous.

Next to the door sat the infamous Octi. He was postured erect in freshly starched bib overalls. His head was bobbing forward as though he was nodding off. Micro-slit eyes revealed that he was giving it his best shot to remain conscious for his granddaughter's graduation. Octi had always held a special place with me. He was the first farmer that I had met on my first day at the feed mill. Octi was always his own man, never letting the crowd sway him. I couldn't help but let my mind drift, remembering the time Dad tried to put a feed seminar together. We had only been in Arcadia for a few years, and Dad thought that he'd better market himself or provide a service that the big Co-op competitor in town didn't. One of the services he knew that he could provide was consulting, and he started it off by offering a feed meeting down at the mill one evening.

It was springtime, and Dad knew that this new high-tech feed seminar would be a timely event. The farmers were starved for education, and the fields were too wet to do much else. So the date and time were set. A poster-size registration sheet was tacked up to the office door, hoping the RSVP would make for an accurate head count. The posting had been up for about a month, with minimal response generated.

224

"You's gonna have beer dare?" was the most commonly asked question.

One Saturday morning, Norbert Zigweed stopped in for some fertilizer. He noticed the registration sheet and promptly put his name on the first line. After he left, Dad could hardly contain his enthusiasm.

"Imy, this is almost as good as having Adolfus Sopenski's name up there. Norbert farms up on the other side of Devil's Hill, just shy of Lookout Curve."

"Don't they have those names backwards?"

"Huh?"

"Well, shouldn't it be Devil's Curve, and Lookout Hill? Doesn't that make more sense?"

Dad gave me one of his distant looks.

"Anyway, Norbert's got a degree from UW River Falls in agriculture. Now we should see some names pop up on the board!"

Farmers continued to stop and review the reservation log, some staring for quite a while before walking away.

One Saturday morning, Clifford Rantsner even went as far as to pretend to sign up, then scooted out the door when he claimed that the pen hanging from the twine next to the poster went dry.

"Yeh hay, I'll go git my pen dare. I'll be right back."

Clifford shot out of the door and headed for his truck. Once we heard his pickup fire up and chug away, we knew that another one had suffered from stage fright. Dad stared at the poster as if in deep thought.

"I wonder what the heck we have to do to get 'em to sign up."

"You need a headliner."

Dad didn't acknowledge me, but since that was status quo, I didn't let it inhibit me.

"You need someone like Adolfus Sopenski, an Octi or maybe, let's say, a Lavern Kupietz and Berbage Gemeaza in tandem."

"Well, then get on it!"

"OK Dad."

A week later, Octi stopped by to pick up some fence posts. While in the office, I pointed him over to the reservation poster.

"So Octi, you coming to the feed meeting?"

"Hell no, I got so much stuff going on at da udder place it ain't eben funny. Dat's why I ain't laffin', cause it ain't funny. Get it, pretty funny, uh?"

"Uh, yeh."

"So, who's dis Norbie Ziggy anyway?"

"Well, Norbert Zigweed farms up on the other side of town over Devil's Hill."

"Umm, never been ober dat hill before."

"They say it's a whole different way of farming," Dad said, elated to ignite a farm forum.

"He even went to college," I piped in.

"Well, lots of college boys are jist dat, college boys!"

We stared at Octi, expecting him to expound on that, but he didn't.

"That's right, a lot of those college boys need some good home schooling from real farmers," I added. "It would be great for someone like him to have a mentor."

"Hell mentor, he needs someone ta saddle up besides 'em and give 'em advice, kind of steer him straight, if ya know wat I mean."

"Yea Octi, that's right."

"Yea hey. Well, you know, Wednesday night is bat night anyway, so I guess a guy could clean up and come in and see what he's got goin.'"

"Can I sign you up then?"

"Bet your ass you can. Hey dat reminds me, I need a new ass. Mine's cracked!"

Octi clutched his side after that one, and we all gave him the obligatory laugh. He then stuffed his checkbook in the vest pocket of his bibbers and strode out the door. I stood admiring the poster. I felt as proud as if I had gotten Babe Ruth's autograph. I waited for a hint of praise or gratification from Dad, but, as usual, it never came. So I went out to the mill to start locking up for the day.

Sure enough, in the week before the scheduled meeting, no less than thirty names appeared on the signup sheet. We knew that would happen because Octi was his own man. Everyone else knew that as well, and they all followed.

The evening of the meeting, Dad and I finished placing the heavy wooden planks between the set's of five-gallon paint buckets. We had set four rows, enough to seat at least thirty people. Dad glared at his watch, and I followed him out of the backroom into the adjoining office. We looked out the window to a sea of metal. The lone yard light suspended from the telephone pole ricocheted the defused beam over some twenty car hoods. It resembled a scene from a Mafia action movie. I could imagine all of the mobsters talking among themselves at this clandestine meeting place with no one wanting to risk exiting their automobile.

"Dad, it's 7:30, what do you think they're waiting for?"

"Octi. He said he might run a few minutes late."

Sure enough, once Octi pulled up and hopped out of his truck, the entire parking area from the mill to the corncrib was illuminated with interior lights as the farmers exited their vehicles.

I readjusted my gaze and started to concentrate back on the graduation stage.

The speaker had finally closed, and now it seemed time to get down to business. This was the reason we came here tonight, I thought. In moments, we will be rewarded for 12 years of hard work and dedication. These diplomas wouldn't mean a lot to some of these kids, but to the rest of us, it was almost independence. We had put in our time, survived the idiosyncrasies of the town and now had a license to get out into the real world, whatever that might look like. We had worked hard for the privilege to leave the "Bermuda Triangle," as Steve Laliberty used to call it.

"Clarence Kutlarsh…"

I was getting closer to achieving my goal. It wouldn't be long now before I was called to receive my precious certificate, my ticket out of Arcadia. I closed my eyes, trying to appreciate how awesome this feeling was. The only image that I could come up with was a picture of Clarence, who, when asked by a teacher, "What's Utopia?" responded, "Isn't that just north of Waumendee?"

I smiled to myself, actually wondering what was Utopia, and what did exist north of Waumendee? Well, soon I would finally find out.

"Brent Lecheler"…

I opened my eyes, sprang to my feet and proudly walked up the center isle. I looked to my left, and Dad was actually clapping for me. That made me feel good. Damn, did that make me feel good.

Chapter XXVII

Summer had now officially started, and I had applied to several colleges in the area. It was tough for a kid of my caliber to be accepted at a known-name school. I not only didn't posses a lofty GPA, but my prerequisites were weak, and money was an issue. But like anything in life, if you want it bad enough and visualize through it, you'll achieve it. And I guess I did have an advantage over a lot of kids my age. I cleaned Frankie's barn to the tune of a dollar-seventy-five an hour.

I drove up to Minneapolis, Minnesota from Arcadia one day to survey a school and check out housing. On the way home, I decided to take a detour and drive through the town of Elmwood where I had grown up. I stopped in at my real mother's brother's house, Larry Fieler. Larry was a whimsical looking man interweaving common sense with his quick wit. He and his wife, Sandy, talked me into staying the night. It was good to see them again and catch up on everything. Larry was now the town Mayor, basically by default. Apparently about a year ago, there had been a mud slinging campaign going on with both maverick candidates trying to replace the retiring incumbent. Larry and his family had just come back from a one-week vacation when the telephone rang and a voice resounded, "Congratulations, Mayor."

Larry was bewildered, wondering why the caller imbued him with the distinction of Mayor over this 700-person village. He was informed that a town meeting was summoned on election eve, and everyone decided to vote for Larry as a "write-in" candidate.

That was just part of the crazy news. Apparently, celestial visitors were bombarding the town of Elmwood and surrounding areas. More flying saucers were being sighted than deer, and the townspeople even wanted to build a UFO landing strip. Now this, I thought, was a very interesting topic, especially for such a sleepy little village.

"Uncle Larry, do you really believe in UFO's?"

"I don't know, but there sure are a lot of reports of people seeing them."

228

"Have you ever seen one?"

"No, not personally, but some people with great reputations have reported them, so it's kind of making me wonder."

"What are you going to do about the UFO landing pad thing?"

"Until I see one, I'll take all of the excitement in stride. Even then, I probably won't believe it."

Sandy walked in, feeling guilty for interrupting the fascinating conversation but knowing that she'd be forgiven in a heartbeat.

"Guys, dinner's ready."

After the meal was over, we went back into the living room to lounge and recover from the two pieces of pie each that we scarfed for desert. We talked more about the UFO's and life, in general.

"Well guys, I'm going to get ready for bed."

"Sandy, thanks for a beautiful dinner. Don't you want to stay up and hear more UFO stuff?"

"Yea, like I've never heard it. Heck, I live with it every day."

"Yea, everything loses its luster after while," I said. "Anyway, it's getting late, and I've got to cruise out early tomorrow morning. I think that I'll hit the hay as well."

"The guest bed is made up in the downstairs bedroom."

"Thanks."

"See ya tomorrow."

Sandy walked upstairs as Larry lended an ear toward the static coming from the bookshelf on the other side of the living room.

"What's that?

"That's the police scanner."

Larry jumped off of the couch to turn it up.

"I usually have it on since there is very little police communication in Elmwood."

I started listening, as well, detecting a scratchy sentence or two.

"There seems to be a fire in the lime quarry. Better get the truck up here! It looks like a big one."

"What's your 20?"

"I'm just outside of Butternut Park, heading west up the hill. Should be there in about five minutes. I can't see the flames yet, but I see the glow. Better get 'em both up here."

"Who's that?" I asked.

"That's Ray Smith, Chief of Police, talking to the volunteer dispatcher."

"Well Uncle Larry, on that note, I'm gonna hit the hay."

I struggled to get out of the consuming recliner that I had buried myself into.

"I'm gonna jump in the car and run up to check out that fire. Being the Mayor, it doesn't look good finding out the news second-hand."

"Sounds good. See you tomorrow."

Had I known what was about to transpire that evening, I would have forgone the second piece of pie that made me want to retire for the evening and rode shotgun with Uncle Larry. After I had gone into the guest bedroom, Uncle Larry located his keys, jumped into his car and headed for the lime quarry. Once Larry arrived at the quarry, he almost ran into the police car sitting in the middle of his lane. The squad car sat with no lights on, and the driver's side door was swung wide open. Larry turned on his emergency flashers and ran over to see what was going on. Ray Smith was slumped over in his police cruiser with the police radio microphone lying next to him. Larry's thoughts were interrupted by the blare of the fire truck siren that was approaching from the bottom of the hill. Once it arrived, the volunteer fire fighters helped Larry put Ray Smith into Larry's car to transport him to the doctor's office. One attended to Ray while the other drove Larry's car. Larry stayed behind to drive the police car back into town. But there was one problem. The car wouldn't start. The engine wouldn't even attempt to turn over. With each frustrating turn of the key, there was nothing but dead silence.

With a stalled patrol car in the middle of the road and a fire truck parked right behind it, the lane was closed to traffic. "Traffic jam" could hardly describe the vehicular flow on this rural highway, but Pete Gassy was one of the inconvenienced motorists who encountered the delay that chilly evening. He jumped out of his truck to offer help.

"Let's start by checking the battery."

A quick examination under the hood pointed to melted cables where they connected to the battery terminals.

"That's strange," Pete said in a bewildered tone of voice. Let's pull the plugs and have a look."

Moments later, all eight plugs were lying on the fender of the disabled cruiser. A flashlight inspection illuminated spark plug ends reduced to a molted mass of metal. The protruding electrode was completely fused to the outer perimeter of the plug, as if it had been submitted to an incredibly high temperature.

"Wow. Something went through the electrical system, no doubt. Let's pull the points next, and I betcha we'll see the same thing."

After confirming Pete's suspicion, they placed the parts in an empty shotgun shell box found on the floor of the patrol car. Larry and company guided the cop car backward down the hill until a wide enough shoulder was found to curb it. Larry then hopped in the fire truck and was given a ride down the hill to pick up his car at the doctor's office where Ray Smith had been delivered.

The next morning, I sat wide-eyed as Larry detailed the events of the evening.

"Well, what happened to Ray?"

"I don't know exactly. By the time I got down to Frank Springer's office, he was gone. Doc Springer examined him, and then they hauled him up to Menomonie. We should find out more today."

What had happened to Ray Smith was later published in a book and also featured on the Geraldo Show about ten years later. Ray testified to a brilliant glow emanating from the lime quarry that evening. Thinking it was a fire, he dispatched the fire truck, knowing it would take a little time for the volunteer fire fighters to get to the station. In the meantime, Ray rushed to the scene, ready to assess the situation and perhaps cancel the dispatch.

At the lime quarry, he witnessed a sight almost too incredible to believe. A large egg-shaped craft was hovering over the quarry, extending a laser-like rope that appeared to be extracting some sort of energy from the limestone. The light radiating from this laser was so intense that Ray couldn't look at it for very long. He dropped back into the squad car to report his findings. He remembered that the radio went dead, along with his car. But that's where his tale ends. The next thing that Ray recounted was waking up in the ambulance from the Elmwood doctor's office to Menomonie Hospital. Also reported that evening were a dozen people in the area who lost power on their televisions and had to have them repaired.

The next day, Larry reported the phenomenon to the government agency, "Project Blue Book," who called him back a couple of hours later and interviewed him intensely. They were particularly interested in the eight spark plugs pulled from the

231

cruiser that evening, along with the ignition points. They concluded that a burst of radiation could have caused the ignition system meltdown. They were intentionally vague about details. However, their last question piqued Larry's interest.

"Was their any limestone in the area?"

"Well, that hill is nothing but. Why do you ask?"

"Oh, just wondering."

Larry did what he was instructed to do, ship the components off to a laboratory in Houston, Texas. And as far as Ray Smith? Ray walked around town with a king-size headache, never acting the same again.

"They're in my head. I know they got in my head," Ray was heard to say repeatedly.

A few months later, Ray was taken up to the Mayo Clinic in Rochester, Minnesota for tests. He was diagnosed with radiation poising of the brain and died a short time later.

It was getting late, and I knew that I had to get back home, so I headed for the door.

"Now, I know that you're going to stop in and see Grandma," Sandy said, with a stern look on her face.

"Common Aunt Sandy, as if I need prompting."

I hugged Sandy and trotted to the car. I couldn't wait to get to Grandma's. I had the same excited feeling in the pit of my stomach, much like fifteen years ago. I remembered running over to her house whenever things got crazy. Her carefree demeanor was so comforting.

The elderly citizen home was located on the other side of the village, so it didn't take me but a few minutes to complete the drive. I pulled up behind a short bus that was loading up residents from the home. I ran in to the information desk located in the lobby to insure that Grandma Rosie was not among them. Sure enough, she was not. I scanned the seating area in the foyer, wondering how much she had changed. It had been about five years since I had seen her last. Since we moved away to Arcadia, our communication was reduced to birthday cards to each other.

I spotted a short, average-weighted, dark haired lady sitting in a chair in the sterile lounge. She was wearing glasses and had her hair up in a bun. She was staring in the direction of the TV, as if using it to pass some time away.

"Gramma?"

She responded quickly, looking across the tiled entryway. A brilliant smile lit her seasoned face.

"Well I'm telling you…"

She stood up, and we gave each other a giant-size hug. After a kiss from her on the cheek, her smile said it all.

"You look like your mother more and more. I just wish you could have known her. She was my only daughter, and…"

Her voice faded as it started to crack, and she turned her head to keep me from seeing the tears well up in her eyes.

"How have you been Gramma?"

"Great," she said, wiping her eyes with a Kleenex that had been concealed in her sleeve.

"What's with the bus?"

"They load up all the old folks once a week and take us for a ride, like we've never seen the area around Elmwood."

Just then a spry old man interrupted our conversation.

"Rosie, I don't believe I've met your new date. Even though he looks way too old for you, he's a pretty good looking fellow."

"Imy, I'd like you to meet George Lempky. George and I went to grade school together, then he moved out into the country, and we didn't see each other for years. Now as fate would have it, here we meet again."

George pointed to a seemingly incoherent man slumped over in the chair on the other side of Grandma Rosie.

"See this old duffer right here?" George asked.

"That's old Judge Olsen. The Judge and I grew up right across the street from each other. The Judge was always smarter than me, always getting better grades in school. Well, he went off to college, and I got a job cutting wood. He always made more money doing his lawyering, and, at times, had it easier than I did. But that tree trimming kept me in shape, and who's dancing now, Judge? Uh? Who's dancing now, baby? Uh? Who's dancing now?"

On that note, George Lempky grabbed the front of his suspenders with his thumbs and danced a jig around the Judge's chair, kicking his work boots high enough in the air to produce the brand name on the bottom of them.

"Look at old Geo go now, old boy, look at old Geo go now," George chanted while doing his whacked chicken dance.

233

"Well, I'd like to stay for an encore, but I've got ice cubes to make. Imy, please escort me to my room."

We got up and excused ourselves as we headed for the hallway. As Grandma and I carefully lumbered down the long hall, we were startled by the clamor of an old man whose walker stomped along the tile floor. He stumbled past us in a big hurry.

Grandma Rosie stopped, took in the scene, and turned to me with that big smile of hers. I knew exactly what she was laughing about. She and I had an unusual bond in finding humor in everything, from all-star wrestling when I was six years old to now some thirteen years later.

"Why is he in such a big hurry? Like, where does he think he's going?"

Her eyes danced, and we both laughed in perfect synchronization. I was in tune with her, knowing they were all put here to pass their time until death.

After some time in Grandma's room we had covered the old times, the now times and just a bit of politics. When I kissed her goodbye, I knew it would be the last. Not because I would never come back again, but I just knew it was the last time that I would see her alive. Like I said, Grandma Rosie and I were in sync. Six months later, I would come back to say my last goodbye to my best friend who stood by me growing up. No one knew how close our relationship was except us. Even though my step-mom chastised her in my youth, Grandma never interfered with our family matters, and, at the same time, she never held out on her outpouring of love for me. This love gave me something to hang on to, and I'll never forget it.

Chapter XXIII

A little fuss from Nicholas caught my attention, and I immediately awakened from my childhood past. He repositioned himself in my arms, then locked onto a deep gaze in my eyes. His long eyelashes never blinked as his "baby blues" looked into mine, as if he had just witnessed my entire flashback.

I continued to rock him, thinking that the motion would lull him back to sleep. He turned his head straight, continuing to keep his big blue portals open. It was as if he could sense what I was thinking and was digesting it all as I was.

I sat there trying to figure out how a father could be so cold toward his own son. I never got into trouble and tried countless times to please him. As innovated as I was in trying to be the model son, it never worked.

I couldn't imagine acting ambivalent toward Nick. I can't hold him for more than a few seconds without planting a kiss on his forehead. I laugh with him when I change his diaper and hold him tight when he is inconsolable. Any concern of his is a concern of mine. I missed him when I was away and run to him as soon as I'm through the door. My family is the most important thing in my life.

I looked down at Nicholas, noticing that he was not the least bit sleepy. We both stared at the closed entertainment cabinet in front of us, neither of us making a sound. I was aware of an eerie unease. I guess the subconscious reminiscing of my upbringing surfaced memories that I had long since suppressed. And while I thought that I had escaped the trappings of my family years ago, my own family was causing old emotions to be exhumed.

Chapter XXIX

It was just a year ago that I decided to take a trip back to my hometown. I had been back there many times before but only for short stints, usually just to see my friends.

I decided to drive to Arcadia from Denver and make it more of a vacation for my wife and me. We stopped in Minneapolis where I had attended college and spent more than ten years as a working professional. After visiting a few close friends, we made the three-hour trek to Arcadia.

Doreen had never been there before, mainly because we were so newly married. Since my brother Tom was the only family member to attend our wedding, it was great to have her meet the rest of the family and see the area where I grew up.

We pulled up in front of subsidized apartments that were built in the middle of town some 25 years ago for senior citizens with fixed incomes. We anxiously walked from the car to apartment #7 and gave a courtesy knock before entering. Dad inched up slowly from his chair and grabbed his cane to balance himself so that he could greet me properly. He held out a wobbly hand, then gave me an uncomfortable hug.

Feelings rushed through me, leaving me totally at a loss for words. Guilt, pity, sorrow and anger were all present, tugging at me simultaneously from all angles. This once powerful man who seemed to be bigger than his family was reduced to a shaking recluse. This man who I shared a life with appeared to be a total stranger. But whose fault was it? Why did this have to happen? This person who didn't need anyone, especially me, now needed everyone, including me. I would buy my life back in a heartbeat if things could be different, but deep down I knew it would only be a waste of money.

After giving Mom a big hug, I walked over and gave my brother, Tom, a hearty handshake. Doreen had already met Tom at the wedding, where they spent virtually no time together. As Doreen was shaking my brother's hand, he expelled a fart that was so loud and long that it sounded like a king-size sheet being ripped down the middle. My cosmopolitan wife was unaccustomed to such crude antics and was befuddled by how to respond. She didn't know if she should politely pretend that nothing had happened or act like a hometown girl who was unfettered by such acts of vulgarity? Sensing her discomfort, I immediately chastised my brother, which gave way to thunderous laughter around the room. And that was Doreen's initial indoctrination into Arcadia and my family.

After a few minutes of idle conversation, Dad started getting down to business.

"Farmers just don't know how to plow anymore. Dig, dig, dig. Everyone's digging! First they plow. Then they disk. Then they drag. How the hell is this field gonna hold any moisture? It's not dirt anymore, it's sand..."

This is just great, I thought. For the first fifteen years of my life, we had absolutely no relationship or anything in common whatsoever. Here I had moved away, established a life of my own, and he still responds to me as if I farm the next forty acres over. He was getting worse each year. He started talking farm with Tom after I had left and continued to talk it with whoever would listen. I just couldn't figure it out. Why couldn't I ever have a relationship with this man? He was intelligent. He could be funny. He was well spoken. He could be kind. But he just couldn't relate as a father, only as a farmer.

A knock at the door interrupted the farm lesson for the day.

My sister, Linda, walked in the door past Mom and Dad and gave me a big squeeze. After introducing her to Doreen, we starting catching up on lost time. After some small talk concerning how Doreen and I had met, we got down to some current events.

"So how do you like living out in the country now?" I asked.

"You know, we absolutely love the peace and quiet, but the commute with the kids back and forth for school activities does get old."

"Who bought your old house?"

"Rollie and Evey Skribner."

"So you move from town to the farm, and Rollie moves from the farm to town."

"Well, they're old and need to move closer to the services."

"How long did you have your house on the market?"

"Funny you should ask. A week before we were going to list it, Bob's nephew said something to Rollie that we were thinking of moving. The next day, we get a phone call asking if they can see the house after church that Sunday. So, Sunday morning they drive up and get out of their truck. They ring the doorbell, and I go out to the front hall to greet them. When I opened the door, Rollie busts through me like a running back bulldozing through a linebacker. He runs down to the basement and proceeds to clang on the furnace. By this time, Evey has made her way in. I take her coat and ask her what's wrong with Rollie. She said that nothing was wrong, he was just looking at the house. I had just hung her coat up in the closet when Rollie shoots past me again, like a cow heading for the barn. I watch as he jumps in his pickup and pulls off. I ask Evey again what's wrong with Rollie, and she again says nothing. He loves it, she said, and I just want to see it for myself to get some decorating ideas.

'But Evey, Rollie didn't see the house. He just ran down to the basement and made some noise.'

'Hey, as long as the furnace and hot water heater are in good shape, and the joists haven't sagged, he's happy.'

After a couple of hours of nonstop conversing, it was time for Doreen and me to get some sleep. Linda was on her way along with Tom and his wife, Lori, who were going to go to her house to spend the night.

Later that night after saying our goodnights, Doreen was replaying her first impressions that members of my family had made on her. To no surprise, my brother Tom's name surfaced.

"Now, how was I supposed to respond to that? Was I supposed to say, 'good one'? Should I have had one stored up to come back with? Do I pretend that I didn't hear it? I mean, what do you do when someone does that? That is so rude!"

"Well Doreen, welcome to Arcadia."

The next day was Saturday. We woke up and sat around the living room, trading conversation. Tom and Lori arrived in time for breakfast after making the short jaunt from Linda's house. Tom was full of news and shared it all.

"You know, Adrian Krysner put a jet turbine on his tractor, and now she goes like a raped ape. In fact, at the last tractor pull, he couldn't flame her out, so he jumped the end of the runway, heading straight for the Broiler plant."

"What happened?"

"Well, the P.A. announcer immediately deputized everyone there a stakeman, so anyone sober enough to run tried to chase him down to add more weight to the sled."

Doreen now had put down the newspaper, appearing to be interested in the story.

"Well, did they get him?"

"The tractor went down the park road, pulling the sled behind that was loaded with stakemen. Sparks were flying from the skid…

"Then what?"

"Well, the whole works bailed, and the rest of the shooting match went right through the metal-sided wall into the chicken storage room. It was funnier than heck. Out comes Adrian, totally covered in feathers, just like in one of those old-time movies. Then chickens started to escape, nearly emptying the holding bin. Alby Kribec tried to pull over a high-racked chicken truck that was parked alongside the building to block the hole in the sheet-metal, but the yard-birds all scattered by the time he found the keys. Chickens ran around this town for months before they captured 'em all."

"Well, Doreen, I guess some things just never change."

"Yea, and I always thought you made this stuff up. Did any stakemen get hurt?" Doreen asked.

"Na."

Dad was listening from the recliner. A knowing smile warmed his face. Either he thought the story was funny, or he was having a farm flashback.

"You know, they don't use stakemen anymore. Now they have a skid with a weight that moves further up the sled as the tractor goes forward. Now no one can cheat this way."

"Well, that doesn't sound like fun," Doreen chided.

The telephone rang, and Dad hobbled over to get to it.

"For you, Tom, I mean, Imy."

His mind was just a little bit slower these days, however, he was still pretty sharp for an 84-year-old who had suffered a stroke four years earlier.

"Hello."

"Imy, heard that you were coming home from my mom. So I drove down to meet that wife of yours."

"Hi Wayne."

"I'm going to my cousin's wedding. So maybe you can come up to the new Country Club for the reception and see some of the gang. I know Lib and Bim should be there."

"Yea, I think my parents were invited to it as well. As long as they're going, we may as well tag along, too. I don't know what else we would do anyway."

"Well, it's an eleven o'clock wedding, so I'll see ya up there."

"Sounds good. Let me check with the boss, but we'll probably see you there."

"Later."

Mom had just walked into the kitchen from the bedroom.

"Who was that?

"That was Wayne."

"Oh, Margie told me that he's coming down for that Ruecorn wedding. That should be big. I know we'll probably go. Why don't you and Doreen come along with us?"

"Well, Doreen, what do ya think?"

"Doreen, if you don't want to go, why don't you come to Linda's with us?" Lori asked. "This way we can all go through those family pictures that we've been trying to sort out."

"Hey, sounds good to me," Doreen replied. "Besides, I don't know those people anyway, Imy, and this way I can spend time with Linda. We can stop out and see Wayne on Sunday."

"OK, sounds like a plan."

Now every Polish wedding in Arcadia, which meant practically all weddings, were an all-day affair. They usually started at eleven o'clock on a Saturday morning. The reception would run from 1:00 until 5:00 PM. Following the reception, the wedding party would end up downtown to go bar hopping while the farmers would go home to milk the cows. The celebration resumed with a dance that started at 9PM and wound up around midnight. It was as traditional as the seventh inning stretch at a baseball game. That's just the way they do it. Always have and always will.

Tom and Lori left with Doreen, while I drove Mom and Dad to the wedding. At the church, I helped Dad along as the three of us walked down the center isle looking for a pew. My parents always sat on the left-hand side, about a third of the way from the front. A

240

few seconds later, Wayne walked in, genuflected, and, with a grin, planted himself beside me.

"How's it going, Boss?" Wayne whispered.

"Great. How you've been?"

"Good. Where's the wife?"

"She went up to my sister, Linda's. We'll stop by tomorrow so you can finally meet her."

"Sounds great. Wait till you see this circus."

"What do you mean?"

"Well, the groom and groomsmen are from out of town. They all went out drinking last night, and none of them had tried on their tuxedos until less than an hour ago. Apparently, the guys had met at the church only a short time ago to change into their tuxedos that a friend of the bridesmaid's had picked up from the distributor in LaCrosse. Since the boys were too busy partying, no time was set aside to try on their tuxedoes."

"How bad?"

"I only saw one of them, and it's pretty funny. This should be a good one."

About a minute later, the music started, and a bridesmaid glided softly down the center isle, in search of her complementary groomsman. He appeared from the front vestibule, wearing suit pants cropped about two inches higher than they should have been. He was taking minute steps so as not to accentuate this fashion faux paux.

Another bridesmaid entered from the back of the church and began her long journey toward the altar. Again, a groomsman appeared from the far side of the church, walking gingerly so as not to rip out the crouch of his suit pants. The pants reminded me of peddle-pushers from the 60's. He was wearing the waist so low that you couldn't help notice the crack of his butt through his white shirt. My eye was drawn to the silver timepiece inconspicuously exposed on his huge wrist. The apparent ill-fitted suit raised the cuff of his coat sleeve to the middle of his forearm. A sheepish grin lit his face, rousing my curiosity as to whether he was excited about the event in which he was participating or simply laughing at the spectacle that he was making of himself. Whatever the reason, Wayne was right. The groomsmen looked comical, and I was glad that I came.

A minute later, the bride was announced and began her regal promenade down the isle. Her groom entered from the side, drawing snickers from the guests as he made his way to the altar to meet the woman of his dreams. You couldn't help but notice that his pants were about two sizes too small. He was an abundant man, and his beer belly flopped over the narrow-wasted pants that were inched down below his hips. The suit coat was putting up a good fight to conceal his belt line, but it was slowly losing the battle. The pants were sliding lower and lower with each step he took. In a subtle yet fruitless attempt, the groom stopped once and pressed his forearms against his hips to hike them back up. The zipper was down all the way, displaying nothing but the white undershirt in the shape of a V. He had cleverly maneuvered the cumberbun, trying to mask this area that is usually covered by trousers. His trousers were so short in length that flesh was detected between the top of the socks and the bottoms of the pant legs. When he arrived at the altar and turned to accept her hand, she blushed and looked as if she had just seen a clown. In many respects, she had. Random giggling finally subsided when the Priest came and escorted them both and hid them behind the front of the altar.

After the ceremony, we went up to the New Country Club for the reception dinner. I saw a few of my high school buddies there and had a chance to catch up with what was going on in Arcadia. Two old classmates of mine, Lib, now a doctor, and Lard, a policeman, were there.

"Did you hear about what happened to Carl Libenski?" Lib asked.

Carl was a classmate of mine. We had met in forth grade, and he was the first kid over at my desk talking to me. I also remember the school picnic that year. We were playing softball, and Carl had a small leather case of three little cruets filled with booze. After every swing of the bat, he would turn around and have a swig from one of these dark colored liquids. The older he got, the more that it seemed that alcohol played a big part in his life. Once he graduated high school, he happily adopted the nickname Carl Can.

"No, what?"

"Well, he had a horrible accident. I guess, once he got up to the hospital, he almost died."

"Well, that doesn't surprise me. Everyone who registers in there with anything more serious than a broken fingernail puts their life at risk."

"Seriously, the reason it was almost fatal was because of his addiction to alcohol. It was so severe that they had to intravenously feed him with alcohol during and after surgery for him to survive."

"Well, I knew that he liked to drink. But I thought he was just like most people around here, a "case-a-night drinker.""

"No, I think he really had a problem," Lard added. "In fact, during a State Patrol convention a couple of years ago, they were discussing heavy drinking and at what level someone's classified as impaired, legally intoxicated or inebriated. A blood alcohol level of 0.1 is legally intoxicated. I learned that anybody between 0.14 and 0.2 should be put in the care of a responsible party. Anybody over 0.24 should be taken to a hospital to treat alcohol poisoning, and 0.3 or over should be rushed to urgent care because time is of the essence. Anyway, our buddy, Mike the cop, stopped Carl, had him get out of his car and commanded him to walk the centerline. Since he appeared drunk, not only having a little difficulty walking the straight line but also slurring his speech, Mike decided to give him a breath-o-lizer test. One blow into the device pegged it to the max, and Mike thought his equipment might need calibration. Since we had all gone to school together, and Carl didn't appear that drunk, Mike gave him a break. The next day Mike calibrated his breath-o-lizer and found it to be well within specification. In fact, he checked it right up to the maximum read which is 0.4 blood alcohol level."

"So, like Carl should have been dead at that level?"

"Yea, and to Mike's disbelief, Carl seemed to be somewhat sober, so much so that Mike let him drive home."

"Wow."

After a decent meal, a few of us were talked into going downtown to Tricky's Tavern, apparently still the popular place to be. My parents headed for home, so I rode with Wayne as we made our way down Main Street. On the way there, we passed the bride and groom, obviously on their way to the "bar hopping" phase of an Arcadia wedding ritual. They were in a manure spreader being pulled by a massive John Deere tractor. Signs adorned the sides of their rural limo reading, "We're really spreading this wedding" and "Get a load of this." Both bride and groom were waving to people with beers in hand, celebrating the happiest day of their lives. Most brides couldn't be talked into a manure spreader, especially after the attire fiasco that had taken place. Oh well, a match like this will last a lifetime, as it should, I thought.

A few minutes later, we pulled into the parking lot of Tricky's Tavern. I worked my way through the crowd up to the counter to buy a round for the guys.

"Wha 'chew drinking?"

"Ahh, excuse me?"

The voice sounded vaguely familiar, but I couldn't put a name to it.

"Wha 'chew drinking, buddy?"

I stared, seeing only a pair of hands removing a dirty glass that someone had just placed on the bar.

"PeeWee?"

"Yea."

"Oh boy. OK, just give me four draft beers, please."

"Comin' right up".

As I looked around, I noticed that nothing had changed. I remembered it exactly as it was when I was 8 years old. The only difference appeared to be the aged and tattered sign that read "Tricky's Tavern, Where good friends meet." I glanced over at the end of the bar, remembering how I had eagerly jumped up and established a perch so many years ago when I had come down here with Aloyzie Sookla. My mind raced, thinking about how I could remember that odd, one-time relationship with a drunk welder, yet could hardly remember a one-day event with my own dad. Why we could never be close was always the million-dollar question. My thoughts were interrupted with PeeWee setting four cold glasses of beer on the bar.

"One-sixty."

I pulled out two dollars and plopped them on the bar. I grabbed three of the beers and passed them over to Lib.

"Hey, you forgot your change!"

Since I took his remark as sarcasm because of the paltry tip that I had left, I grabbed another dollar and tossed it on the bar.

"How many more beers do ya want?"

"It's a tip."

"Did one tip? Just grab the glass, and I'll fill ya back up, buddy."

"Just keep it."

"For what? It's your money."

"Buy yourself a beer with it."

"I work in a bar. I get all the beer I need."

"Alright, alright, I'll take it back then."

I grabbed the beer soaked dollar bill and put it in my pocket. I stood there and looked around, knowing that I was just killing time so I wouldn't have to spend more time alone with Dad. It was ironic that I looked forward to coming one thousand miles to be with him, yet I couldn't convince myself to go the one-mile to be alone with him. As long as we were not alone and other people could create a diversion, I was OK.

But Tricky's Tavern was equally unsettling. How could so many people spend so much time wasting time? Everyone was drinking and talking up a storm, but no one was relating. It was just bar talk. Talk about what they're gonna do someday, stuff that was wrong with the country and why the world is so screwed up.

"Wayne, take me back to the house. I've gotta go home and see Dad."

When Wayne dropped me off at my parent's place, Mom was sitting in her favorite easy chair, staring at a blaring television. A smoldering cigarette occupied an ashtray full of butts.

"Oh, you're back already?" Mom asked in her husky voice.

"Yea, you know, we have so little time to spend, and we live so far away that it seems such a shame not to spend more time with you and Dad instead of in a bar with my friends."

"That's good."

Mom appeared happy that I came back early, but was slightly disappointed that the cigarette smoking would have to cease with me in the apartment.

"Where's Dad?"

"He went up to the antler convention at the new armory."

"What the heck is an antler convention?"

"Well, I don't know, but Irv Ganchow came by and picked him up."

Now, Irv was a name out of the past. Irv was my driver's education teacher, whom we called "Swerve" and for a good reason. Irv was a great teacher and highly respected, although he couldn't drive a straight line if asked. Irv was a good man, and it was great that a guy twenty years younger than my dad would take such good care of him. Both were active Legionaries, and that common interest that they both shared created a bond of friendship.

"He shouldn't be gone too long. By the way, did you hear about Benny Weegs?"

"No, what happened?"

"Well, you know Benny lives right next door to Ogden."

"Yea, he's always lived right next door to Ogden."

"Well, anyway, I guess he was feeling so depressed that he walked next door to Ogden's barn and shot himself. Then the milkman comes to drain Ogden's milk tank and sees the body. Well, the Milkman thinks that it's Ogden and runs into Ogden's house to call 911. In the meantime, Ogden comes home, sees the milk hauler's truck and walks into the barn to talk to him. Ogden sees the same body and, of course, thinks that it's the milkman. Ogden runs into his house to call 911. And as he rounds the corner into the kitchen, he runs right into the milkman who is on his way back to the barn. Well, since both men thought the other was dead, they screamed bloody murder as they collided in the kitchen. After things calmed down, they went out to identify the body."

"Wow. Even a simple suicide in Arcadia has a twist."

A few minutes later, Dad walked in the door, and in no time at all, we were sitting there discussing farming issues again.

"Everyone wants more cows."

"Let's grab a bite to eat, Daddy," Mom said, sensing my boredom.

"No sense working yourself into a tizzy."

Since it was getting late, I decided to make a run up to the Root Beer Stand to get dinner to go. I returned with everyone's favorite burger. We sat down to eat a quiet dinner. Nothing had changed much. Once food was involved it was serious business. As soon as we finished eating, there was a knock at the door.

"Come in!"

In walked Lard and Palutichi, both wanting to see if I was going to head back up to the New Country Club for phase two of the nuptial celebrations.

Dad seemed excited to have a new audience and eagerly had them sit down for awhile. He sat there deep in thought, as if premeditating a one-liner to kick off a farm debate.

"Farmers think silage is the all purpose food."

Everyone stared at the carpet, obviously not knowing what to say.

"Cows need protein. They think, just because you have corn, beans and hay that that's all you need. But the cows need concentrate, they need vitamins and minerals..."

He continued to preach as he stood up right in front of their chairs making sure that he drove the point home.

"Daddy, the kids want to go out."

Both Lard and Palutichi, a police officer and math teacher respectively, sat wide-eyed, agreeing with everything that was said. I don't know if they concurred or simply didn't know what else to do or say.

"Well, alright then. I just get so worked up trying to get this message to mainstream farmers."

"Bye, Mom and Dad. I'll be home early."

"OK, see ya when ya get home."

It was Sunday morning, and I had just gotten up from a restful night's sleep. Doreen had spent the night over at my sister, Linda's, house, and I was going to meet up with her after church. I was exchanging morning pleasantries with Mom and Dad when the telephone rang.

"I'll get it."

I sprang up from the chair to grab the call.

Doreen was on the line with that little giggle in her voice. "I'm looking at the Arcadia News Leader, Thursday's edition, and guess what happened on this date twenty five years ago?"

"Imy Lecheler is proven the smartest man in town?"

"Stout Gouch wins the Fall Creek chicken catchers award." Doreen went on reading, "Stout was a little over forty, but still had it. He loaded up the monster trans-hauler, not to be confused with the stack rack chicken truck, in three hours and ten minutes. Stout chased, loaded and stacked his way into the record books mainly because of his handicap."

Stout had a muscular problem that caused him to droop from the shoulder on his right side.

"The condition of actually carrying your right hand just inches from the ground would be a detriment to most people, but not to Stout. Stout turned a deficit into an asset, and this posture earned him the most coveted award Fall Creek has to offer."

"I can get more chickens on the run, not only because of the way I walk, but I'm stout with a low center of gravity," Gouch said as he picked up his trophy in between innings of the softball tournament during the Fall Creek Chicken Chaser Days.

Doreen, at this point was heaving with laughter.

"Can you believe it?"

"Yea. You're in Arcadia."

A couple of hours later we walked into St. Stan's church and took the usual seat. I held on to Dad's arm as he maneuvered cautiously with the help of his cane. I realized that this was one of the first times that I'd ever touched him in a helping and loving way. It felt strange, and I could tell that it felt uncomfortable for both of us. As Mass continued, we were informed that videotape of the Bishop would be played in lieu of the sermon. The uninspired crowd looked as if it had just settled in for a sixteen-minute nap when a NFL Pre-game show flashed across the monitor. This sure beats the annual letter from the Bishop, I thought. As the announcer diagrammed a touchdown pass to a wide-open receiver, the church crowd erupted with life. The priest moved quickly to recover from his fumble. A low groan spread throughout the church as the priest hit the switch and the tape player started to run.

As the Bishop droned on, my thoughts wandered back to Dad. A warm rush overtook me as I thought about the closeness I felt in helping him down the church aisle. I always thought Dad would live forever and that we would develop a loving relationship down the road, but time was against us. If a meaningful relationship were to exist, I would have to start it. I put my arm around the back of Dad and sat there feeling as uncomfortable and awkward as I had the first time that I had put my arm around a date. Dad looked over at me and smiled. I smiled back at him. I began to rub his massive shoulder, and he sat totally content.

After church, Dad said that was the best Mass he had attended in ages.

"That priest is getting so much better. People say he's boring, but he's a good man. I really got something out of him today."

I sat behind the steering wheel with a big smile on my face. Hey, if he wants to give credit to the priest, so be it. But we came a long way that day. We came a long way.

We stopped at Linda's house to pick up Doreen before driving over to Memorial Park where a special service was being held that Dad wanted to attend. Linda mentioned that she had another obligation to fulfill. Her husband, Bob, wanted to get some things done before raccoon hunting that night, so Doreen jumped into the car, and we were on our way.

When we arrived there was upwards of one hundred cars parked in the lot. We got out and walked down the sidewalk, admiring all of the monuments that were dedicated to local Arcadians who had served during the various wars. I always thought it odd that people would wait until a person died before they honored him.

We followed our ears to the amphitheater. After glancing at several stone statues and plaques, we sat down on the lower bleacher to take in some of the dedication program. Dad leaned on his cane, intently listening to the speaker talk about our heroes lost in battle.

The Color Guard lined up in formation to execute a twenty-one gun salute. The men were all about my Dad's age, most of them WWII veterans. I combed their faces, seeing if I recognized anyone from the days when they did those programs at the high school.

The Color Guard captain belted out the "fire" command, and one senior member was literally knocked over by the kick of his gun. He lay there for a brief moment. But like the soldier he was, he flipped over and started to get up. He put the stock of the gun on the ground, using it as a cane and proceeded to crawl up the gun barrel, as if he were a gymnast climbing the hanging rope. About half way up, a comrade limped over and held his rifle out as if he were rescuing a quicksand victim with a stick. The program was stalled until both veterans were back in position and ready to fire again.

Mom looked incredulously at the Color Guard.

"Honestly, these guys should be in walkers," she hacked.

A few more shots were fired, and the Color Guard stumbled down the sidewalk in formation to the parking lot, signaling the end of the event.

I wondered what Dad was thinking, seeing his own out there, struggling to get through an event because of their age. Dad had been the Commander of the Legion and had done so many civic events right up until his stroke a couple of years ago. He was reduced to sitting on the sidelines, and I could tell that it was killing him.

Back at the apartment, Dad grabbed a package and told me to follow him into the bedroom. He parked his walker against the bed, then took the matted bag he was carrying and emptied the contents onto the bed. The bag had contained some old monochrome pictures that Doreen had brought back from Linda's. I sat on the edge of the bed close to Dad, allowing him full narration. We talked about Dad's war days, the farming days, right down to the pickups and tractors that he owned. At the end, we talked about how he lost my real mother to cancer and how he thought he needed to give up farming to keep us together as a family. We reminisced about times when I was an infant and different family situations. He apparently remembered everything about us, but for whatever reason, he just seemed to have shelved it for the last forty-some years.

The next day came, and Doreen and I said our good-byes. Once we headed for the door, Dad reached for the remote control in order to turn off the TV. He leaned on his cane while inquiring how long of a drive was it to Denver. As soon as conversation faded, he asked question after question, intently listening to every answer. I was taken off guard with the dialect, totally shocked with this inquisitive man. However, deep in my heart, I felt he was delaying the inevitable.

I shook Dad's hand as I always did, but this time he grabbed me close for a hug. He didn't let go for over a minute. When I walked to the door, his eyes welled up, and tears flowed down his cheeks. This was the first time ever that I saw him cry. In retrospect, I should have turned around, embraced him and told him how much I loved him and needed him, but I didn't know how. Instead, I turned and headed for the door. Not wanting to make direct eye contact, I casually commented,

"I'll come home again real soon, Dad."

I walked to the car thinking, had I become just as emotionless as I always perceived my dad to be? Or had he always loved me in ways that I didn't understand?

Chapter XXX

It had been four weeks since we had returned from Arcadia, and things were back to their hectic pace. Work was busy, and I was trying to get the house ready for winter. My mind was occupied by a project at work, and I was spending a lot of time at the office. My desk was a mess, as usual, and I was feverishly searching for a design review that a vendor had sent to me. A group of team members stood in the doorway of my office, impatiently waiting for me.

"Imy, we need that review for the ten o'clock conference call."

"I know it came across the fax machine yesterday. I saw it and put it on your desk."

"Well, that's the first problem. Look at his desk? What desk? It's like finding Waldo."

"Alright guys, give me just a minute to see if I can locate it. I'll be right out so we can jump on that conference call."

"Imy, we'll transfer the call to your extension as soon as it comes in so you can take it here."

"Thanks."

I stood up to obtain an aerial view of my desk, searching under everything to find this fax. I knew it was important, and I needed the data during the forthcoming call. After a minute or two of turning over everything, the telephone rang, and I grabbed it, thinking of an excuse to buy some more time.

"Imy Lecheler, and I'll be right with you. Let me put you on speaker so I can scribble."

"Imy, I've just got terrible news."

"Who's this?"

"It's Lori, your sister in law."

My heart stuck in my throat, and I swallowed hard. I took the phone off speaker and reached for the handset.

"What?"

"You're dad died this morning. Imy? He got up this morning and had breakfast, and you're mom found him later on the bedroom floor."

Without saying another word, I hung up the telephone, dazed and momentarily paralyzed. I reached in my drawer and slipped on a pair of sunglasses, hiding my tears. I hadn't cried in over forty years; it simply wasn't the logical thing to do. I couldn't let anyone at work see me cry. I grabbed my lap top computer and headed for the door.

"Imy, I've got them on speaker over here. Did you find the report?"

I brushed past my boss who was standing outside my office door and headed outside, unable to utter a word. Inside my Jeep, I drove down the road with no clue where I was heading. I pulled over at a remote gas station and turned off the engine. Sitting there, staring blankly at the pumps, I just couldn't help but think about all of the time we wasted trying to get to know each other. I reflected on the effort that I had put out trying to bond with this man. We waited forty-two years to do it. If I could rewind the clock, I would. But I couldn't. With all the things I'd achieved in life, I had neglected this one, the most important one.

Doreen and I headed for Arcadia the next morning and met up with the family. The funeral was held at Woyzney's, the new funeral home on top of the hill. So many people and friends came to honor Dad and comfort our family. Dad looked incredible in the casket, with the casket lid open, displaying a farm scene painted inside. How appropriate, I thought.

The next day was spent back at the funeral home. After the wake, we all went down to the bowling alley for dinner, since it was the only restaurant of the three in town that was open. Dad would have loved to have been there. Family and cousins from all over that he hadn't seen for thirty years showed up to offer their condolences. I saw Aunt Bertha's sisters, and they both recognized me. The last time we had seen each other was when I was three years old.

The next morning, family members congregated back at the funeral home. We were told to go in and view the casket one more time. We just stood there motionless with no one uttering a word. There wasn't anything left to say to anyone, let alone to Dad. The funeral director solemnly closed the casket, as an awkward silence filled the room. Six pallbearers placed Dad in the back of the hearse. As it proceeded slowly to the church, we followed, one by one, headlights on low beam. Within a block of the church, I could hear the church bell clang to a lonely hollow rhythm. The procession traveled around the outer edge of a full parking lot, stopping at the front doors. I pulled up behind the hearse and slowly exited the vehicle. Chilled silence was interrupted only by the echo of the bell, along with the haunting whoosh of the huge pulley connected to the bell rope.

The casket was lowered down on the church walk as the family filed behind. Each of us donned sunglasses to mask any tears as we made the last walk with him. After all, we were just trying to act as emotionless as he was. A twelve-man Color Guard lined up in formation on one-side of the sidewalk. They stood perfectly still, engaged in a full salute with their right hand, and in their left, holding a rifle by the long barrel as the stock rested on the ground. I recognized most of the faces as the old guys at whom we laughed because of the less than perfect execution during Color Guard drills. Today was different. It wasn't funny anymore. They were here to bury their dead, just like they always did. If they were lucky enough to live on after the war, they would still be there for a fallen soldier, no matter how old that the soldier was. It was their duty. It was their honor. It was their life. Today, was notably different. Everything about them was perfect. Men in their late seventies standing at attention, not moving a muscle.

We entered the church and proceeded to the front pews and took our seats. The priest started Mass and talked about Dad's humility.

"Arnie didn't want me to bring him communion at home anymore. He would say, 'Father, you're so busy.' That was Arnie. Always independent, always his own man."

He went on to say how Dad was the perfect Catholic, remarking on his perfect church attendance and how he always made it a point to bury the dead. I had to agree. Dad was a rock that could never be swayed. He didn't drink, cheat, gamble or chase around. He was unflappable, as straight as an arrow. He never bad-mouthed anyone and lived up to his favorite saying: "If you can't say anything nice about someone, then keep your mouth shut."

However, I couldn't understand how a person so aligned with the Catholic Church couldn't display love for his son, or family for that matter.

Following the service, the procession drove over to the cemetery for the burial. Friends and family stood around the grave as the priest read a prayer. The Color Guard did their twenty-one gun salute in perfect unison. Two Color Guard drill team members rolled up the American flag and presented it to Mom while a third Guard read a prayer.

"This is my flag. This flag…"

The Color Guard member read on as John Gamoke came up from behind and put an arm around me.

"I've heard this prayer before. Your Dad wrote this prayer and read it at my dad's funeral two years ago."

Suddenly, the bugle sounded as Taps was played. Like a levy, I broke down into tears and sobbed openly. Before now, the last time that I had cried like this was when I was four years old, and my great uncle Dorsey threatened to amputate my teddy bear's legs at the knees with a butcher knife. I felt so embarrassed. Dad wouldn't have done this, but he wasn't around any more to police my actions. I had to finally feel my emotions, no matter how good, bad or indifferent they seemed.

After the funeral, we somberly proceeded back to the church basement to eat lunch. I had already received a call on my cell phone from my friend, Andrea, saying that she had her assistant call in an order to send pies for the funeral lunch.

"Imy, I found out that they don't make pies in Arcadia."

"What?"

"Yea, I had Michelle call to order pies for the funeral lunch, because we know it's your favorite. The local bakery said that people don't take pies to a funeral in Arcadia. They take coffee cakes. So we sent up a few of them."

As soon as I walked into the church hall, my eyes instinctively looked around for Upherzine Rebarchick, the old lady who used to take the two-mile hike to attend every funeral luncheon. John Gamoke walked up with a smile, knowing who I was trying to spot.

"She was at my dad's funeral two years ago."

"Is she still alive?"

"Probably not, or she'd be here."

Just then, a man walked up and politely waited for a pause in my conversation with John. I turned to politely acknowledge him. He held out his hand and shook mine. He was a good-looking man about mid-to-late fifties. He had dark hair, a moustache and wore glasses.

"I'm George Wienzel."

"I'm Imy."

"Yea, I know."

I recognized him as one of the Pallbearers, but I had no idea who he was.

"I knew your dad for over thirty five years. I stopped in at the mill one day just to pick up some baler twine. I started talking to him about a few things, and before you know it, we became friends. The next time I stopped in there, I found that I could talk to him about some of my problems. I had just lost my wife to cancer and was having a hard time raising my family while trying to farm. Relatives were eyeing my kids, knowing I didn't have the money or time to raise them properly. I was losing both my family and farm and had nowhere to turn. When I started talking to your dad about it, he surprisingly had been through the same thing. I used to live on faith alone after a visit with him at the feed mill. The days turned into weeks, and I was able to make ends meet. What I thought was bad for my family, Arnie convinced me was OK. I was able to hold the relatives at bay, and with Arnie's constant farm coaching, I was able to make more money. I had been working the farm too much. Arnie used to say everyone spends too much time tilling the soil. I reduced my time to a third and had the best crop ever. Your dad was my dad, and I just thank you for letting me share him."

"Did you drive a black pickup?"

"Yes, I did. I drove that thing for twenty years."

Wow, I thought. At least Dad was a father to somebody. I guess he just needed someone who really needed his expertise.

I shook George's hand again and wished him well.

"George, any son of his is a brother of mine."

I dropped his hand and gave him a big hug.

George walked away, and I stood alone for a moment. If Dad had passed anything down to me, it was my ambivalence or lack of expressing emotion. Everything in this weird world was suddenly starting to make sense. Dad was able to love this man as a son, and both Dad and George were better men because of it.

Back at the apartment, Mom had me go through my things that I had left behind in a bottom drawer of a chest. I pulled out the weathered red scrapbook that housed my family memories through all of these years. There were mostly black-and-whites of Betsy and Tom. Since Dad never appeared too interested in their lives either, it was up to me to record them. I had bought a Bazooka-Joe Camera years ago with fifty bubble-gum wrappers and fifty cents. There was a shot of Tom pounding carpenters nails into the old stump that Dad had brought home from the mill. Tom was no more than three-years-old at the time. He was able to pound each nail as straight as an arrow into the petrified piece of wood. From that point on, we knew that Tom would take up the vocation of woodworking. There were oodles of pictures of Betsy, as well, along with all of my friends. Oddly, there were no pictures of Mom and Dad. Toward the back of the book there were a few ribbons that I had won running track in High School. I thumbed toward the front of the book, running into a news clipping of Green Bay Packer headlines: "Pack thwarts Vikings 13-10." I remembered that game like it was yesterday. Dave Hampton returned a kickoff one hundred and three yards for the winning score. I returned the yellowed piece of history back in its place when I noticed a wrapper on the floor. I picked it up and tossed it into the waste-paper basket. As I stared at the dark brown Snickers wrapper, a feeling went through me so violently, I started to tremble. I sat on the edge of the bed, staring into the trashcan. After an entire lifetime with my father, this is what I had to show for it. Yet, this experience summed it up. Even though Dad struggled to show any emotion, he did prove his love in many other ways. His family's priorities were always first and foremost. He never had anything we didn't. He was tough, unemotional and physically abusive, but that's all he knew. He worked like a dog, but he never spent anything on himself. And in the end, he thought he was a fabulous father.

I picked up the candy wrapper out of the trashcan and crumpled it in my pocket. It might not be much, but it was something. I walked down the hall to the living room and handed the scrapbook to Tom. He received it with a surprised look on his face.

"Imy, don't you want it?"

"Na. They're mostly of you anyway. Besides, I got what I wanted."

I patted the outside of my jeans' pocket to a crinkling sound.

"I got what I wanted."

Chapter XXXI

I woke up to a kiss on the forehead. Doreen had just walked in from her meeting.

"Did you boys enjoy your time together?"

"Well, I can't speak for Nick, but I think so."

"So what did you guys do?"

"We both sat here thinking about what kind of relationship we want to establish between us."

"And what kind of relationship did you guys come up with?"

"Well, I don't know if Dad realized it, but he did teach me a valuable lesson on relationships. I'm taking that lesson and applying it to us."

"Well, I hope you always feel free to show emotion toward Nicholas."

Nicholas swung his head, adjusting his gaze away from Doreen and stared me down as if looking for a reply. I brushed his hair aside, giving him a kiss on the forehead.

"You can count on it."

"Reenie?"

"Yea, honey."

"Will you do me a favor?"

"Sure. What?"

"I remembered that I can't make the tech conference next week, so mark down one more guest for Nick's party."

"But in the past, you've lived for that conference."

"I didn't have Nicholas in the past, and it's about time that I start living for him."

Doreen walked around the corner of the kitchen with a smile on her face. She hugged Nicholas and me at the same time.

"I love you, Imy Lecheler."

"I love you, Reenie."